Watching Jim Crow

Console-ing Passions

TELEVISION AND CULTURAL POWER

Edited by Lynn Spigel

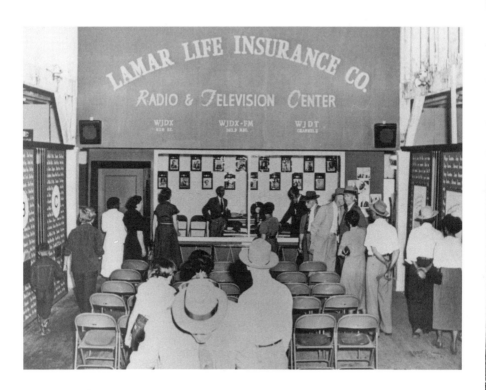

STEVEN D. CLASSEN

Watching Jim Crow

THE STRUGGLES OVER MISSISSIPPI TV, 1955-1969

Duke University Press Durham & London 2004

© 2004 Duke University Press

Printed in the United States of America on

acid-free paper ∞

Designed by C. H. Westmoreland

Typeset in Times Roman by Keystone

Typesetting, Inc.

Library of Congress Cataloging-in-

Publication Data appear on the last printed

page of this book.

A shorter version of chapter 2 appeared as
"Standing on Unstable Grounds: A Reexamination
of the WLBT-TV Case" in *Critical Studies in
Mass Communication* 11(1) (1994). Portions of
chapter 3 appeared in a different version as
"Southern Discomforts: The Racial Struggle
over Popular TV" in *The Revolution Wasn't
Televised: Sixties Television and Social Conflict,*
edited by Lynn Spigel and Michael Curtin (New York:
Routledge, 1996).

Frontispiece: Live audience and studio of
WJDX radio program, 1953

TO KATHLEEN

CONTENTS

ACKNOWLEDGMENTS

It is impossible for me to imagine this work apart from my frequent conversations with colleagues and the many new friends I have met along the way. And it is equally impossible for me to adequately measure or acknowledge all of their generous critiques, comments, encouragements, and suggestions.

In Mississippi, dozens of individuals spent hours telling me their life stories — stories that have truly changed and enriched my life. If this project had stopped after this fieldwork, my visits to Jackson and other parts of Mississippi would still have been time very well spent. My heartfelt thanks to everyone I interviewed, but especially Barbara Barber, Dr. Gordon Henderson, Mary Ann Henderson, Dr. Aaron Shirley, Dr. Jeanne Middleton, Austin Moore, George Owens, Ruth Owens, Aurelia Young, and Ed King. Ed, thank you for an abundant supply of stories, papers, manuscripts, and good southern hospitality.

Juanita Jefferson was an extraordinary woman and friend, marked by her love for God and her fellow humankind, and I am very sorry she will not see this work in publication. Aaron Henry, Hewitt Griffin, and Sam Bailey also passed away in recent years, but not before offering to me their considerable wisdom and insight.

At Tougaloo College, the Lillian Pierce Benbow Room of Special Collections is a little-known treasure-house of archival materials pertaining to the Jackson movement of the early sixties. Librarians Odell Dockens and Clarence Hunter were wonderful resources there. Thanks also to the hard-working staff at the Mississippi Department of Archives and History, particularly librarian Anne Lipscomb, and to the State Historical Society of Wisconsin. Everett Parker, retired director of the United Church of Christ, Office of Communication, was most charitable in his contributions to this project by agreeing to multiple interviews in New York City.

The faculty of the Communication Arts Department at the University of Wisconsin — Madison, past and present, particularly Julie D'Acci,

Michele Hilmes, and Michael Curtin, have been a consistent source of encouragement — offering advice, modeling superior scholarship, and providing supportive friendship. This book had its origins in my doctoral dissertation at Madison, directed by John Fiske. I could make many fond remarks regarding John, but simply put, he demonstrated all the qualities a mentor and professor should possess, including extraordinary insight, graciousness, and an abiding enthusiasm for the work of his students.

The department at Madison provided a terrific environment for research and writing. Jeff Sconce, Kevin Glynn, Pam Wilson, Chad Dell, Lisa Parks, Aniko Bodroghkozy, Shari Goldin, Matthew Murray, and Moya Luckett all endured presentations of my early research, and contributed in ways tangible and intangible. Outside of the department, frequent conversations with Marshall Crossnoe and Cam Anderson afforded warm friendships and perspective.

In recent years I have been teaching in the California State University system, first in San Bernardino and presently in Los Angeles. At San Bernardino, I received ready support and encouragement from my chair, Craig Monroe; from Dean Bev Hendricks; and from faculty colleagues Scott Rodriguez, Meryl Perlson, and Susan Finsen. At Los Angeles my critical studies colleagues, Robert Vianello, Enrique Berumen, Kelly Madison, Suzanne Regan, and John Ramirez, have walked with me the final miles of this project, and I'm very grateful to them. Particular thanks to Kelly, Suzanne, and John for reading and commenting on parts of the final manuscript.

John Dittmer generously read the final manuscript and made important corrections and suggested changes. Tom Streeter has been a wonderful friend, critic, intellectual catalyst, and supporter throughout the several years of this project. Lynn Spigel has patiently read various versions of this research too many times — beginning during the early Madison years — and has offered her remarkable talents and insights far more often than I can adequately recognize. Thank you, Lynn.

Finally, my wife Kathleen has not only contributed to the work and shaped it, but lived with it and read every page multiple times. Her belief in this project was often more steadfast than my own, her support unfaltering, and her laughter, perspective, and grace a wonderful antidote for a writer's stubbornness and anxiety.

Acknowledgments

Reconstruction

The broadcast complex that houses WLBT-TV remains today where it has always been, a few blocks outside the modest cluster of skyscrapers that defines downtown Jackson, Mississippi. Built in the 1950s a short distance from prominent businesses and seats of government, the center's managers have long enjoyed proximity to political and economic power. But as the years have passed, station planners have faced the problem of updating the center's aging physical plant and technologies. The architectural results are an eclectic mix—a layering of the new upon the old—as a consequence of repeated remodeling projects. While the station's original brick facade remains at the public entrance, behind it the furnishings have been dramatically changed to reflect contemporary needs and concerns. Familiar spaces remain but have been transformed: the cramped dressing rooms and viewing areas built to keep "Negro performers" apart from white audiences have been radically redesigned for contemporary uses. Traces of a past station remain, reconfigured for the present.

Much the same can be said for WJTV, Jackson's first television station. Broadcasts on WJTV began in January 1953, eleven months before WLBT, and the station remains at its original site, reconstructed to keep pace with contemporary audience and industry expectations. More than fifty years after their initial construction these communication centers continue their roles as powerful cultural institutions marked by manifold changes in ownership, business affiliations, personnel, and programming. The stations offer news, entertainment, and representations of the social world. They also serve as tangible reminders of a painful past.

Aligned at their conception with white supremacist and segregationist interests, as newborns WJTV and WLBT complemented an already

WLBT-TV and WJDX radio, Jackson, Mississippi.

intimidating white power bloc including prominent business leaders, bankers, politicians, clergy, and police departments determined to thwart integrationist or "black freedom" advances in the fifties. Facing the growing conglomeration of powerful cultural and economic institutions in Mississippi at that time, many civil rights activists opted to delay their tactical offensives. Others simply bypassed the state and its segregationist strongholds altogether, seeking more fertile spaces for social change.

But some did not — and in this book I focus on these agents of change and the discourses animating their bold campaigns, particularly on the fronts of television and public entertainment. I offer a detailed description of the civil rights activities targeting the segregationist programming practices of Jackson's television stations from 1955 to 1969, and examine their significance in terms of state regulation, racial politics, and cultural history.[1]

These campaigns defined late-fifties and early-sixties TV programming less as a "wasteland" than as a strategic battleground, and they stressed popular entertainment as crucial to social change. In 1955 Medgar Evers and the NAACP began seriously to confront the stations, petitioning the broadcasters and the Federal Communications Commission (FCC) for the inclusion of more (progressive) integrationist and African American personalities and perspectives in the stations' pro-

Watching Jim Crow

gramming. In the years that followed, resolute black Mississippians and activists allied with New York's United Church of Christ to work to alter local television. Eventually their efforts changed the programming of both WLBT and WJTV, as well as WLBT's ownership. Alongside these struggles, a small group of intrepid college students and staff enacted a "cultural and artistic agitation" campaign designed to isolate the racist coercions accompanying public segregationist entertainment. As I will show, this small-scale cultural offensive prompted a wider scrutiny of racist practices in Mississippi and provoked a segregationist backlash aimed at one of the nation's most popular television programs.

Federal regulators, activists such as Evers, and powerful segregationist institutions all recognized the power of televisual representations early in the civil rights struggle. For example, in 1962 the FCC took the unusual step of reprimanding eight Mississippi television and radio stations, including WJTV and WLBT in Jackson, for their "biased" coverage of the rallies and violent riots surrounding the event of James Meredith entering the University of Mississippi. While mindful of its apparent clash with First Amendment liberties, the commission pursued this regulatory course by asking each station to justify its relevant programming and detail its adherence to broadcasting's "fairness doctrine." Although they took no further substantive action against the broadcasters at the time, the regulators signaled the Kennedy administration's sensitivity to the multiple political concerns put in play via TV and radio.

During the Meredith admission crisis, Fred Beard, general manager of WJDX radio and WLBT-TV, exhorted his audiences to resist "the evil and illegal forces of tyranny." He went on to state: "Governor Barnett needs the support of every true and loyal Mississippian. I know that he will receive full support. We can all stand with him and say 'Never!' "[2] Medgar Evers, however, persistently attempted to rebut such remarks and add integrationist or African American perspectives to Jackson's broadcast editorials and reports. In May 1963 Evers lobbied, as he had many times previously, to appear on local television in an equal-time response to segregationist voices. He did so on May 20. Less than a month later Evers was murdered in his driveway by a man who had watched in the darkness for him to arrive at his Jackson home.

Mississippians close to Evers and his cause have long speculated, while not necessarily asserting a causal link, on the relationship be-

Medgar Evers delivers a response on WLBT-TV to segregationist Jackson mayor Allen Thompson on 20 May 1963. Evers states: "What does the Negro want? He wants to get rid of racial segregation in Mississippi because he knows it has not been good for him nor for the state. . . . But whether Jackson and the state choose change or not, the years of change are upon us." (Photo copyright Bettmann/CORBIS)

tween Ever's local broadcast appearance and his death. Jackson writer Eudora Welty is among those who have done so, penning a powerful story that places the reader in the point of view of Evers's killer. In Welty's "Where Is the Voice Coming From?" the assassin is clearly angered and inspired to kill by the sight of a black man's face on television, and he bitterly remarks: "His face was in front of the public before I got rid of him, and after I got rid of him there it is again — the same picture. And none of me."[3] Welty writes that she "knew" the murderer, "not his identity, but his coming about, in this time and place."[4] She certainly knew the impact of Evers on segregationist-managed television: the image of the eloquent, intelligent, and respectful black spokesman for integration, "entering" into thousands of segregated white living rooms in south-central Mississippi for the first time, was undeniably powerful and even shocking for some. It was a moment recalled by many I interviewed — a representation prompting powerful stories and memories that endure to this day.

Changing segregationist television in Jackson was not straight-

A Jackson *Clarion-Ledger* editorial response to Medgar Evers's May 20, 1963 televised address.

forward or easy. The intersecting activities of multiple, differently motivated agents and rights campaigns were necessary to prompt local television's transformations. The dramatic changes in television in Jackson, in full flower by the seventies, did not start within the industry, the FCC, or some enclosed circle of technological experts. Rather, they were sparked by the friction of race rights activists joined to liberal advocacy intervenors and some agents of state regulation. All were vitally motivated by larger social concerns. Then, as now, local television and popular entertainment performances were often recognized as crucial sites of political and racial struggle, where social identities and fundamental notions of human dignity were at stake.

During the period addressed in this volume, race and rights activism was explicitly connected to local television and entertainment practices as well as notions of a new "consumerism," prompting progressive social change alongside regulatory retrenchments. "Consumerism" was a key sixties trope, mobilized strategically by different interests in very different ways, and explicitly connected to broadcasting, race, and politics. For this reason, the concept receives considerable scrutiny in the pages that follow, where I am especially interested in showing, in

Michel de Certeau's words, "the models of action characteristic of users whose status as the dominated element in society . . . is concealed by the euphemistic term 'consumers.' "[5]

In line with the architectural metaphor outlined earlier, this book represents a layering of present over past — a reconstruction of sorts — employing the traces, interpretations, and constructions of the past to address enduring social problems. The struggle over representation on local television screens, and the rights of citizens to represent such concerns before the industry and state, today remain vital activities to democracy, even as they were decades ago. Basic representational issues, such as portrayals of difference and different cultural groups, as well as authority within the powerful state and corporate institutions of broadcasting, were not neatly resolved in a civil rights past but rather brought to the fore as issues of continuing concern and debate.[6] The divergent ways in which these concerns have been addressed reveal the disparate visions of democracy and social justice in conflict yesterday and today.

By echoing recent cultural studies scholarship I hope to persuade readers that television is more than a technical apparatus and/or a set of industrially produced texts. Rather, it is "something people do": a complicated set of social practices, both forming and formed through various modes of state and social regulation.[7] In this project I offer a close examination of these social practices at a particular time and place, and point to the ways in which federal broadcast regulation in the United States has been historically aligned with "white privilege," or what George Lipsitz calls our society's "possessive investment in whiteness."[8]

Rather than simply speaking of some distant past — "the sixties" — that harbors the racism of old, the stories offered here inevitably ask important questions of the present — questions that bring the dynamics of one historical moment together with another. As John Durham Peters has put it, paraphrasing Walter Benjamin, "the present becomes intelligible as it is aligned with a past moment with which it has a secret affinity."[9]

The dangers of the present are manifest in myriad ways, particularly concerning the concept of race. This project is written against the backdrop of these problems. In 1968 the Kerner Report — part of the study of the National Advisory Commission on Civil Disorder — concluded that social institutions, including broadcasting, were contributing to the creation of "two societies, one black, one white — separate and unequal." Thirty years later, a group founded to continue the commission's work concluded that the report's dire warnings had indeed "become reality."[10] The divisions of more sophisticated racisms continue, often growing wider and more complex.

I often heard this concern voiced while living in Jackson. For example, as I interviewed African Americans in the city during the 1990s I heard dispiriting comparisons of present and past challenges faced by black communities. Dr. Aaron Shirley, a physician deeply committed to public health among the city's poor, offered this perspective:

Shirley: I think the challenge before us now is greater than back then, with what's going on among young black males. I think the answers back then were just so obvious, but now . . . it's frustrating to get a map and plot out all the homicides that occurred in Jackson [last year] and the causes. It's just unbelievable. . . . All but three occurred in the same area. The ages, the incident, the spot, it's unbelievable.

Classen: What ages, are they young?

Shirley: The average . . . victim is twenty-seven, black, killed by someone he knew, or she knew. Killed by someone who lived in the same neighborhood.

Classen: Were drugs involved in a majority of those homicides?

Shirley: Could have been. Well, a majority were not related to drug transactions. They're likely to have drugs or alcohol involved in the condition of the victim or the perpetrator. The typical murder because of a drug transaction? Very few.

Classen: So whereas in the 1960s you kind of knew the foe, and knew what you had to do — in the nineties, you're not exactly sure who the foe is, and what the foe is?

Shirley: Way back in the forties, early fifties, Smith County was a place where a number of blacks were lynched. I was never afraid to drive through Smith County. To walk around Smith County, any time of the day or night. But now, the neighborhood I grew up in . . . I would find it difficult walking around that [Jackson State University] neighborhood. It's different, much, much different. I grew up in the Jackson State area.

Classen: Off Lynch Street?

Shirley: On Pascagoula. It was two blocks off Lynch . . . as junior high and high school youngsters, we walked to the movie and ice cream parlor. Didn't even have a lock on the front door, really. My mother had a little screen door . . . and we bought another house and moved out of that house. We had aluminum siding, it was a two-story house. . . . After she sold it she moved out. I'd go over there quite often, we had a clinic for school children. And the people had pulled the aluminum as high as you can reach — got stripped. You see people picking up aluminum cans. That's not to beautify the area.

Classen: It's not an antilitter campaign.

Shirley: No . . . I find it difficult walking around in that neighborhood. I'd go over there in the daytime.[11]

Later in my fieldwork, I went to the home of the Reverend Willie Lewis. Lewis is a lifetime resident of the state and has spent years in a variety of professions, including work as an ordained Christian minister. When, based on my previous conversation with Shirley I explicitly asked him to compare the 1960s and 1990s, Lewis answered along the same lines as Shirley:

Lewis: Now the one place where you have it worse is, I'll tell you this now, in 1963 you knew your limitations. You knew you couldn't go but so far then. Because the sign told you — don't go there. Now . . . the sign is not there, so you are walking into it, but it is still worse than it was then, but you don't know.

Classen: You still what?

Lewis: It's just as bad or worse now, but the sign is not there. If you walk in, you understand, but you've still got the same arms against you, and you don't know they're against you. How would you like right now if you go on out that door and know somebody's got a gun, and is going to shoot you? Well, you'd be kind of scared about going out that door. But you think, ain't nobody got a gun, why not walk out? And the time you walk out you get shot, that's what we got going now. The better we are now, we got more opportunity opened up to us now than we had in those days. Because you have such things like salesmen and managers. We didn't have nothing like that. . . . That is better, but the worse part about it is that some of the folks that got those opportunities have turned their backs on from whence they came.[12]

While the observations of Lewis and Shirley highlight the continuing problem of racism, they also point to the different forms racism takes relative to those most evident in the sixties. They refer to a racism that is not overt or publicly "signed," but rather what Stuart Hall terms "inferential"[13] — that which insidiously advances the discourses of white supremacy, by, for example, subtly recoding racial meanings. As Lewis remarked, "you've still got the same arms against you, and you don't know they're against you." In speaking of an innocent person walking out of a door only to be gunned down by an unknown, unexpected assassin, Lewis uses an illustration chilling in its realism. What he dramatically calls attention to are discourses of the present that hide racist signs of the past.

While "modern" or "inferential" racism manifests itself in multiple, ever-changing ways, it most often looks and sounds very different from the vulgar racism of Jim Crow; operates along axes that are not simply black/white; and continues to be powerfully racist in effect — in part precisely because its crass heritage has ostensibly been jettisoned. Often couched in claims of neutrality, equality, or race blindness, such practices routinely pronounce an antipathy or hostility toward the political agendas and leaders of people of color, alongside the claim that racism is a problem of the past and no longer inhibits achievement.[14]

Conservative backlash against affirmative action as well as other legacies of the sixties freedom movement has been prominent and powerful since the seventies. On the terrain of law, years of conservative Supreme Court and federal administrative agency rulings have disassembled important formal safeguards for people of color and narrowed the rights and legal recourse of citizens of ordinary means.[15]

Conservative-fueled state referenda, such as California's Propositions 187 (also known as the "Save Our State" measure) and 209, have aimed at the elimination of affirmative action programs and the denial of important state services to immigrants, employing arguments regarding the "costs" of illegal immigration to "ordinary" citizens. Steeped in myths of rugged individualism and nostalgic meritocracy, as well as the formal language of race blindness or neutrality, such race-sensitive lawmaking has been a sorry hallmark of recent years, cynically mobilized by xenophobic political campaigns. As Roopali Mukherjee has shown, such policy events point to the "ways in which the public policy process served [and serves] as a critical site for the production and legitimation of particular [racialized] knowledges."[16]

Many of these racially coded campaigns and initiatives are "known" to Americans primarily via television and electronic media journalism. More precisely, audiences "know" about these political activities in large part due to the representational work of television stations and journalistic operations that increasingly are bureaucratized arms of enormous commercial corporations. But by federal government measures, in the midst of the recent trend of corporate concentration and conglomeration, "minority" ownership and control of television properties over the past decade has not only not increased but actually decreased. The U.S. Department of Commerce's Year 2000 National Telecommunications and Information Agency report on broadcast ownership concludes that "minority" ownership of television stations in the United States is less than 2 percent — the lowest level measured in the last decade. The document solemnly underlines concerns about the loss of diverse sources of information relevant to minority communities and the lack of outlets for local issues.[17]

Within this context, this history is motivated by a desire for a reinvigorated democracy that truly engages more citizens and stimulates progressive change, particularly in the sphere of American race relations. If such change is to happen, certainly the histories and practices of key state and cultural institutions, and different understandings of these institutions, must be more widely debated. Perspectives and voices long marginalized must be more thoughtfully heard. It is my hope that some of these voices are heard here, and that because of these voices the historical yet enduring strategies of racial supremacy and marginalization are further scrutinized. In turn, this might lead to what Kobena Mercer has described as "the construction of a wider system of alliances and equivalences that [strengthen] . . . new forms of democratic agency."[18]

SCHOLARLY RECONSTRUCTIONS

The 1960s were a heady time for those on the liberal front of U.S. broadcast reform. As media historian Willard Rowland Jr. has summarized, during these years many believed the promises of "social responsibility" approaches to U.S. radio and television broadcasting were being revitalized in a series of legal regulatory and activist challenges to the status quo.[19] Key among these challenges were those aimed at Mississippi broadcasting. Thus, scholarly stories regarding Jackson television, particularly WLBT-TV during the 1960s, have been written elsewhere, and this is understandable given the dramatic, important issues and players involved. In these narratives, civil rights,

Watching Jim Crow

broadcast policy, consumerism, and identity politics all explicitly or implicitly intersect and interact.

During the fifties and sixties the popular media institutions of Mississippi and the South were sites of pitched warfare. What conservative forces within Mississippi and other states perceived as a cultural invasion was fought against with determination and dedication to the status quo and a particular southern "way of life." Segregationist politicians, business people, and civic leaders recognized broadcast stations as key fortresses against this "invasion," and fought long and hard alongside like-minded media managers. On the other side, citizen rights activists faced tremendous institutional obstacles, threats, and resources but in the end prompted significant changes in broadcast representation as well as other aspects of everyday life.

Particularly in fights surrounding the licensing of WLBT-TV there were dramatic performances involving racial politics and state regulation. Significant changes in federal broadcast licensing regulation, as well as federal administrative agency law addressing citizens' legal status, were outcomes of the station's licensing fight. Because of this, it is common to find a few paragraphs regarding the "WLBT landmark" in undergraduate texts addressing broadcast history or policy and regulation. These historical summaries point to WLBT-TV as involved in a long-lived, precedent-setting legal case in which the U.S. Court of Appeals for the District of Columbia repeatedly ruled against the Federal Communications Commission and finally vacated the station's license in 1969.[20]

For decades the court of appeal's oft-cited arguments and rulings have had an impact far beyond the city limits of Jackson or the state of Mississippi. In the years immediately following the protracted WLBT licensing fight, citizen activists used these legal precedents, in concert with other lobbying efforts, to launch numerous broadcast licensing challenges. In 1969, for example, black citizens in Texarkana, Texas, with the assistance of the Office of Communication of the United Church of Christ (UCC), negotiated an agreement with local station KTAL-TV that addressed concerns including programming and news coverage, as well as black employment. This was just one of the first local campaigns explicitly modeled on the WLBT license challenge, including the strategies of station monitoring and the filing of a formal "petition to deny" relicensing. Scores of similar citizen actions followed. What some observers termed the "broadcast reform movement" was born, due in no small part to the success of strategies first employed in Jackson.

Beginning in 1969 and on into the early seventies, the "number of media reform groups mushroomed," according to Kathryn Montgomery, as did the number of station licenses challenged.[21] Montgomery has traced the dramatic increase in formal licensing petitions, and she states: "In (fiscal year) 1969 two were filed; in 1970, 15 petitions [to deny licensing] were filed against 16 stations; in 1971, 38 petitions were filed against 84 stations; and in 1972, 68 petitions were filed against 108 stations. Though very few stations actually lost their licenses, the 'petition to deny' became a powerful weapon of intimidation."[22] In 1971 the industry organ, *Broadcasting* magazine, snipped: "It is hard to find a community of any size without its organizations of blacks, Chicanos, Latinos, liberated women, activist mothers, or other concerned types negotiating for stronger representation in broadcasting."[23] Mindful of the WLBT and KTAL precedents, many of the stations challenged entered into KTAL-type agreements in exchange for withdrawal of formal petitions.[24] While management concessions regarding employment and programming were often modest, and certainly reformist, the changes achieved were significant and the empowerment of the underrepresented was made tangible, thus sparking wider activism.[25]

Many ethnically and racially defined groups fought during this period for more progressive broadcast representation. The NAACP and Congress of Racial Equality (CORE) continued to pressure the networks and local affiliates. The National Latino Media Coalition, La Raza, Justica, and the League of United Latino Citizens fought to address the concerns of Mexican Americans and Latin Americans, and antidefamation groups, such as the Italian-American League and German-American Antidefamation League, challenged televisual representation. Importantly, these actions opened opportunities for "minority" employment, and were a catalyst for FCC equal employment initiatives.

However, the moment for this grassroots activism was short-lived. By the mid-seventies it was declining in scope and power as the victim of multiple countervailing trends, including increasing industry resistance, FCC intransigence, and a rising technocratic ideology, in addition to the inherent limitations of its reformist vision.[26] The movement had never sought to fundamentally change broadcasting structures but rather just to work within them. The movement's significant gains, made, for example, in employment, suggested to many that existing systems "worked" and more radical alternatives need not be considered. And, as indicated by Robert Horwitz, without altering such structures "media reform will usually be short-lived."[27]

Willard Rowland Jr.'s excellent study of broadcast reform makes exactly this point, briefly noting that the WLBT licensing challenge was itself the product of converging social concerns, rising "out of the spreading civil rights movement." Rowland further observes that the focus of the rights movement had at the time of the station challenge expanded to become closely identified with "the anti-war movement, countercultural expression, and consumer rights."[28]

In this project I take some of Rowland's cogent observations and ground them in the pluralistic memories and practices of longtime Jackson residents and activists. At the same time, I recognize the pitfalls of personalist or formal explanations for various historical and legal decisions, because such explanatory schemes obscure important social patterns and configurations of power. Broadcasting in Jackson did not change simply because of the actions of heroic individuals or groups of dedicated activists, although both were necessary. Rather, powerful social discourses, joined to multiple agents and institutions, prompted significant change in local practices. Rather than asking which personal or legal qualities or actions brought about historic ends, I aim to examine the relationship of specific social and cultural forces to changes in television, regulation, and representation.

Along the same lines, segregation and racism are poorly explained if they are simply attributed to a few individualized subjects. Thus they are examined here not primarily as character traits but as sets of historically reproduced ideas and practices. Racism promotes particular interests "that are always racial but never purely so, and that function by putting racial difference into practice."[29] Assigning the title of "racist" to certain champions of white supremacy may be accurate but it lacks explanatory value, and it too neatly individualizes and isolates that which is fundamentally social. Such a derogatory title affixed to a particular state, such as Mississippi or Alabama, also homogenizes diverse populations and pays too little attention to the ways in which discourses articulating race, gender, class, and other social differences work across a variety of formal geographic boundaries.

Although scholarly treatments addressing the broadcast station battles claim to have a primary concern for, and focus on, the cultural welfare of black Mississippians, most simply reproduce histories that highlight the perspectives of northern activists or powerful industry and government officials. In doing so, these studies provide further, sadly ironic, evidence that the voices and everyday perspectives of black Mississippians have too rarely been deemed worthy of further investigation. In contrast, African American voices are a point of focus in this work. Attempting to address past historiographic omissions, in this study I underline the importance of placing the "official" accounts of the station challenges that are offered by scholarly and legal institutions against the "unofficial," or "official" yet marginalized, stories of local African Americans.

I also focus on Jackson-based civil rights activists and their supporters rather than on FCC regulators, attorneys, or those who stood with white segregationist campaigns and activities. Certainly the opposing camps in the station fights did not divide neatly along racial lines, and among the bravest of all Mississippians in the civil rights struggle were the white Mississippians who fought for integration and racial justice. These activists offer concrete demonstrations of how whites can take a stand against white supremacy and privilege. With this focus, I hope to offer a better understanding of how those in the historical struggle against white supremacy and privilege understand and interpret a particular past.

WRITING HISTORY AND LAW

Detailing the struggles surrounding television in Jackson requires that points for narrative beginning and ending be marked, voices be selected, and spheres of discourse be chosen for focus. Chronologies and histories, like the physical plants of the broadcast stations, are constructed within the dynamics of particular cultures, times, and places — layering present interests, anxieties, and concerns over the always interpreted traces and fragments of the past. As Nancy Partner has explained, "history is a hermeneutic of fragmentary present texts which makes them yield something intelligible and larger than themselves. The hermeneutic necessarily involves layers of figurative interpretation, creating of present odds and ends a metaphoric world called 'evidence,' and then working out within its confines intricate patterns which force silence and time to take form."[30]

As self-evident as the "truth" of any particular paper trail, historical document, or record may appear, such texts have meanings that are dynamic, variable, and socially contingent — meanings that are articulated and naturalized by history's architects at their moment of interpretation. Historical truth is not simply passed whole and intact through some timeless apolitical channel, but, like a television studio, is built piece by piece within particular times and places, based on what is deemed most relevant, interesting, and important. So, for example, most histories dealing with sixties Mississippi and WLBT tell a particular type of lawyerly story focusing on central legal characters and federal court rulings, introducing and concluding these dramas with explicit discussion of the salient legal precedents established.

As "new historians" and critical theorists such as Hayden White have observed, the process of writing history inevitably involves placing a chronological and teleological framework on a fragmented, plural reality.[31] Moreover, recognition of history writing as an always interested, and contingent, exercise of power recommends modesty, honesty, and self-reflexivity on the part of the historian. The historian should not hide behind the past the present that produces and organizes it; rather, historiography should be an explicit building of "genealogies" — histories of the present — examining the past for insights today.[32]

Writing this particular history of the present has required dialogue with various texts, memories, and people that all resist abstract categorization. This resistance, moreover, has prompted me to make changes in my research scope and conceptualization, and more fundamentally, in my understandings of race, politics, and writing. Such interactions inevitably prompt change, because we always depart from an honest, engaged dialogue somehow different from when we entered. Certainly this has been true for me. Oral history telling and sustained conversation are potentially radical enterprises for the parties involved, and such a project can only touch on the richness of the dialogues experienced and the changes prompted.

While this work started as an examination of a broadcast licensing challenge, my varied conversations continually underlined the point that life is not lived within limited research conceptualizations — which are always inadequate and partial. Dialogues prompted my consideration of wider social contexts and of the relationship between racial representation and what sociologist Pierre Bourdieu has termed "habitus." Habitus, in Bourdieu's conception, points us to the dynamic, everyday intersections of structure and action, society and the individual.[33] In distinction to traditional materialism, it refers both to the conditions in which one lives, and to the ways in which one lives within these conditions — looking at how people and practices within social conditions act on those conditions and vice versa.[34] And while such contextualizations are admittedly partial, they offer perspectives and potentials less narrow in my mind than when I started this work.

In previous examinations of the WLBT challenges, the federal government and its official legal processes are the narrative center around which the broader context of watching Jim Crow television has been placed.[35] But if television is something that people do, a complicated social activity of everyday life rather than something constructed and contained within official, legitimated understandings, then such narrative foci are rather obscure and backward. This fact became particularly clear to me as I engaged longtime Jackson residents in their oral histories. My understandings of Jackson television, abstracted from policy and history texts, often were received as strange or irrelevant by those who had "lived" local television. A different, more richly textured view of television is available when its practices are contextualized within everyday routines, rhythms, and memory making.

Like the writing of history, the writing and articulation of law is always political, involving the construction of a particular frame or point of view through which reality, life, and human behaviors are viewed. "Law" is best understood as a complex of interdependent social practices — an inevitably human and thoroughly social enterprise.[36] Thus, the boundaries and redefinitions of "law" are never secure or finally established but rather are fundamentally social and dynamic, and the continuous renegotiations of these borders (often evident in popular texts and practices) are a key concern and focus of energy. Within an increasingly pluralistic society including disparate cultures and senses of history, it is inevitable that differing notions of history and law — their purview, purposes, and meanings — are produced and performed. Legal "truth," like historical "truth," comes out of specific cultural and social contexts, and exhibits a power contingent on its relationship to time and place. Thus it comes as no surprise, for example, that African Americans less than two centuries removed from legally legitimated and supported slavery would in many instances hold conceptualizations of law at odds with dominant, predominately white, courts and governmental agencies.

16

Viewed through these lenses of context and history, law has been and continues to be a key site for social and cultural conflict. What is deemed lawful, true, and trustworthy is defined as such within a particular discursive context. Although formal institutions continually invoke the "blind neutrality" and political independence of procedures and outcomes, law and its varied operations have no life independent from the discourses that constitute their authority and status. And certainly the same can be said of the vital components, such as evidence and testimony, of legal procedure and decision making. The relative importance and definition of these components are historic and dynamic.

Key to the maintenance and legitimation of state law's authority is its proclaimed detachment from the hurly-burly of political power. In a manner similar to official policy making, law is most often declared to be qualitatively different from politics. Mainstream discourses of law associate it, at least in the ideal, with rational, controlled, disinterested decision making, expert knowledge, and a concern for the general welfare. Law's autonomy is pronounced in its tidy detachment from other related social phenomena. Aligned with science, rationality, neutrality, and predictability, law is juxtaposed to a politics defined as narrowly partisan, uncertain, and self-interested. This is a pervasive construction that, according to Alan Hunt, "sees in the doctrine of separation of powers the most powerful ambition of liberal legal theory, namely, to ground and to secure a firm separation between law and politics."[37] On the other side, it is claimed, is politics, with its play of the wills, constant compromise, lack of expert insight, and privileging of special interests over the larger social good.[38]

Contemporary liberal discourses extract policy making and law from their historical place and reify processes that have demonstrated marked patterns of interest. These discourses fail to recognize law and policies as built within the frames of particular times and places, and instead encourage understanding of policy making and law as somehow escaping the dynamics and implications of social power. As I demonstrate here, within such discourses public claims are made regarding law's apolitical consistency, rationality, and objectivity that collapse under their own weight.[39]

Within recent years critical race scholarship has worked to circulate alternative understandings of history and law. At their foundation, these understandings break away from dominant legal liberalism through an embrace of counternarratives or "outsider" knowledges. They accept the standard teaching of street wisdom: law is essentially political.[40] Perhaps even more important, these practical, experiential knowledges are accompanied by a refusal to separate the politics of law from the politics of race, class, gender, and everyday life. In other words, law is recognized as more than the sum of its formal institutions — the sets of rules, courts, attorneys, bureaucracies, commissions, and policing and coercive state agencies. It is conceptualized as of a piece with dominant social formations, regulations, and practices that work in the exercise of social power.

Critical theorists of race and law such as Patricia Williams, Derrick Bell, and Kimberlé Crenshaw make the point that, in Crenshaw's words, "rather than providing some kind of firm ground to challenge racist institutional practices, formal notions of equality, objectivity, neutrality, and the like [have tended] to obscure the way that race is experienced by the vast majority of African Americans in this society."[41] To the degree such notions and grounding positivisms position African American stories and understandings as "subjective" and consistently "outside" the realm of "objective" legal frames, they operate as limiting knowledges and discourses. These critics point out that in the articulation of rulings and procedures privileging race or color blindness, contemporary liberal institutions fail to recognize the covert, as well as overt, social practices that constitute racism and instead offer formal alibis for a refusal to confront white supremacy.[42]

Critical theorists of race also argue that law as a dominant, legitimating narrative of omission and marginality cannot be ignored or left to its internal devices. Rather, progressive agents, employing strategic counternarratives, must undertake the decentering challenge of interrogating its privileged discourse.[43] Such an interrogation cannot be substantial without a fundamental rethinking of law and its contemporary conceptualizations, and this is where scholars from a variety of backgrounds and disciplines have focused their efforts. As Williams and Bell repeatedly point out, and as my project concretely demonstrates, what is "inside" and "outside" of law is one of the most fundamental and significant questions of legal study and analysis. Indeed the central, continual task of American legal and regulatory institutions is the legitimation of "law" via its redefinitions and delimitations. As mentioned earlier, the boundaries and definitions of "law" and "the legal" are always at stake.

Still, the question of what is inside or outside of law, or the closely related query of what is official or unofficial, is more complex than some theorists suggest. In part this is due to the nature and everyday operations of official legal institutions that produce complicated hierarchies of acceptance, inclusion, and power. As this study demonstrates, the binary oppositions of inside/outside and official/unofficial, while perhaps rhetorically effective and strategically important, also obscure as many legal power dynamics as they reveal. For example, as I investigated FCC materials and the volumes of papers deemed part of the agency's "official" report on WLBT-TV I found, not surprisingly, that not all official knowledges, or voices considered "inside" the formal hearings and judgments of the commission, were equally valued. Indeed, many African American voices were included in the official FCC dockets and station reports yet were almost entirely ignored, literally marginalized by relegation to document appendices or used only insofar as they legitimated commission decisions. While deemed "official" and "inside" the procedures and hearings of a dominant legal institution, such voices and perspectives were clearly marginalized in other ways. They may be considered "outsiders" allowed "inside," the unofficial become official, only to find that, as one media historian has put it, that "entrance is not acceptance," and further, "that acceptance itself is a problematic concept insofar as it requires an authority — that is, someone that can confer acceptance upon the supplicant."[44]

The histories surrounding Jackson television point to this enduring problem, as well as to the deeper racial dynamics at play. The dismissals or silencing of African American counternarratives and testimony described in this volume connect with other local instances today, calling attention not only to the elite, technocratic nature of state policy making and law and efforts to police their boundaries and definitions, but also to their historical whiteness.[45]

"DO YOU HAVE A FEAR OF KNOWING NOTHING ABOUT US?"

Although a central goal of this project is to broaden participation in the telling of historical stories and the making of contemporary cultural assessment, such a goal makes historiography more complex. Certainly not all of the stories offered to me aligned neatly with one another, which prompted difficult editorial decisions. Further, stories offered sometimes clashed with the documents stored in local archives, which prompted further editorial as well as evidentiary considerations. In making these historiographic decisions, I chose to highlight themes and concerns that converged in my reading of oral materials alongside long-ignored or marginalized sections of official documents. But in terms of where they disagree, both the archival document and the oral account offer productive perspectives on important pasts. Both reflect the disparate concerns and visions that must be addressed in a fuller understanding of race and politics in the contemporary United States. The search for common or converging themes should not obscure the value of studying such differences.

In recognizing my own role in the construction of the histories presented here, I have often reflected on how notions of racial progress informed my own perceptions and writing. Within post-Enlightenment Western cultural contexts such notions are commonly bound up with historiography and certainly with oral histories, because these projects necessarily speak to perceptions of the present, the past, and the ways in which change has occurred or "progressed." Still, as present/past comparisons of racial relations are foregrounded by white writers in dialogue with African Americans, it must be recognized that such comparisons are located within a longer history of whites asking blacks to assure them that things are indeed "getting better."

Certainly I could have been viewed as yet another historian looking for the reassurance of progress in American race relations. Undoubtedly this is a dynamic running through my project and the conversations that I represent here. Some interviewees told me forthrightly that I would receive historical accounts very different from those exchanged within the black community. In making such comments they highlighted, among other things, the dialogic dynamics of oral historiography.

What was striking to me was that even as a white outsider who might be viewed as one seeking reassurances of racial progress, I often did not receive them. Most often I was told that although the forms of oppression had changed and some opportunities had opened, the evidence of better times for African Americans was uneven and at times nonexistent. And, I was pointedly told, racial struggle continues. I frequently heard remarks made along the lines of those cited earlier by Aaron Shirley and Willie Lewis. Another interviewee, Henry Kirksey, was one of several black Mississippians who told me that although today racism is more dignified and "palatable," or not so much "out in the open," it is "like a cancer that's growing like hell and eating away and ultimately it will have a devastating effect, and it is already having that. . . ." Remembering his boyhood, Kirksey remarked, "It was difficult in those times for blacks, almost as difficult as it is today, and that's saying a hell of a lot."[46]

Kirksey, a former Mississippi state senator, underlined the fact that racial struggle continues today. He linked such conflicts, past and present, to a variety of contemporary institutions, including television — remarking, for instance, how poor blacks watch television with its advertisements for the middle class and "want some of what they see." And although lacking education and jobs, he continued, "there is another way — you can get a gun and you can get it." Again, he pointed to how the poorest neighborhoods of Jackson reap the violent consequences of representations not of their own making.

Kirksey also reminded me that local television's racist representations and practices were, and continue to be, thoroughly integrated with other experiences in everyday life involving employment, education, housing, voting, and economics. Instead of reassurances regarding the passing of old racisms and problems or discrimination, what I took away from my conversations with Henry Kirksey and others was an increased awareness of racism's complex and dynamic nature. Those who have long borne the brunt of racist power live with its subtle yet devastating appearances today, and they point to its presence. Others say that the United States, with a few exceptions on the extremes, is no longer plagued by systemic racism, and they point to the abolishment of legal segregation and other formal rules as proof. For many, the dominant myths of racial progress ring true, as do understandings of racism as monolithic — as something unchanging, obvious, and crass. But such understandings are, at best, dangerously naive. And listening to those who have experiences speaking to the consequences of fluid, dynamic, inferential racism is one way such understandings might be changed.

Talking with relative strangers at length regarding the past is a rewarding and taxing activity, fraught with historiographic and political problems, some of which I discuss in chapter 5. It is a most productive way of not only broadening historiography but also of widening the line of questions prioritized. I quickly discovered that the very best and most productive questions would come not from me but from those I interviewed; I then used these queries in subsequent conversations.

The questions asked by the interviewees demanded that I remain self-critical and reflexive in my interviewing. This was certainly ex-emplified when I first visited the home of Juanita Jefferson. Until her death Jefferson was a compassionate, strong figure in her neighbor-hood and local church, a longtime resident of Jackson who had worked alongside other black Mississippians in the sixties struggles. Her cour-age and commitment to her Christian faith, family, and social justice were clear from our first minutes of tentative acquaintance, and our mutual respect and friendship grew during the visits I made to Jackson. In 1992, after a few brief phone exchanges, we had the first of our long conversations in her living room, which ended with her inquiring about my position as a historian entering strange new homes:

Jefferson: You know I often wonder, and I'm serious, how do you all feel to come into our homes? Do you really feel comfortable or do you have a fear of knowing nothing about us? Can you kind of get a feel or imagination by talking on the phone to people or [do you have] fear of going into a home that you know nothing about? Now the reason I asked you that [is] because I have to kind of really talk to you to kind of get a feel before I feel comfortable to say "yes, you're welcome to come." See there has been a time that you received those calls, they were not good for you. And so I just wondered if you all as visitors to the state had that kind of feeling or felt that way, kind of go through a test.

Classen: Well, I think the main discomfort I feel is part of me . . . feels badly about coming into people's houses. Not so much because I'm afraid of being in their houses but because I wonder if it seems like an intrusion to them. You know a little bit of it . . . the history you're talking about, you know, where white people have often times kind of inserted their selves into black lives for bad purposes and I don't know if much of that exists any longer. But part of me feels like, here I am a historian coming and asking you to share part of your life with me. I'm saying I'd like you to tell me about your life and share your life with me. Well that's a pretty intimate thing.

Jefferson: A lot of them don't let you in do they?

Classen: Yes, some of them say no. . . . I say to people, "I don't want to steal something away from you that's precious, and if it feels uncomfortable for you, you shouldn't do it." And I don't know of any other way to write history other than doing this, but it has that risk involved of me saying "I'm going to take a part of your life," and that's the main thing I feel.

Jefferson: Well, you know, I admire you all's courage to go out to do this and the least I can do is share what little bit of knowledge I have about it with you, to let you know. Because you've never lived in Mississippi and you don't know what it's like to live here, and I have been here all my life. But as to that view, where are you from?

Classen: Wisconsin.

Jefferson: Wisconsin? How will the news get back there from somebody that has lived through it if somebody don't come in and ask for it? It has to be somebody to tell the news and it has to be somebody to pick up in Wisconsin and say, "Well I'm going to work to see that that does not happen here, we are not going to allow this to intrude and invade in on us and to crush people down as they have been in other states."[47]

I appreciated this bit of conversation at the end of a long interview, particularly for the generosity it made manifest. And this expression of goodwill epitomized much of my experience talking with Mississippians whom I did not know about a still-sensitive and painful past. Juanita Jefferson's desire to aid others at risk for "intrusion" and "invasion" outweighed the risk and intrusion that I represented coming to her home as an out-of-state stranger. We had talked on the phone on a few occasions until she felt comfortable inviting me into her home. She explained she had finally been able to imagine who I was, and had then felt comfortable making the invitation. She had imagined the relationship between two people of different ages, races, gender, and geography as one of alliance rather than opposition.

Looking at her question in retrospect, I did have more fear in those moments than I was willing to admit. Alongside my very awkwardly expressed fear of unethically appropriating the stories of others,[48] the stark poverty and physical conditions of some neighborhoods in Jackson also prompted my anxiety. I found the poverty in parts of Jackson startling, with its areas for public recreation and leisure in terrible disrepair. Many of those (although certainly not all) with upper-middle class or higher economic status left the city years ago. The suburbs, with their contemporary malls, new roads, and good public schools and well-funded private academies, welcomed the predominantly white professional upper-middle class as they moved away from Jackson. The consequences of such urban flight are sadly familiar across the United States, and Jackson is not exceptional in this regard, but such dynamics in an already poor state effectively further disadvantage those who have always been poor. This dilemma describes the material environment and situations for many remaining in predominately black west Jackson.[49]

When asked to compare the present to the sixties, Juanita Jefferson said "it's a lot better, but not what it could be, or should be." She talked about the problems outside her front door — including the crack dealers who would walk around outside her home and stand on a nearby corner, and the flooding that would occur periodically on her street and, just as routinely, be ignored by the city. She talked about how the high entrance fees to various fairs, clubs, and events continued to operate as a racial gate or point of discrimination, keeping African Americans outside even though such opportunities are ostensibly open to all. Jefferson's comments invited reflection on how "entrance fees" of various sorts discourage entry to various spaces, institutions, and properties. Thinking back on the lunch counter sit-ins of the 1960s, she remarked:

> Jefferson: They thought they were really going to stop it [the movement] if they were tough everywhere that blacks went to be served. But you know, it's not today what it could be, because so many places . . . you go in there, and we're not sitting together, and they will sell you the same food for one price and mine is another price, and my price is more than your price. Because I'm not wanted there, but they can't say "You can't come in," and they can't say, "You have to be served at the back door" anymore. There were many places, and I'm sure you've heard it from others, that you could not go to the front door to be served. You could not ride the city bus by going in the front door, you had to hand the driver your money and go to the back door to get on. . . .
>
> Classen: You say some of that still exists today? In terms of giving different prices to different people?
>
> Jefferson: Yes.
>
> Classen: So it's more subtle, but it still exists.
>
> Jefferson: Right, that's right. And in a lot of places the prices are so high — they know we can't afford to go there, because we don't have the money, because we don't make it.[50]

Having lived in Jackson's neighborhoods for almost fifty years, Jefferson's thoughtful comments, along with the others cited earlier, suggested to me that the substantive dialogue of whites and blacks regarding racial justice, while very rewarding in this instance, was not likely to occur in everyday life. Various segregations — economic, racial, and otherwise — continue to disincline citizens in Jackson and elsewhere to engage in dialogue across these social lines.

Such an observation underlines the dangers of the present, because interracial alliances and more substantive, frankly difficult, dialogues are vital to better address white supremacy and our nation's historical and contemporary investment in white privilege. And, before one reifies dialogue or attaches magical, salvific powers to the processes of human communication, it is paramount to recognize the historical position of whites as those who have listened too little and dictated too long the terms of interracial dialogue. Dialogue, for all of its positive and progressive potentials, can be thoroughly imperializing and oppressive. As Peters has remarked, communication is "more basically a political and ethical problem than a semantic or psychological one."[51]

In an admittedly partial way, I hope this project bears evidence of substantive dialogue and historiography that is synthetic — motivated by questions and concerns learned by listening and by encouraging consideration of media habituses very different from my own. Increasingly I am convinced that listening to historical stories that embed media practices within lives lived whole, and the contemporary questions they bring and prioritize — stories that connect television and industry practices to larger social contexts and recognized problems (e.g., poverty, crime, underemployment, healthcare access) — is one way that communication scholars and policy makers might evade some of the dead ends and limitations of existing historical and policy discourses. As I interpret some of the comments that follow in this study, they invite such conversations by questioning contested notions of racial identity and racial progress and by linking them to local broadcast ownership and programming responsibilities.[52]

Certainly such an approach cannot be disconnected from particular ends or goals. I am not proposing a "neutral" means of information gathering nor prioritizing such means over particular ends. As Ien Ang has reminded us, the scrutinizing of media audiences is never an innocent practice, and one "cannot afford ignoring the political dimensions of the *process* and practice of knowledge production itself."[53] On the contrary, I am proposing that concerned citizens and activists find ways to escape the deadening and detached legal liberalism that espouses "neutrality" — so evident in the communications policy mainstream — and with the goal of social change place a more holistic focus on enduring problems.

In the conclusion of *Television and New Media Audiences*, Ellen Seiter observes that social scientists, particularly anthropologists, have "bemoaned their lack of influence over policy matters," and she goes on to describe a series of recommendations to address this lack.[54] While Seiter's focus is on the connection of media ethnography and public policy, and while my project makes no claim to be social scientific or ethnographic, I share her interest in rethinking the relationship between reflective qualitative audience studies and policy making. Audience studies such as Seiter's, whether employing ethnography, oral histories, extended interviews, and/or other forms of substantive dialogue between the researcher and audience, represent the potential to revitalize and refocus "policy" research, prompting further investigation of alternative questions and perspectives. As she notes, media studies would be well served by adopting Clifford Gertz's research goal "to enlarge the possibility of intelligible discourse between people quite different from one another in interest, outlook, wealth, and power, and yet contained in a world where, tumbled as they are into endless connection, it is increasingly difficult to get out of each other's way."[55]

This project begins with an examination of specific civil rights and consumerist discourses in order to contextualize the early struggles over Jackson broadcasting. In the first chapter I provide a brief historical overview of early Jackson television and the cultural, political, and other institutions that influenced its construction, including the Citizens' Council (founded in Indianola, Mississippi) and the notorious Mississippi State Sovereignty Commission. I also introduce the early petitions and efforts made to change local programming practices.

In the second chapter, "Consuming Civil Rights," I specifically examine how the disparate discourses of sixties consumerism intersected with concerns regarding race and civil rights in the legal challenges to, and court considerations of, WLBT-TV licensing. This examination of popular consumerist discourses and their articulation in a widely read 1966 U.S. Court of Appeals decision shows how conflicting consumerisms were mediated by legal institutions in an attempt to address increasing social and racial tensions. Further, it demonstrates how the dominant discourses of liberal consumerism, pronounced in the halls of lawmaking, formally displaced issues of race.

In chapter 3, "Trouble around the Ponderosa," the struggle over "consumerism" is moved from the spaces of federal courtrooms to the streets, fairgrounds, and performance halls of Jackson. In the chapter I trace the early years of the Jackson Movement, a local direct-action effort organized and carried out by activists primarily on the fronts of consumer rights and popular culture, including a discussion of the varied movement communication strategies. One campaign allied with this movement, which was initiated by a handful of Tougaloo College students and staff under the name the Culture and Arts Committee, receives particular attention as a grassroots intervention mounted with very limited sources and planning yet with significant impact, including dramatic consequences for local public entertainment, television advertising, and viewing.[56] For example, one production targeted by the Tougaloo activists was *Bonanza* — one of the most popular television series of the sixties — and this chapter describes how the program became a cultural touchstone for key political players and dialogues regarding changing race relations in south-central Mississippi. By focusing on these interventions I make the point that the legal challenges aimed at WLBT and WJTV were integrally connected with other struggles on the terrain of popular culture, and that television had considerable significance for integrationist efforts outside the narrow questions of journalistic representations and broadcast licensing.

Chapter 4, "Programming/Regulating Whiteness," moves chronologically to 1964 and to a specific discussion of WLBT's programming and the complaints that African Americans lodged against local television. Through an examination of these popular and legal texts, as well as formal and informal grievances, I offer a glimpse into the common, enduring strategies of white supremacy and supremacist representations of race. I also offer a critique of the official handling and dismissal of black complaints, through my examination of the Federal Communication Commission's official responses to the marginalized voices and perspectives of local African Americans. With this focus I demonstrate how ostensibly neutral, expert-centered policy making works as a technology for the constitution of race and racialized subjects.[57] A "genealogical" study is offered, explaining how institutions of law make thoroughly political decisions regarding the nature of evidence and proof while formally denying considerations of everyday contexts, social power, and race by basing their rulings on assumptions that provide formal justifications for the dismissal of particular voices and perspectives.

Moving away from the examination of the "official" legal texts, in the next chapter I offer the memories, perspectives, and concerns of activist Mississippians regarding historical struggles on multiple cultural fronts, including those of local broadcasting. Chapter 5 is based on more than two dozen extended interviews and oral histories that I recorded in Mississippi primarily during the summers of 1992 and 1993. In light of these histories I offer a discussion of how African Americans watched white supremacist television, talked about it in their own communities, and viewed its evolution. While the questions I initiated were narrowly focused on local media practices, the subsequent queries and remarks of those I met are reminders that television and radio are but parts of a whole, a habitus, and that television is indeed not simply consumed but rather is actively made and remade within people's lives: that is, something that people do.

Chapter 5 begins with a discussion of popular memory, dialogue, and historiography. The interview excerpts that follow illustrate some of the dynamics attendant to oral history, but they also provide a glimpse into the historical contexts in which local television and popular culture became fronts for progressive social change. Memories of the WLBT challenge, the legal and FCC interventions, as well as the evolution of local television are foregrounded. Among the concerns raised is how racial identities are defined and connected to issues of property — particularly media properties and licensing. The voices in this chapter repeatedly remind readers how the past and present are thoroughly intertwined and imbricated within the other. Or, more poetically, as Mississippian William Faulkner penned: "The past is never dead. It's not even past."[58]

In chapter 6 I conclude by taking a brief look at the rapid changes and challenges in Jackson's local television market, especially in light of the problem of declining minority broadcast ownership. There, I return to a focus on the historical discourses of consumerism, looking at the implications of this activity more than three decades after the sixties consumer movement. In particular, I highlight the complexities and pitfalls within consumerist discourses, as well as the strategic employ-

Watching Jim Crow

ments of dominant "consumer" nominations and discourses during the period, and the refusal to be limited or contained within them.

The stories of struggle surrounding Jackson television are multiple and rich with meanings, and they provide narratives of hope for progressive movements alongside clear acknowledgments of the barriers and obstacles to such change. And, amid their hopes and cautions, they consistently remind us how race and racialized identities are bound up with the practices that constitute U.S. television as we know it today.

CHAPTER 1

Broadcast Foundations

During the mid-fifties as the black freedom fight prodded some institutions, cities, and states toward progressive change, Mississippi, in the words of one activist, "stood still."[1] In the wake of the Supreme Court's 1954 *Brown v. Board of Education* decision, which made de jure school segregation illegal, the strident proponents of the segregationist status quo retrenched, white-on-black violence escalated, and efforts were redoubled to establish the state as a virtually unassailable bastion of white supremacy.[2]

In response to the *Brown* decision, Mississippi's segregationist Citizens' Council quickly formed. The council rapidly grew in size as well as in political, social, and economic power to become one of white segregation's most important social formations. According to Charles Marsh, it "rallied around the notion that the South had again become a victim of ravenous federal expansion."[3] The trope of "invasion" was regularly and passionately invoked, referring to incursions by the federal government, northerners, and others outside Mississippi, soliciting memories of a devastated southern culture and landscape scarred by the Civil War. By March 1955, 167 local Citizens' Councils were reported in Mississippi, loosely affiliated into a state organization.[4] Within two years the group boasted a membership of eighty thousand and was publishing a newspaper, the *Citizens' Council*, and after 1961, a journal, the *Citizen*, which "offered a wide range of pro-segregationist opinion, from Paul Harvey reprints to quasi-scientific accounts of black inferiority to biblical defenses of white supremacy."[5] Federal Bureau of Investigation director J. Edgar Hoover, certainly no friend to civil rights activists, described local Citizens' Councils as new organizations that "could control the rising tension or become a medium through which tensions might manifest themselves."[6] If by "controlling the rising tension" Hoover meant that the use of intimidation and coercion might silence some rights activism, he was prescient on both counts — the council worked to both "control" and inflame racial tensions.

In Jackson the council quickly grew in power and prominence, and enjoyed having some of its most vocal and powerful supporters in positions of media management. Frederick Sullens, editor of the *Jackson Daily News*, spoke for many angry Mississippians when, in response to the *Brown* decree, he said, "Mississippi will not obey the decision. If an effort is made to send Negroes to school with white children, there will be bloodshed. The stains of that bloodshed will be on the Supreme Court steps."[7] As many Mississippians, including some whites, celebrated the Court's statement, viewing it as, according to Myrlie Evers, a "voice of change, of impending liberation, of challenge to the central fact of any Negro's life," white supremacists "developed a siege mentality so pervasive it encompassed virtually every citizen and institution."[8] In Mississippi in the mid-to-late fifties a "racial orthodoxy" and "homegrown McCarthyism" flourished, consistently reinvigorated by media managers such as Sullens.[9]

In response to systemic repression and escalating violence within the state, efforts at "winning the franchise" stalled. The number of registered black voters shrank. Several prominent black leaders were forced out of Mississippi after finding themselves repeatedly targeted by financial institutions and/or violent thugs. As Sam Bailey, one of Medgar Evers's closest friends and an early NAACP activist, explained to me early in this project: "All the segregated laws that you had, and anytime when a white man killed a Negro, he got more time for killing a rabbit. All seasons were for killing a Negro in Mississippi."[10] Facing such terror, NAACP branches around the state began to disintegrate.[11] The Reverend George Lee, Lamar Smith, and Emmett Till were killed, and Till's case drew widespread, even international, press attention. Still, none of these men's killers were convicted of their crimes. Reflecting on the murder of fourteen-year-old Till, Anne Moody wrote in her 1971 autobiography, *Coming of Age in Mississippi*, that "before Emmett Till's murder, I had known the fear of hunger, hell and the Devil. But now there was a new fear known to me — the fear of being killed just because I was black. This was the worst of my fears. . . . I didn't know what one had to do or not to do as a Negro not to be killed. Probably you just being a Negro period was enough, I thought."[12]

Even in the midst of such fearful times the hard-fought gains and

Watching Jim Crow

spirit of empowerment founded in the earlier years of rights struggle could not be quickly snuffed out. As historian Charles Payne has observed, a focus on the decimation of Mississippi's activist leadership during these years is misleading, "obscuring the fact that the return on racist violence was actually diminishing. . . . Blacks could still be intimidated but not as easily or as completely as had been the case."[13]

Contrary to the impression left by many sixties civil rights histories, the *Brown* decision, cheered as it was by many African Americans, was often viewed as a less important catalyst for black activism than the 1955 murder of fourteen-year-old Emmett Till and its mediated treatments. Amzie Moore, perhaps the most highly regarded and enduring leader of rights activism in the Mississippi delta, dated the beginning of the modern movement in the state from the time of the Till trial, and many younger black activists identified themselves as the Till generation.[14] Graphic pictures and descriptions of the Till murder and trial circulated in popular magazines like *Jet* and *Look*, as well as in large daily newspapers, prompting readers to further involvement in the struggle. Joyce Ladner, a student worker active with the Hattiesburg NAACP during the fifties, remembers looking at the *Jet* photos and that "we asked each other, 'How could they do that to him? He's only a boy.' "[15] Press coverage of the tragedy and injustice cast Mississippi's segregation in a new light, and to a larger, more diverse audience. Journalist David Halberstam has called the Till murder "the first great media event of the civil rights movement."[16]

Certainly as early as the Till trial, prominent white supremacists recognized such popular media coverage as problematic and, in turn, learned the value of informational and representational control. Key segregationist groups, such as the Citizens' Council, understood representations of Mississippi outside of Mississippi as vital to in-state operations. Thus, for example, when press accounts announced that CBS-TV planned to air a Rod Serling–authored *Playhouse 90* loosely fictionalizing the Till tragedy, the program's sponsor, U.S. Steel, was quickly targeted by nearly three thousand letters of segregationist complaint. According to the *Pittsburgh Courier*, Serling's script was subsequently "cut, revised, and twisted because of U.S. Steel's fear of economic pressure."[17] Serling complained that his script had been chopped up in an environment that was "like a room full of butchers with a steer."[18] Branches of the Citizens' Council responded enthusiastically, editorializing that "all objectionable TV shows could be eliminated if more people would write their protests to the sponsors of these shows . . . [We] wish to thank . . . members and friends who helped in protesting against this proposed anti-South, pro-Negro propaganda show."[19]

Complementing such national and network-targeted efforts, a network of Mississippi radio stations, along with Jackson's two highest circulation dailies, formed a crucial part of what University of Mississippi professor James Silver termed the "vigilant guard over the racial, economic, political, and religious orthodoxy of the closed society."[20] Bolstering this guard, two new Jackson television stations, WJTV and WLBT, came on air, playing a major part in the campaign for "massive white resistance."

Both stations were licensed and began service in 1953, following the 1948–1952 federal freeze on licensing new stations by the FCC. Because of the freeze, it was not until this relatively late date that the southern states of Mississippi, Arkansas, and South Carolina enjoyed operative television transmitters,[21] and Jackson residents, particularly business leaders, publicly expressed excitement regarding the potentials of local TV.[22] As early as 1951, Wiley Harris, manager of Jackson's first radio stations, WJDX and WJDX-FM, met with P. K. Lutken Sr., president of Lamar Life Insurance Company, to consider a TV station for Jackson and to begin readying for the postfreeze licensing process.[23] Having made such preparations, in the three years following the FCC freeze Mississipians rapidly built six television stations, the first of which were WJTV and WLBT in Jackson and WCOC in Meridian. On 22 October 1952 the *Jackson Clarion-Ledger* proclaimed that "WJTV will alter the patterns in Jackson life," and the station's first general manager, John Rossitor, anticipating the outlet's inaugural broadcast, told city leaders and educators that television would "bring the world into your home and accent friendliness among neighbors in this city and state." In January 1953, WJTV began broadcasting on UHF channel 25 (later moving to VHF channel 12) as the state's first television station. On 28 December of the same year, WLBT-TV began local service on channel three.

The CBS-affiliated WJTV was built and owned by newspaper money — namely, the Hederman family's Mississippi Publishers Association, owner of the *Jackson Daily News*, the *Clarion-Ledger*, and the *Hattiesburg American*. Thomas and Robert Hederman were powerful businessmen, not only by overseeing the state's wide-circulation

Lamar Life Broadcasting signs a contract in 1959 with Ideco Company to build a new, more powerful antenna. Left to right: J. Roger Hayden, Ideco Company; P. T. Lutken, president of the Lamar Life Broadcasting Company; Fred L. Beard, general manager of WLBT and WJDX; and John L. Pausch, Ideco Company.

dailies but also by serving as presidents of the Jackson Chamber of Commerce and as members of multiple corporate and educational boards.[24] The owner of WLBT, which ran primarily NBC network fare, was Lamar Life Insurance and Lamar Life Broadcasting — two local corporate entities owned, quietly and at a distance, by the Murchison brothers of Dallas, Texas. Closer to home, the station included among its prominent and politically connected board members Robert Hearin, chairman of the First National Bank of Jackson. As television operations began at channel three, Fred L. Beard succeeded a retiring Wiley Harris as the general manager of WJDX radio and WLBT-TV.

The local managers of WLBT and WJTV were definitely competitors, and not always on the friendliest of terms as broadcast operations began. Early on in their contest for television dominance, the Hedermans were angrily accused of censoring programming information submitted to the Jackson dailies by the staff of WLBT.[25] The easy access of

WJTV to, and use of, the state's most prominent dailies was a point of contention. However, on the topic of the overriding concern of racial segregation and preservation of the southern "way of life," the two media corporations were steadfast allies. Dominant racial politics were even inscribed in the new station architectures. A *Jackson Daily News* article announcing the new WLBT studios reported "the new building is one of the finest television-radio installations in the South. . . . In the center of the building is a large studio for audience programs which can seat 100 persons on the ground floor and 150 more in a special viewing balcony enclosed with glass. . . . Another unique feature of the station is private dressing rooms and viewing platform for Negro performers so that they may visit the station and take a dignified part in its activities."[26]

The Citizens' Council was thoroughly ensconced throughout local media management. The Hederman family continually highlighted and worked to naturalize council positions via the airwaves and print. At WLBT, General Manager Beard, a particularly outspoken council member, was often perceived as exceptionally militant in his beliefs and expressions, but held a position of leadership in the Jackson branch of the council. Some of Beard's braggadocio ultimately undermined his passionate cause.

This is not to say that there were not significant political and ideological differences among white Mississippians. Some, for example, distanced themselves from public firebrands such as Beard, but felt powerless to resist the racial and cultural orthodoxy of the time. Class position, political affiliations, and religious alliances separated whites in significant ways. Ku Klux Klan members and other radical segregationists were routinely considered less than respectable and lawful by the primarily middle-class supporters of the Citizens' Council. And there were also divides between conservative segregationists and self-identified "moderates" who believed that segregation was unjust or just economically unsound, but who were uncomfortable with a full embrace of integration. Thus, even while such differences existed their practical manifestation remained widespread white support for the segregationist status quo.[27]

With widespread white support, and their handpicked men at the helm of local media, the Citizens' Council attempted both to guard powerful communication outlets and to reproduce "respectability" for its race-based politics. The council's strategy was to thwart integration by using the legitimated institutions of traditional party politics, law, and journalism. Citizens' Council director W. J. Simmons maintained regular communications with Fred Beard and other media managers. Years after leaving WLBT, Beard testified that council leaders would frequently call the station to complain about NBC or other network programming and ask for airtime to present opposing views. In response to such "respectable" racist activism, black activists such as Medgar Evers, Mississippi's NAACP field secretary, sometimes remarked that the council was "the Klan in suits."[28]

In 1955, the state council organization started producing fifteen-minute films under the moniker of Citizens' Council Forum Films. The films were made in a talk-format series titled *Citizens' Council Forum*, and were distributed as a syndicated TV program throughout the United States. The program, which was obsessed with the combined "threats" of racial integration and communism, had direct ties to Mississippi state government and was allocated tens of thousands of taxpayer dollars during its first years of existence, including, of course, tax dollars from black taxpayers. By 1961 council director Simmons issued unconfirmed reports that the *Forum*, in radio or television format, was shown or heard on more than three hundred stations in forty-one states.[29]

Forum, which used "Dixie" as its musical theme and nominated itself as "America's number-one public affairs program," usually featured interviews with politicians, segregationist leaders, and authors. Its televised version began with a graphic logo of American and Confederate flags criss-crossed and encircled by the words "state's rights, racial integrity." One of its standard ending segments announced: "We Americans are threatened with the loss of many of our hard won freedoms: The historic right of each sovereign state to govern itself without interference from political courts; the right of the individual to choose his associates without the prodding of federal bayonets; and the right of each citizen to make up his mind in the American way, free from propaganda."[30] Given Mississippi's "closed society," this last statement was rich with irony. But the reproduction of such themes did reiterate a sense of federal invasion and national disrespect sincerely perceived.

The program worked to bring high-status defenders of Mississippi's "state's rights" before the camera and microphone. Clearly, the show's agenda was not only focused on the distribution of white supremacist information but also on the provision of credibility and respectability to such arguments. *Forum* used an aesthetically simple interview format in which producer Dick Morphew would appear with one or more noted conservative spokespersons. Although structured in a fashion similar to network news panels or public affairs offerings, the program was very narrow in topical scope and consistently offered discussions of integration and communism veiled within the language of "state's rights" concerns. The program also offered a frequent critical focus on northern or federal "threats," as well as the problem of northern "news management." The guest list included personalities such as scientist Carleton Putnam, author of a treatise on black inferiority; the U.S. Senate's anti–civil rights point men, Strom Thurmond and John Stennis; and Edward Hunter, chairman of the Anti-Communist Liaison, who made an appearance to discuss "news management by communist sympathizers."

In order to work as an official organ alongside these council efforts, in 1956 the State of Mississippi created the Sovereignty Commission, with a mandate "to do and perform any and all acts and things deemed necessary and proper to protect the sovereignty of the State of Mississippi, and her sister states, from encroachment thereon by the Federal Government."[31] Despite the claim by some that this creation of the Mississippi legislature was not originally intended to "operate with a CIA mentality," once in operation the commission was quickly recognized as serving two primary, interrelated functions for white power — public relations and surveillance.[32]

The Sovereignty Commission was perhaps best known, and feared, for its spying activities. Commission files recently opened by court order have revealed to the wider public the terribly widespread, vulgar, and damaging nature of commission surveillance and misinformation. The state agency amassed reports and files on tens of thousands of citizens, many containing investigator or informant speculation or hearsay regarding sexual practices, infidelities, and "illegitimate" children, as well as other assorted behavior marked as deviant. Alongside this surveillance, the commission also spent considerable resources trying to rehabilitate public impressions of "Mississippi." It carefully scrutinized, and intervened in, popular media representations of the state and its segregationist fight.

Throughout the fifties and sixties Sovereignty Commission communication efforts spoke of a "Paper Curtain" existing in America. In

Governor J. P. Coleman and WLBT news director Dick Sanders discuss election returns in 1956.

Framing the South, Allison Graham explains this metaphor's motivating anxieties: "Like the Iron Curtain in Eastern Europe, the Paper Curtain was the creation of communist-inspired ideologues, an impenetrable wall of lies extending along the north side of the Mason-Dixon Line. Hollywood, not surprisingly, was a member of the Paper Curtain conspiracy, filling its movies with subversive white degeneracy, black superiority, and even miscegenation."[33]

In attempting to work behind the "curtain," Sovereignty Commission directors made a point to socialize with, and lobby, television network and journalism leaders, such as the National Editors Association, for positive or "corrective" portrayals of Mississippi.[34] In addition, public relations emissaries were sent to northern states to give lectures regarding the virtues of "the most lied about state in the Union."[35]

On request from the commission the only newspapers available statewide, the Jackson *Daily News* and the Jackson *Clarion-Ledger* (with a combined circulation of approximately ninety thousand), routinely terminated news stories deemed "dangerous" to state "sovereignty" and published materials attacking integrationist efforts.[36] As owners and publishers of both dailies, the Hedermans worked closely with Sovereignty Commission directors. One commission director, Erle Johnston, frequently supplied the Jackson newspapers with commission-written stories and editorials, as well as advice to editors such as Jimmy Ward at the *Daily News* on how to address and frame new civil rights events. Sovereignty Commission files also show that Tom Hederman of the *Clarion-Ledger* regularly received the confidential reports of at least one commission director and expressed concern when such documents were not made immediately available to him.[37]

Much the same could be said for the relationship of the commission to Jackson's television and radio stations, as various state organizations coordinated their activities with cooperative station managers and scrutinized broadcast representations of the integration fight. The stations commonly recycled on-air versions of the Hederman press. This was particularly blatant on WJTV, as long-time newscaster/weatherman Bob Neblett made a regular practice of reading and commenting on *Daily News* or *Clarion-Ledger* articles — in ways still remembered within Jackson's black community as particularly noxious. In such a climate, verbalized threats of censorship, penalties, or intimidation from segregationist state agents were not the daily norm for broadcasters or newspaper workers. As a former Mississippi resident put it, the state government "did not resort to the heavy-handed tactics [of controlling media content] employed in totalitarian societies: censorship laws, troops storming newspaper offices, jailing or killing editors who did not follow the party line. It did not have to."[38]

It was in this environment, and against such powerful coalitions, that Medgar and Myrlie Evers, Aaron Henry, Ruby Hurley, Ruby Stutts Lyells, Reverend R. L. T. Smith, Amzie Moore, Gus Courts, Dr. T. R. M. Howard, and Reverend George Lee, along with other black residents of Mississippi, continued their fight, in alliance with a small number of white Mississippians, for full citizenship and civil rights.[39] In the mid-fifties, in the aftermath of the *Brown* decision and the Till murder, Jackson television was just in its infancy, but many, including those in the Citizens' Council as well as newly appointed NAACP field secretary Medgar Evers, had imagined what local television might become.

Watching Jim Crow

The disparate campaigns in the sixties for civil rights across the South were not solely carried out by a few national charismatic leaders, although these figures often served vital, courageous roles. Rather, the campaigns primarily were the work of less-publicized local activists and citizens, many of whom have neither produced official records nor been the subject of official historiographical focus.

Existing accounts of broadcasting and sixties civil rights change, with a focus on media professionals (such as brave journalists) and national movement leaders, routinely fail to recognize local or less-publicized activities and activists. Certainly the televised campaigns of Martin Luther King Jr., Stokley Carmichael, Malcolm X, and other black leaders, as well as network coverage, were crucial to social change, but the less-publicized efforts laid foundations for the national exposures, leaders, and campaigns. To understand the relations of broadcast representations to civil rights it is essential to historicize the mediated struggles of the sixties by acknowledging earlier campaigns, in the fifties, conducted by a handful of deeply committed integrationists and African Americans who attempted to attract the attention of the national television networks and use local media to attack Jim Crow.

For example, in Mississippi both Medgar Evers and his brother Charles were part of these early efforts. Both served in the military during World War II and returned to their home state with a renewed determination to challenge white supremacist segregation. Charles became one of the state's first black disc jockeys at a small radio station in Philadelphia (northeast of Jackson), where he used his on-air opportunity to regularly exhort the African American community to claim their franchise too long denied: to pay their poll taxes, register, and vote. Evidence of Evers's impact came quickly, and white retaliation against the disc jockey and his employer began immediately — Evers was threatened with assassination and forced to resign after a short on-air term. Still, his activism helped empower local black citizens in Mississippi in the fifties, and as a leader in the black voter registration drive he was acknowledged as at least partially responsible for the addition of an estimated two hundred names to the voting rolls in one of the state's most militantly white supremacist regions.[40]

In the years preceding his assassination, Medgar Evers also directly challenged the powerful cultural institutions of segregationist Mississippi. After accepting the assignment of NAACP field secretary in 1954, Evers gathered and publicized reports about racial injustice throughout the state. During the late fifties, as Mississippi seemingly "stood still," Myrlie Evers remembers her husband worked tirelessly to bring the battle for local civil rights to the attention of journalists and local broadcast stations. She has written that Medgar "literally dragged reporters to the scenes of crimes"[41] and continually issued press releases that countered segregationist narratives. Increasingly, during the late fifties and early sixties, the national and network press came to recognize Evers as an important information resource. National and network reporters called him from out of state following up on reports of dramatic violence, and the Evers name became integrally attached to the integrationist fight in Mississippi.[42]

Evers also fought on the legal and regulatory front by establishing a record of complaint against Jackson broadcasters that would later be mobilized to affect significant change. The NAACP's traditionally conservative approach to Jim Crow emphasized changing laws before taking direct action. In Mississippi, this meant that some serious miscalculations were made regarding the effectiveness of legally based campaigns — miscalculations that underestimated the power, threat, and ready illegality of white resistance while also overestimating the federal government's commitment to segregation's end.[43] Evers was frustrated as the NAACP national office largely withdrew from his state, refocusing its energies and resources on more immediately promising regions and simultaneously discouraging efforts to cooperate with other civil rights groups.[44]

Still, Evers and others recognized the representations offered by the popular press and broadcast outlets as key to their fight, and they sought ways to change existing media practices. Following the NAACP's focus on the enforcement of law and regulations, Evers and his NAACP colleagues began in the mid-fifties filing challenges to segregationist broadcasting practices.

In 1955 J. Francis Pohlhaus, counsel for the Washington bureau of the NAACP, filed letters of complaints with the FCC against WLBT-TV and its companion radio stations, WJDX-AM and WJDX-FM, requesting, among other things, that the FCC take action toward revoking the stations' licenses. The civil rights organization argued that the general manager of the stations, Fred Beard, should be investigated immediately because he was "incapable of operating a station in the public interest." In support of this assertion were published accounts of Beard protesting the NBC network decision to present a black actor in a leading role in a dramatic program, and of Beard complaining that radio and TV were "overloading the circuits with Negro propaganda." Also in these accounts was the report that the general manager had bragged to the Jackson Citizens' Council that he had "cut off" an NBC *Home* program segment with NAACP attorney Thurgood Marshall by disguising the intentional interruption as a technical problem with a televised "sorry, cable trouble" sign.[45]

The NAACP argued that these stations were not serving the public interest and had clearly failed the "fairness" test of providing coverage or spokespersons for both sides of publicly important controversial issues. Management of WLBT replied that the station had tried to maintain a "hands-off" policy on the issues of segregation and integration by refusing to provide airtime to either side in the debate. In part the station reply letter read: "The policy not to provide time to either group was established by both television stations (WLBT & WJTV) in this market to prevent the stations from becoming involved in this issue."[46] For its part, the FCC took no significant action in response to the petition. Instead, the commission stated that the complaint would be considered when WLBT next filed an application for renewal of their regular license in 1958.

The Jackson stations seemed unfazed by this initial legal challenge, and they continued to practice a "curious neutrality" in addressing racial integration.[47] For example, in September 1957, immediately after President Dwight Eisenhower appeared on national television to explain his actions supporting the integration of a school in Little Rock, Arkansas, WLBT and WJDX omitted the national anthem that traditionally started each broadcast day and in its place aired spot advertisements for the Citizens' Council that warned: "Don't let this happen in Mississippi, join the Citizens' Council today."[48] The elimination of the anthem was a gesture steeped in meaning, because it came at a time when segregationist Mississippians were increasingly of the view that governments outside their own state were against them; that those outside Mississippi were not fellow citizens but rather malevolent interlopers threatening to break apart a cherished, distinctive way of life.

Shortly after the national anthem incident, in response to the stations' thinly veiled politics and a particular instance of supremacist ventriloquism, field secretary Evers again petitioned the FCC and WLBT-TV. In October 1957, in response to the airing of *The Little Rock Crisis* — a program featuring a panel of established segregationist politicians, including Mississippi senator James Eastland — Evers requested that a "group of Mississippi Negroes" be given airtime to "accurately and pointedly express the feelings of the Negro on this very vital issue." Evers pointed out that the original show had three white men expressing "what the Negro wants and doesn't want" regarding racial integration.[49] WLBT flatly denied Evers time.

In 1959 the FCC published its response to these programming concerns. In this licensing review of the 1955 and 1957 complaints the commission echoed their 1955 decision, opting to take no significant action against WLBT but instead renewing the broadcaster's license while admitting that the station's past programming content was "not entirely clear." The commission secretary wrote that the body had concluded that the station's "isolated honest breaches" of the commission's fairness doctrine did not warrant license revocation or further commission action.[50] The commission's response reaffirmed both its historical alliance with the broadcast industry as well as its particular ways of "knowing." Basing its judgment on admittedly incomplete knowledges, absent of any investigation or hearings, the regulators comfortably defaulted to the status quo. Of course, the omission of black Mississippians from local broadcast programs were far from "isolated honest breaches," as any serious opponent of segregation could, and later would, testify. But such testimony and lived experience, as I show in the next chapter, were routinely ignored or discounted as a legitimate way of knowing, suffering from its lack of conformity with bureaucratic "fact finding."

After failing to receive airtime through the regulatory appeal process, Evers also petitioned the industry directly, contacting not only Mississippi newspapers and broadcast stations but also prominent national periodicals and television programs, arguing that "the plight of the Mississippi Negro" was not well understood. For example, in 1958 Evers wrote to Dave Garroway of NBC's *Today* program, requesting an opportunity to appear on the show. Evers's specific argument was that Mississippi's governor and WLBT's news director had, in concert with other southern whites, offered only a "distorted and slanted" view of the conditions faced by black Mississippians. "The Negro's point of view," as the field secretary put it, was not being seen or heard in local or network presentations.[51]

But even national and network press attention was not easily gained. As Myrlie Evers later wrote, the problem her husband confronted was that the northern as well as southern press dismissed Mississippi's brutality toward African Americans as an "old story . . . unless there were some new twist to make it newsworthy."[52] The struggles and brutalities within Jim Crow were indeed old, but just as old was the limited range of televised voices and perspectives offering description and analysis. Throughout the fifties and into the first years of the sixties, the rarity of televised black personalities discussing this oppression made their appearance an incredibly, almost shockingly, powerful new experience for television viewers, particularly in some Deep South states.

Evers persisted in his requests. In July 1962, in response to the *Citizens Council Forum* program, he wrote to WLBT manager Beard again requesting airtime. Evers evoked the legal force of the FCC's fairness doctrine, which obligated stations providing commentary on controversial issues of public importance to make reasonable opportunities available for "opposing points of view." Evers argued that a definite point of view was represented by *Forum*, and that "both sides of the issue [of integration] should be aired." In correspondence with Evers and the FCC, the station simply claimed that integration had not been addressed on *Forum* but rather only discussions of "state's rights" and presentations by "personalities of current interest to the American people." In response to the station's refusal, Evers began to hint at the larger legal challenges the station would soon come to face, writing that "our application for equal time will be appealed to the highest authority."[53]

Meanwhile, Evers's colleague in the fight for airtime, the Reverend R. L. T. Smith, was running for elected office and thus making frequent appeals to those in high authority. In 1961 the Jackson grocer and minister declared himself the first black candidate for the U.S. Congress from Mississippi since Reconstruction, and he approached local television stations WLBT and WJTV regarding the purchase of political campaign airtime. Late in the year WJTV aired candidate Smith's thirty-minute presentation, including his explicit call for black voters to pay poll taxes and register to vote. When Smith approached WLBT station manager Fred Beard, the latter not only refused to sell Smith the time sought, but vaguely threatened the minister and suggested that he should run his campaign by appearing and speaking only at black churches. In response, Smith took his campaign request to powerful Washington institutions and politicians in letters that also noted that WJTV was now resistant to selling him more time, following WLBT's lead. After months of appeals to the FCC, the National Democratic Party, President Kennedy, and others including Eleanor Roosevelt, the station felt enough pressure to relent and grant Smith airtime.[54] Candidate Smith was given thirty minutes on WLBT on 4 June 1962 — one day before the congressional elections, which he lost to archsegregationist incumbent John Bell Williams.

These official legal petitions and challenges by Smith and Evers, following the model of legal remedy long established by the NAACP, provided powerful and empowering images of articulate African Americans to audiences, but offered only an extremely small representation of black discontent with the segregationist status quo. Evers and Smith certainly were not the only black Mississippians fighting against Jim Crow, but both were frustrated by the lack of support from others within Jackson's clergy and black middle class. Scores of black Jacksonians stayed a considerable distance away from the NAACP, Evers, and the direct-action campaigns. The risks of visible opposition to supremacist segregation were evident everywhere — not only to individuals but to entire families. But Evers and Smith, with others highlighted in this volume, opted to take very public, vulnerable positions of leadership because they were deeply convinced that popular mass media would be a powerful instrument in their fight against injustice.

By 1963, defamatory segregationist images of Evers and his integration campaign were in wide circulation. However, his voice was virtually never heard in mainstream media within the state unless it was via a Citizens' Council production that decontextualized and caricatured the leader, placing him in the most unflattering and threatening of poses. So it was consequential and unsettling to the segregationist status quo when Evers, in one of his most visible actions, formally challenged, and appeared on, WLBT-TV in 1963 as part of a campaign for increased desegregation in Jackson.[55]

On this date, many Mississippians heard the NAACP leader speak, in his own voice, for the first time. White segregationists who had never allowed "Negroes" in their living rooms watched an articulate black

Watching Jim Crow

Mississippian come into their homes in a direct address. Evers was calm, poised, and eloquent in his aired presentation. Speaking in response to the previously aired address of Jackson mayor Allen Thompson, Evers concluded: "But whether Jackson and the state choose change or not, the years of change are upon us. In the racial picture things will never be as they once were. History has reached a turning point, here and over the world. Here in Jackson we can recognize the situation and make an honest effort to bring fresh ideas and new methods to bear, or we can have what Mayor Thompson called 'turbulent times.' "[56] Such early black activism provided precedents and temporary tactical openings that could be exploited later in the sixties as the challenges against local Jackson television were argued in the more formal, and often distant, spaces of officialdom. As both Medgar and Charles Evers knew early on, broadcasting and regulation of the airwaves were vital to the struggle not only over the representation of race and rights but over a different way of life.

Certainly this struggle was not confined neatly to Jackson or Mississippi. Troubling patterns of racial representation had emerged during the early years of television, not only in local southern markets but also on the national scene. As the Kerner Commission study summarized in its statement to President Johnson, viewers of network and local television had, among other things, seen a world that was "almost totally white in both appearance and attitude."[57] And as the commission went on to note, not only was the visibility of African Americans generally low, but when blacks did appear on the screen they were represented as whites saw them, not as they saw themselves.[58]

Such observations had uncanny salience in Mississippi and throughout the South. Especially as civil rights conflict and change increased throughout the region, the strategy of omitting or ignoring integrationist or black perspectives grew in practice. Some individuals reflecting on that time have remarked that audiences often would not have known of civil rights activism within their own cities had not network coverage been broadcast after local newcasts.

Certainly this observation held true for citizens of Jackson. For example, Jackson physician Aaron Shirley told me: "In the early 1960s folks had television . . . television was an essential bit. As bad as the newspapers were, television at least you got from the national perspective. They had to carry the evening news. So many times we learned more about Mississippi watching NBC or ABC news than we did watching the local programs. . . . We watched the locals too. And it'd just make us angry. To get a better focus we would watch NBC, ABC, and the *Today Show*."[59]

Bill Monroe, a former news director in New Orleans, wrote about similar conditions in Louisiana, stating that "the frequent and pronounced bias of many southern stations against the Negro side of the story was of massive proportions. Some southern stations would not use film showing police brutality even though their own cameraman had shot it. The customary justification for this kind of suppression was that the use of the film might increase tensions and lead to demonstrations and disorders, two words often used interchangeably in the South."[60]

In Jackson, stations WLBT and WJTV offered prime examples of this concealment. For example, WLBT sent camera crews out to film local white violence against black students, and dutifully shipped the dramatic footage to NBC headquarters while steadfastly refusing to air the same footage locally. Given this censoring norm, on the rare occasions that integrationist arguments or dramatic scenes of white supremacist violence were aired, there were strong reactions from all sides of the struggle. For example, Clarie Collins Harvey, a prominent black businesswoman and civil rights leader in the Jackson area, remembers the significant, powerful impact of public meetings carried by local television stations for the first time in 1965, as the stations felt federal licensing pressures and the Mississippi committee of the U.S. Commission on Civil Rights hearings were aired:

> I think, for the first time, many people realized that the stories that they had been hearing were not just fabrications of the imagination of a deprived people . . . [but] that these were things that were actually happening. Many people that did not come out to hearings sat at their television and heard a Negro person in Natchez, Mississippi, talk about the fact that he was never in any civil rights movement, not anything, but just because he was colored and maybe he might be "contaminated," he was used as an example for the colored, the colored community, and taken out and was stripped of his clothes and was flogged and beaten and poured — Castor oil was poured down his throat — and he was shot as he ran . . . you know, and you could see that the man couldn't be making this up. . . . And people for the first time realized, well now, maybe there is something to it. Maybe there are things going on in my state that I didn't know about.[61]

Watching Jim Crow

Fearful of losing sponsor or audience support, stations throughout the South resisted such damning images emanating from broadcast centers and worked for further independence from the national networks and other professional organizations. During the early sixties many southern member stations of the National Association of Broadcasters (NAB) voiced resentment regarding "integrationist" or provocative network fare, as well as their unhappiness with the leadership of the new NAB president, LeRoy Collins. Collins, a Democrat and former governor of Florida who took the presidency in 1961, often aligned himself with Kennedy administration initiatives only to be thwarted by a conservative board of directors.[62]

Regional groups such as Monitor South emerged during this period and worked to coordinate station rejection of shows deemed unfriendly to the segregationist status quo, arguing that station managers should, for example, preempt network documentaries that probed civil rights law and activism.[63] Some stations went so far as to threaten secession from the NAB to form their own regional alliance — an affiliation to combat network programs seen as being "against the South."[64]

In the midst of these economic and cultural anxieties, many station managers adopted an ironically aggressive "hands-off" policy toward the treatment of civil rights or the fight for integration. Typical of this "studied neutrality," as historian J. Fred MacDonald has termed it, was a 1958 policy statement from a Virginia television station, WAVY-TV, announcing that its staff would not " 'editorialize, give an opinion, or predict any future development relative to the integration issue.' Further, the station underscored that interviews with local school officials and members of local and state government, 'will be handled so that no side or definite stand will appear to result from the questions asked by our newsmen.' "[65]

Viewed within this context of professional practice the actions of the Jackson stations can be characterized as less exceptional than some academic accounts imply.[66] For example, when WLBT general manager Fred Beard issued a 1962 memo to his staff explicitly reminding them that programs with references to racial integration or segregation were *not* to be aired, his actions were typical of many other station managers throughout the South. Also typical were the station's preemption or exclusion of network fare deemed "too dangerous" for the public. Network news executives, such as Fred Friendly at CBS, complained loudly to the FCC about southern affiliate refusals to air public affairs programming dealing with civil rights that had been provided by the network.[67]

It is worth noting that while southern stations carried network affiliations and network programming, they often enjoyed the option of choosing their evening fare from multiple television networks. For example, WLBT carried a primary affiliation with NBC and a secondary affiliation with ABC, and used this dual alliance, as well as liberal access to syndicated sources, to offer programming that was deemed comparatively less controversial or dangerous. WJTV had primary affiliation with CBS but also at various times used the facilities of the ABC and Dumont networks. This juggling of network resources and programming as well as the consistent omission of integrationist or black perspectives were common, routinized professional practices. As these strategies of preemption, omission, and aggressive "neutrality" were increasingly practiced, they were also increasingly interrogated, and southern broadcasters found themselves in growing tension with not only factions of the NAB but also the FCC.

The Federal Communications Commission, for its part, stepped up its scrutiny and investigation of southern stations in the early sixties, particularly after the violence during the admission of black Mississippian James Meredith to the University of Mississippi in Oxford in fall 1962. The commission notified eight radio and television stations in Mississippi that their coverage and editorializing regarding the Oxford incident was considered biased and solicited station comments. Alongside this somewhat toothless gesture, the commission, in July 1963, also issued a public clarification and restatement of broadcasting's "fairness doctrine," pointedly noting that the law required broadcasters to present black perspectives when broadcast programs addressed racial integration. The commission repeated the point that the doctrine required broadcasters, as part of their fiduciary responsibilities, to give reasonable opportunity for opposing parties to speak regarding such important, controversial issues. This regulatory reiteration, aimed at particular Mississippi stations, was to serve as a key component in later challenges to the licensing of WLBT and WJTV.[68]

In immediate response to this published commission clarification and de facto reprimand, prominent southerners such as Senator Strom Thurmond simultaneously attacked the fairness doctrine and the FCC, claiming that southern broadcasters were being targeted by such fed-

Watching Jim Crow

eral policy. Thurmond took to the floor of the U.S. Senate to denounce the fairness doctrine as "a most dangerous threat to freedom of thought and the right of the public to have more than just the left point of view presented over the nation's airwaves."[69] The president of the Mississippi Broadcaster's Association wrote a letter in September 1963 to E. William Henry, chair of the FCC, arguing "I do not think a radio or TV station located within the limits of the continental United States should be singled out for special treatment, good or bad. It is my understanding that eight licensees of radio stations in Mississippi have been singled out for special attention because of an unfortunate incident in our state."[70] Indeed, within the year, the two most powerful Mississippi broadcasters, Jackson's two television stations, WLBT and WJTV, would be "singled out" by civil rights activists for license challenges. Formal petitions to deny licensing of the two stations were filed with the FCC in April 1964, naming the primary petitioners against relicensing as Reverend R. L. T. Smith, a prominent Methodist minister and Jackson businessman; Dr. Aaron Henry, president of the Mississippi NAACP; and the Office of Communication of the United Church of Christ, led by Dr. Everett C. Parker. Parker, along with attorneys Orrin Judd and Earl K. (Dick) Moore, were primary strategists for the formal administrative law licensing challenges, which began in 1964 and culminated in 1969. However, as this chapter has shown, the challenges to the stations were multiple and started before the intervention initiated by the United Church of Christ.

CHAPTER 2

Consuming Civil Rights

On September 2, 1963, five days after images of Martin Luther King Jr. and the March on Washington appeared on television screens,[1] Mississippians were offered another picture of civil rights struggle. Station WLBT, an NBC affiliate, aired without commercial interruption *The American Revolution of 1963*, a three-hour network documentary. The show was, one network executive explained, "a program of unprecedented length and placement, pre-empting . . . our entire schedule of programming that night."[2] Host Frank McGee, an NBC correspondent, set the tone for the program's treatment of the civil rights struggle by stating that in attempting to "define this revolution, . . . in the South an immediate goal [of rights activism] is equal entrance to, and service by, places doing business with the public — what might be called consumer rights as easily as civil rights."

Long before McGee spoke, Ella Baker of the Student Nonviolent Coordinating Committee (SNCC) had announced that southern direct-action interventions were about more than better service, lodging, and meals. As she put it, "the current sit-in and other demonstrations are concerned with something bigger than a hamburger. . . . The Negro and white students, North and South, are seeking to rid America of the scourge of racial segregation and discrimination — not only at lunch counters but in every aspect of life."[3] Still, McGee's rhetorical frame equating civil and consumer rights was understandable, resonating as it did with mainstream middle-class concerns regarding "consumerism," which were voiced during the early sixties by prominent institutions including Congress and the Kennedy administration.

From just outside Jackson, Tougaloo College president A. D. Beittel wrote to NBC news executive William McAndrew to commend overall *The American Revolution of 1963*. He noted, however, that parts of the documentary — specifically those providing vivid images of recent white-on-black violence in Jackson — had been curiously interrupted and omitted by WLBT. During the moments dealing with local reaction and aggression, a "technical difficulties" sign appeared on screen, blocking audio and video at the precise moments the piece "hit home."[4]

In the months preceding the airing of *The American Revolution*, Tougaloo students had held a lunch counter sit-in at the downtown Jackson Woolworth's. For more than two hours the activists, later joined by Tougaloo professor John Salter and President Beittel, were variously and viciously abused. Some were kicked, hit, beaten, and doused with mustard and catsup. Some of the brutality of the attacks on students politely requesting service during the lunch hour was recorded by affiliate WLBT, and the damning film was shipped to NBC headquarters. This footage would later comprise a portion of the NBC documentary — which then would be blacked out by the very station that provided the footage. Beittel knew all too well what local audiences had not seen.

Such blackouts of news materials were common in Jackson television, particularly in the programming of WLBT and WJTV, thus marking powerfully through omission materials deemed dangerous to white supremacy. Particular interventions involving "consumption" were not to be represented or broadcast. In Jackson and elsewhere, concerns regarding "consumer rights" and their popular representation were intersecting the politics of race and civil rights and were to play a key role in the regulation of Jackson television. The dynamic and interactive definitions of consumer and civil rights were shaping, and being shaped by, local television.

"DON'T BUY SEGREGATION"

In 1962, even as President Kennedy was announcing what he called the consumer's "bill of rights," including a "consumer's right to be heard," African Americans were testing their voices and power as consumers in states notorious for racial violence and oppression. In the small delta town of Clarksdale, Mississippi, black activists persistently boycotted merchants that had a history of racial discrimination. This grassroots effort, led by local resident and NAACP state president Aaron Henry, was maintained for several months and had a significant economic impact on downtown businesses.[5]

In the central part of the state, beginning in the last weeks of 1961, the Jackson Movement purposed to change "business as usual" in the capital by boycott and direct action designed to ensure that "Negro consumers . . . [be] treated as they ought to be — as first class citizens."[6] The movement, comprised largely of local teens, targeted prominent white-owned Jackson businesses where they insisted that basic employment and consumer rights be extended to African Americans and that the abuse grimly familiar to black customers in the white marketplace be confronted and addressed.[7]

By winter 1962, Jackson had become the site of a sizable grassroots effort aimed at pressuring stores and services dependent on black patronage. The Jackson Movement had initial leadership from the North Jackson Youth Council of the NAACP, a group of young students advised by Tougaloo College professor John Salter, and also received additional guidance and support from prominent black Mississippians, including Aaron Henry, Reverend R. L. T. Smith, Reverend G. R. Haughton, and NAACP field secretary Medgar Evers.

Organizer Salter had been impressed by recent direct-action campaigns outside the state and was eager to mobilize the local black community.[8] On November 30, 1962 the official bulletin of the North Jackson Youth Council, the *North Jackson Action*, put its readers on notice: "The boycott is now official . . . picket lines and mass meetings are definitely set." The periodical's front page highlighted "a brief statement of grievances" discussing the problem of employment discrimination, and continued: "Negro consumers are forced to use separate restrooms, separate drinking fountains, and very frequently are forced to use separate seating facilities in the stores. Often, they are forced to stand. Negro customers are the last to be waited on. In any dispute between a clerk and a customer, the customer is always wrong — if he or she is a Negro. Many of the white businesses are members and supporters of the viciously anti-Negro White Citizens' Council — whose national headquarters is in Jackson. . . . Brutality, levied against Negro people, has frequently occurred in the stores of white businessmen."[9]

Attempting to draw further attention to these practices downtown, picketing demonstrators joined the selective buying efforts in December, just in time to impact holiday shopping. The Youth Council organized a systematic phone-calling campaign and pamphlet distribution strategy to inform the black community of its actions and goals. Salter recalls that almost sixty thousand leaflets were distributed in the first six months of the campaign, and that "boycott workers had spoken at length in almost every Negro church in Jackson — and most of these churches had been visited many times."[10] Because police harassed or arrested those engaged in the distribution of boycott information, student workers used unusual, sometimes secretive, techniques such as carrying materials in paper bags, umbrellas, and under their coats and moving quickly through different parts of Jackson.[11]

These extraordinary covert communications efforts were necessary in part because the "mainstream" print and electronic media of Jackson provided virtually no opportunities for black voices to be heard or for pro-movement arguments to be made. In the first years of the decade, requests for "fairness" or contrasting viewpoints in stories addressing segregation and integration were routinely ignored, and many civil rights activities were simply not reported. Instead, the two largest-circulation Jackson dailies published caustic attacks on the federal government and on civil rights activists. The Jackson *Clarion-Ledger* and Jackson *Daily News* were egregious in this regard, even when compared with other daily papers within the state.[12]

The two newspapers offered loud condemnations of the boycott and ran ads urging readers to patronize businesses downtown. For example, one 1963 *Clarion-Ledger* headline referred to a similar campaign in Alabama as a "Negro fuss."[13] Full page *Clarion-Ledger* ads proclaiming "why your downtown merchants deserve your support!" listed as reason number one the fact that "no other group offers a more unified backing of city, county and state law enforcement agencies in the preservation of 'our way of life.' "[14]

Even as the highest-circulation newspapers urged defeat of the boycott, a white segregationist group named the United Front printed and distributed thirty-one thousand leaflets detailing "what you should know about the Negro Boycott of Jackson." The newspapers picked up and recirculated the pamphlet's arguments, such as the view that "radical Negro organizations" had instigated a boycott against "reputable business firms" and were engaging in "un-American activities." Further information included a list of businesses "under pressure," including the downtown merchants on Capitol Street as well as Barq's Bottling Company, Jitney Jungle stores, and McRae's department stores.

The arguments concluded with an appeal: "We need your active support in combating activities that oppose the free enterprise system and a free democracy. There is much work to be done."[15]

In the sphere of electronic media, the connections between white businesses downtown, the state's most powerful politicians, and the two Jackson television stations were quite clear. Both stations were owned and operated by community leaders aligned with segregationism. Fred Beard, WLBT-TV's general manager, was a prominent member of the Jackson Citizens' Council, as were many downtown businessmen and prominent state lawmakers.[16] The NBC affiliate also had a "Freedom Bookstore" on its premises, which was filled with Citizens' Council and white supremacist literature. Further, both stations had a close economic relationship with Citizens' Council businessmen and downtown stores in terms of long-term advertising accounts. In short, the stations had very powerful economic and political allies, and only the marshaling of considerable political and legal resources would bring about changes in broadcast practices.

It was local broadcasting's allies that were under direct attack during the Jackson Movement. Businesses important in terms of broadcast advertising revenue were among those hit by the direct-action campaign. Shaken by the activism, some within this economic power structure argued that the boycotters were plainly destructive and ill focused. Countering this perception, in January 1963 the movement issued a concise, clear list of demands: "(1) hiring of such personnel on the basis of personal merit without regard to race, color, or creed; and promotion of such personnel on the basis of both merit and seniority without regard to race, color, or creed; (2) an end to segregated drinking fountains, an end to segregated restrooms, and an end to segregated seating; (3) service to all consumers on a first come, first served basis; and (4) use of courtesy titles — such as 'Miss,' 'Mrs.,' and 'Mr.' — with regard to all people."[17] In the same month Evers reported to the national NAACP office that the boycott efforts were "60–65 percent effective."[18] After another boycott campaign coordinated by the Jackson Movement ended in 1964, the organizers reported that "more than 23 stores" had been forced out of business due to the movement's selective buying activities.[19]

With such activism the Jackson Movement, while acknowledging the need for equality in the sphere of production (hiring and promotion), focused on the problems of local black consumption.[20] Lizabeth

Cohen, in her analysis of this civil rights activism, observes the existence of a postwar politics of consumption "oriented around blacks' rights as consumers, not just producers," and argues that "although access to jobs remained on the agenda of civil rights activists in the early sixties, they now saw consumption and production rights as . . . intertwined."[21]

Certainly more was at stake in the minds of the Jackson boycotters than the issue of "the consumers" of Kennedy's speeches. While articulating "civil rights problems" during the selective buying campaign, Jackson's activist leaders such as Reverend R. L. T. Smith put the issue of the "denial of human dignity" at the top of their public complaints, and at mass meetings in Jackson's churches they called for local recognition of "freedom and human dignity."[22] Clearly this call was associated with the concrete experiences of African Americans shopping in downtown Jackson, where they were denied access to bathrooms and water fountains and often were ignored by white employees. Attacks on human dignity were multiple and were resisted in multiple ways. As longtime Jackson resident Juanita Jefferson explained to me: "At the Emporium we blacks could go in and buy a dress or a pair of shoes but we were not allowed to try it on or bring it back if it didn't fit. Why shop there? We didn't have any money. . . . And so a lot of people, friends of mine, they had the white people, white ladies, go pick out what they wanted and had the white lady to go purchase it for them. . . . I didn't believe in that. I never did that because I felt human, same as you, and if I can't walk in the dressing room and try this dress on, I don't need it. And I never had anybody go purchase anything for me. If I couldn't do it for myself, I didn't need it. I don't care how much I wanted it — I didn't need it."[23]

Refusals by blacks to cooperate with such indignities were evident not only in specific shopping spaces but also in the broader public sphere, finding rearticulation in criticisms of supremacist broadcast practices. In the months after the Jackson Movement disbanded, the petitioners challenging WLBT's license testified that the station undermined black dignity by failing, for example, to use courtesy titles in addressing black personalities and events.

These locally grounded concerns and demands were quite different from those articulated by President Kennedy earlier in 1962 on behalf of what he called the "American consumer." The president identified four primary consumer concerns and corresponding "rights": (1) the right to safety — which dealt with protection from hazardous goods; (2) the right to be informed — which was concerned with protection against fraudulent, deceitful, or grossly misleading information in mediums such as broadcast advertising; (3) the right to choose — concerned with "access to a variety of products and services at competitive prices"; and (4) the right to be heard — an assurance "that consumer interests will receive full and sympathetic consideration in the formulation of governmental policy, and fair and expeditious treatment in its administrative tribunals [such as the Federal Trade Commission and FCC]."[24]

Such pronouncements could be understood as both expansive and restrictive. While the president's speech provided a symbolic alliance with the "American consumer" and symbolically expanded "consumer rights," it also set implicit limitations on the government's interests in these matters. As one of his speechwriters put it, Kennedy's announcement of these rights served to "define and limit the field of consumer protection and to identify legitimate policy choices vis a vis consumer markets."[25] Aside from a cautious endorsement of consumer representation, the executive statement established as paramount the assurance of safer goods and "improving the level of consumer satisfaction from a given level of expenditure."[26]

Historians have widely regarded Kennedy's embrace of consumerism as politically shrewd but substantively shallow. The chief executive's speech addressed the type of consumer protection initiative judged by politicians and their pollsters to have broad, although not necessarily deep, middle-class endorsement.[27] Although the administration did not hold such protections as a high policy priority, it was recognized that "consumer protection" legislation was well received by targeted voters and the costs of reform could be passed on to the private sector.[28]

By focusing on consumer satisfaction derived from favorable economic exchange, Kennedy implicitly defined the "American consumer" as individualized and autonomous, enjoying free access to the marketplace independent of the social divisions and constraints experienced every day by thousands of Jackson shoppers. Missing was the movement's recognition of a basic need to affirm the human dignity and worth of consumers.

The Jackson Movement had issued their own version of a "bill of rights" for consumers, arguing that an entire class of citizens had been

Watching Jim Crow

abused within and excluded from the "free marketplace." At the same time, Washington's political discourses symbolically erased social differences in consumer experiences, employing the equalizing concept of "the consumer," and worked to reestablish the vision of a fundamentally fair marketplace that balanced the interests of individual consumers and producers.

Certainly, segregated consumers had been influenced by the consumerist discourses of the period, as is evident both in the Jackson Movement's newsletters and more widely throughout the South.[29] However, the meanings of consumerism were appropriated differently and specifically in response to crises such as those experienced in Jackson. It is clear that the direct-action campaigns such as the boycotts undertaken in Mississippi's capital were not at all in line with Kennedy's consumerism. The White House was deeply troubled by such bold interventions, as movement participants brought calls for racial justice to the fore, thereby integrating local consumerism into a far more provocative and destabilizing political force than the administration had desired. On the other hand, the local activists and many other black Mississippians were agitated and uneasy with abstract, formal pronouncements on federal protections — especially those showing little relevance to their primary, everyday concerns.

The Jackson Movement, as well as other direct-action campaigns, were specific articulations of impatience and dissatisfaction. For movement participants, legal and bureaucratic efforts seemed gradualist and often futile. Distrusting existing structures, many student activists, in Mississippi and elsewhere, "assumed that their elders had wasted too much energy on fund-raising, public relations, and bureaucratic minutiae."[30] As James Silver and others have observed, many Mississippi activists were "unimpressed with legalism"[31] and favored the use of grassroots campaigns aimed at problems needing immediate remedy.

It was in this environment that the federal broadcast licenses of the Jackson television stations were challenged. The stations never faced a sustained direct-action campaign, although activists such as Evers, Henry, and Smith had long complained about station programming and had petitioned for change. Rather, the battle over these broadcast properties and their use of public airwaves was waged primarily in the realms of law and bureaucracy, with all of the attendant dangers. In large part because local Mississippians lacked the enormous economic and legal resources necessary for a protracted fight in this realm, the task of the formal licensing challenge largely fell to the legal experts associated with the Office of Communication for the United Church of Christ, headquartered in New York City.

FORMALIZED CHALLENGES

As activists disrupted commercial and traditional consumer practices in Jackson, in New York City the Reverend Dr. Everett C. Parker was studying the possibility of more formal challenges to segregationist television. The church executive and reformer had long been interested in addressing Martin Luther King Jr.'s complaints regarding poor coverage of black activism in southern broadcasting.[32] Late in 1963, Parker, director of the Office of Communication for the United Church of Christ (UCC), traveled to several southern states to talk with African American leaders in Birmingham, Miami, Atlanta, New Orleans, and elsewhere about the possibility of filing official petitions against hardline segregationist stations. The UCC leaders, in line with the protestant denomination's historical commitment to social action and racial justice, supported his quest. Just outside of Jackson, the historically black institution of Tougaloo College was supported by the United Church of Christ and had UCC members on its board. Thus Parker traveled to Jackson, where he met with Tougaloo president Beittel, state NAACP president Henry, and Reverend Smith, among others.[33]

The Jackson broadcast stations seemed particularly vulnerable to licensing challenges. As noted previously, several Mississippi stations, including WJTV and WLBT, had come under increasing FCC scrutiny for their handling of the 1962 Meredith incident at the University of Mississippi, as well as possible fairness doctrine violations. Regulators and civil rights workers suspected that the stations' segregationist cheerleading, combined with other militant voices, had fueled the deadly violence at Oxford and elsewhere throughout the state. Jackson was also regarded as a significant capital of segregationist resistance, and WLBT's management, in the person of Fred Beard, was particularly vitriolic and recalcitrant in its supremacist stance.[34]

Recognizing this recent history, the decision was made. Henry and Smith agreed to act as formal petitioners in a licensing challenge aimed at WJTV and WLBT. The orthodox patterns of segregationist entertainment and news presentation in Jackson were to be challenged again —

Watching Jim Crow

this time through the formal channels of broadcast law and the FCC and employing the resources of a northern reform organization.

Parker traveled south to formally investigate the Jackson stations at the same time that hundreds of northern college students prepared to move into Mississippi. In March 1964, just weeks before the collegians were scheduled to work in the Council of Federated Organization's "freedom summer," Parker's local monitoring coordinators, Mary Ann and Dr. Gordon Henderson, hired more than twenty volunteers from around Jackson to secretly monitor local television. For one week these volunteers quietly traded off shifts at a location disclosed only to them, transferring television sets, reel-to-reel audio tape machines, and specially designed log books into a local home. No one outside of the small group was to know of the monitoring.[35] The volunteers took care to park their cars inconspicuously, and they took other precautions such as preparing diversionary "stories" to satisfy the curiosity of inquisitive neighborhood children.[36]

Such forethought recognized the power of the investigated and the implications of the petitioners' campaign. The monitored institutions, crucial to the maintenance of a particular "way of life," would be guarded on all fronts. Parker remembers being identified and tailed by Sovereignty Commission agents, as well as driving secretively at night down Jackson's streets with the car headlights turned off. Returning north after his trips to Jackson, he found that wire-tapping equipment was attached to the phone line of his New York home. He recalls that when people later figured out where the monitoring was done, "they put so much pressure on those folks that they moved out of Jackson."[37]

In recognition of this hostile environment, one of Aaron Henry's NAACP advisors argued against Henry joining the licensing petition effort, saying "in the first place it wouldn't do any good and in the second place it'd be dangerous ... you try to take these people on, you're liable to get killed. You're trying to really take on people that we can't fight." Parker remembers Henry's response being, "Well, I'm allowed to get killed for a lot of things I do. Give me the petition, I'll sign it."[38]

On April 15, 1964 Henry, Smith, and the UCC officially filed with the FCC two five-page "petitions to deny licensing," asking that the regulators reject the relicensing applications of WJTV-TV and WLBT-TV.[39] In June the small United Church of Christ congregation at Tougaloo College, represented by the college chaplain, Reverend Ed King, signed on as a petitioner, only to later withdraw its participation under pressure from the college trustees.[40] The documents argued for licensing denials by stating that these stations had failed their public interest obligation to serve the viewing community — in particular, local African Americans. Among the charges brought against the stations were: failure to serve the black population in the area, estimated at nearly 50 percent of the total population; failure to use courtesy titles, Miss, Mrs., or Mr., when referring to blacks even though such titles were used for white persons; discrimination against blacks in the presentation of news, announcements, and other program material; discrimination in the presentation of controversial issues, especially in the field of race relations; failure to use black entertainers and other participants in live programs and to announce black community affairs; and an excessive period of time devoted to commercial announcements.[41]

Shortly after filing the petitions the challengers decided to drop their complaints against wjtv. Strategically, they reasoned, they would be better served using their limited resources to target just one outlet, so they chose wlbt because of its particularly outspoken and recalcitrant management. Although the fcc continued to investigate wjtv, along with four other Mississippi stations, looking at their role in the 1962 University of Mississippi riots, Jackson's oldest station escaped increasing petitioner and federal challenges by demonstrating a willingness to change some policies and programming. For example, in response to the 1964 petition wjtv initiated a number of new programs, fired their news director, and broadcast extensive live coverage of federal Civil Rights Commission hearings held in Jackson. On the other hand, wlbt responded to the petitioners primarily with resistance, setting the stage for disputes that would be argued for years.[42] Neither the petitioners nor the stations involved could have anticipated the legal and cultural impression left by this formal, well-aimed blow to the broadcast status quo. The license of wlbt would be the focus of intense legal battles for the next five years, and it would be in a state of contention or interim care throughout most of the 1970s. As I discuss in detail later in the book, between 1964 and 1969 the fcc would issue three public licensing decisions, two pertaining to wlbt, as well as conduct full licensing hearings. The Circuit Court of Appeals for the District of Columbia would twice overturn or remand the decisions of the commission and in 1966 publish a landmark decision that formally challenged the legal status and "standing" of ordinary citizens petitioning federal administrative agencies such as the fcc.

Watching Jim Crow

Regardless of how they were treated by local business, the primary consumers of groceries, clothing, car repair, and the like could clearly be identified in Jackson and Mississippi. But who were the consumers of local broadcasting? And did such consumers deserve federal protections? In this nexus the consumption of groceries and television sitcoms were both issues taken up by the federal institutions of the 1960s.

In the case of the Jackson station challenges, related questions were central — namely, who were the consumers of television, and what rights, if any, did these consumers have? In the midst of a rising national consumer movement, such problems and answers were argued in various legal forums including those within the FCC and in the U.S. Court of Appeals for the District of Columbia. While there was much at stake for the citizens of Jackson in terms of local broadcasting practices, one of the most vital, foundational questions addressed by the court was aimed exactly at the point of "legal standing" — who should have direct access to, and thus power within, the station licensing process? The court's 1966 address of WLBT's licensing controversy[43] is regarded as groundbreaking within the rarefied spaces of American administrative law for its response to this query.

"Standing" is a concept and daily definition crucial to the performance of American administrative law, guiding the official actions of federal agencies such as the Federal Trade Commission (FTC), the Food and Drug Administration (FDA), and the FCC. In essence, to lack legal standing is to lack official recognition. Without it, one cannot seek legal recourse before particular courts of law; without it, one is not "a party in interest." In 1966, the question of standing addressed by the federal court was relatively clear: Who was to be heard or formally recognized by administrative institutions such as the FCC, FTC, and FDA, and who was to be denied such recognition or considered "not a party in interest" by such authorities? The court heard this question, among several others, on appeal of the FCC's 1965 decision granting a short-term renewal of WLBT's license, and the commission's finding was that the citizen petitioners indeed lacked standing.

The court's answer was also relatively clear and was crucial to the reformation of administrative law as well as consumer reform efforts during the late sixties and early seventies — most directly the broadcast reform movement. Within the practice of contemporary administrative law, the opinion is still considered a powerful precedent and is referenced regularly in court opinions and lawyer briefs. But while its importance has been widely noted, what has been less clear to this point is how popular and legal discourses concerning race and consumerism converged and shaped social and legal consciousness in this particular instance.

To understand this issue it is helpful to briefly look back a bit further in broadcast law. Before the challenge to the station's license, both the FCC and federal courts handling broadcasting concerns had granted "standing to intervene" (*locus standi*) only to legislators and those parties "operating in the public interest" that demonstrated sufficient economic injury or electrical interference. Those parties successfully claiming economic injury and electrical interference were invariably commercial and industrial entities. Although the courts insisted that standing was considered in the light of larger public, rather than private, interest concerns, members of the listening and viewing audience — that is, "the public" — were never formally and directly recognized or represented but rather only indirectly heard through the various arguments of industry and government. As one legal analyst summarized, "the courts had apparently given at least tacit approval to the [Federal Communication] Commission's standing construction, for in no instance had standing to contest a licensing order been upheld on any other ground."[44] That is, until 1966 with the release of the court decision regarding WLBT-TV.

Considering the challenge to WLBT, the court's position on standing shifted. Dissatisfied with the forementioned precedents, the court of appeals established that the listening public was now to be considered as potentially "aggrieved" by the renewal of broadcast station licenses, and as a potential "party in interest" would be empowered to challenge license grants and renewals. In granting standing to the appellants, Judge Warren Burger wrote for the court majority, including circuit judges McGowan and Tamm, saying: "Since the concept of standing is a practical and functional one designed to insure that only those with a genuine and legitimate interest can participate in the proceeding, we can see no reason to exclude those with such an obvious and acute concern as the listening audience. This much seems essential to insure that the holders of the broadcast licenses be responsive to the needs of the audience, without which the broadcaster could not exist."[45]

In granting standing to representatives of the "listening audience,"

Watching Jim Crow

the court recognized that it had broken away from previous, more restricted notions of standing, admitting that "up to this point in time, the courts have granted standing to intervene only to those alleging electrical interference . . . or alleging some economic injury."[46] However, now the court had decided to expand notions of public interest beyond those represented in the constricted categories of the past. Claiming a new flexibility and ability to adapt based on experience, the court continued: "What the Commission apparently fails to see in the present case is that the courts have resolved questions of standing as they arose and have at no time manifested an intent to make economic interest and electrical interference the exclusive grounds for standing."[47]

Such remarks show how the court of appeals attempted to distance itself from the FCC's stance by suggesting that the commission had a certain inflexibility that the court was now rebuking by positioning it as detrimental to the public interest. Still, it is important to keep in mind that this rebuke had little justification in terms of legal precedent and formal coherency. Indeed, by the latter measure the commission's decision, not the court's, would seem much stronger. The former's determination was based on well-established and often-cited precedents such as *FCC v. Sanders Brothers Radio Station* (1940), *Scripps-Howard Radio, Inc. v. FCC* (1942), and *NBC v. FCC* (1942). The court had thus repeatedly given, tacitly or explicitly, approval to commission constructions of standing.

In this case, however, the court took great pains to foreground the flexibility and dynamism of standing: standing was defined as a "practical and functional concept." After tracing a case history of standing decisions, the court remarked that "this history indicates that neither administrative nor judicial concepts of standing have been static."[48] And in a passage that pointed to "legal" justifications other than formal process and precedents, Judge Burger wrote that experience linked to implicit common sense guided the court's decision making:

The theory that the Commission can always effectively represent the listener interests in a renewal proceeding without the aid and participation of legitimate listener representatives fulfilling the role of private attorneys is one of those assumptions we collectively try to work with so long as they are reasonably adequate. When it becomes clear, as it does now, that it is no longer a valid assumption which stands up under the realities of actual experience, neither we nor the Commission can continue to rely on it. The gradual expansion and evolution of concepts of standing in administrative law attests that experience rather than logic or fixed rules has been accepted as a guide.[49]

This paragraph clearly points to court justifications outside the formally recognized realm of process and precedents. It explicitly privileges "experience" over formalistic legal logic or "fixed rules." In this rearticulation of law, grounds for standing had uneasily shifted, with little legal rationale available outside of "it seems to be the best decision to make in this instance at this particular time, given the experience of the past years."[50] Disposing of the idea that standing had a natural, inherent, or self-evident meaning, the court's decision serves as a dramatic example of law's social contingency and as a counterexample to claims of law's historical transcendence.

Law's lack of historical fixity has long been observed across the wide spectrum of discourses known as legal liberalism. As Thomas Streeter has written, legal liberalism is a product of Western Enlightenment thought, holding at its core the belief about "the existence and value of neutral, objective forms of language and procedure (the basis for the familiar claim that we should live by 'the rule of law, not men')."[51] Such liberal thought is also taken up in law school training that teaches the importance of distinctly legal reasoning via precedents or the principle of *stare decisis* ("let the decision stand"). Stare decisis instructs practitioners' subservience to prior decisions or precedents, such as in the judicial question of standing. However, even such a fundamental, central concept in American law is hardly determinative. It is undeniably true that stare decisis "neither leads to or requires any particular results or rationales in specific cases."[52] Nor does the practiced logic of stare decisis functionally ensure continuity, predictability, or rationality.[53] Rather, it disguises politics, refusing acknowledgment of social circumstances and dynamics, purporting neutrality and objectivity.

As critical legal theorist David Kairys has put it: "In sum, stare decisis, while integral to the language of legal discourse and the mystique of legal reasoning, serves a primarily ideological rather than functional role. Nor is there any more validity to the notion of legal reasoning when the source of law is a statutory or constitutional provision or the language of an agreement. Courts determine the meaning and applicability of the pertinent language; similar arguments and dis-

Watching Jim Crow

tinctions are available; and the ultimate basis is social and political judgement."[54]

Connecting this to the WLBT case and the 1966 federal court decision regarding which parties were entitled to legal standing before the courts and the FCC, what is clear is that a key legal concept such as standing is a site of continuous social and legal struggle, dynamic through time and place, and that such key concepts at the heart of legal liberalism are fundamentally indeterminate. Eschewing precedents and other existing formal guides, the court focused on the explicitly social variables of industrial and consumer conditions — desired social outcomes.[55]

As some scholars have argued, "standing," whether in the realm of constitutional or administrative law, claims objective a priori status in decision making, but in the everyday world it operates as a type of surrogate for judicial foci on desired ends and perceived merits.[56] In this surrogacy, standing decisions deny their social construction and social specificity, cloaking themselves in an a priori rationale claiming a clean separation from consideration of contemporary social conditions.

Court decisions such as the one handed down in the 1966 WLBT ruling can be seen as stripping the cloak from formal rationale, exposing social and cultural forces at work in such decision making. A more than cursory examination of the precedent-setting decision supports the contention that standing law is fundamentally indeterminate — not determining outcomes in any transhistorical way, but rather serving as a legitimizing justification for judicial activity. We see here a historical moment in which such justifications were thin and revealing — exposing an environment of considerable social struggle including concerns regarding consumerism and race.

TRANSFORMING VIEWER-CONSUMERS

The 1966 court opinion is best understood as explicitly positioned at the intersection of discourses concerning consumerism and racial justice. This is not to suggest that this or any other court decision simply reflects contemporary social concerns. Rather, such formal texts emerge in creative and interactive ways, working on social conditions even as such conditions shape such texts. By issuing such official pronouncements, courts are regulating not only legal but social practices, and performing law for multiple, disparate audiences — audiences that will judge the coherence of such pronouncements based on their resonance with varied, popular concerns and practices.

In the years preceding the 1966 decision, broadcasting had been increasingly defined as a consumer concern. The quiz show scandals and FCC commissioner misconduct had brought the television industry and its regulation into question, and these exploitations of a relatively young and promising medium were widely publicized in the popular press, thus arousing public dissatisfaction.[57] Criticisms focused not only on sponsor scandals and poor programming but also on advertising and the economic consequences of such electronic sophistry in increasing numbers of homes. For example, an early 1960 *Consumer Reports* cover article, titled "Where, May We Ask, Is the FCC?," blasted the commission for its inactivity and "passing the buck," especially in regard to "false and irritating" advertising. The article warned that through the floods of poor programming and advertising on broadcast channels, the industry could "decimate the consumer use-value of all receiving sets."[58] Calling for "the implementation of the consumer position in government," the article nominated television as the nation's dominant consumer concern, stating that "the consumer investment in and the consumer interest in television and radio dwarf that of any other segment."[59]

At the same time, prominent politicians such as presidential candidate John Kennedy campaigned to align themselves with governmental protection of the consumer.[60] Kennedy along with many members of Congress correctly perceived, and played on, increasing public support for federal consumer protection. Politically, a foundation was built for a new cycle of consumer protection legislation that bore fruit during the Johnson administration.[61]

Through a longer view, a rearticulated progressivism was evident. Politicians consistently voiced a mistrust of the increasingly mechanical and impersonal marketplace. Increasing consumer education efforts, fear of propagandistic advertising industries, and the growing public conviction that large businesses as they modernized and mechanized should assume greater social responsibilities marked the time and fueled the rise of the sixties consumer protection movement.[62]

In 1962 the president established a Consumer Advisory Council, which had liaisons with various federal administrative agencies, including the FCC. And in 1964, as Lyndon Johnson established the president's Committee on Consumer Interests, his special assistant for consumer affairs, Esther Peterson, continued the communication between the executive branch and the FCC. During these years, the White House occasionally asked the commission for an account of activities undertaken in the interest of the American consumer. Thus, FCC actions, such as its work on the All Channel Receiver Bill, were called to the attention of the White House and defined as "efforts to help the consumer."[63]

Faced with public anxiety over advertising and claims that ads were increasingly false and pervasive, the FCC, under the leadership of commission chairs Newton Minow (1961–1963) and William Henry (1963–1966), launched campaigns against "overcommercialization" in broadcasting.[64] Congressional members, acting as defenders of the broadcast industry, were persistent in curtailing these administrative agency efforts. However, powerful FCC commissioners believed that the public shared their displeasure with the number of commercials aired and the "ever increasing interruption of programs."[65]

William Henry, FCC chair during the early years of the WLBT licensing challenge, encouraged the commission's broadcast bureau to closely check individual renewal applications for the number of commercials promised in licensing versus the number actually aired.[66] In mid-1964 the broadcast bureau, again with Henry's support, unsuccessfully attempted to take punitive action against specific stations located in Louisiana, Mississippi, and Arkansas that had been accused of broadcasting too many commercials.[67]

With this historical backdrop, the logic of texts surrounding the 1966 court decision come into focus. It is no surprise, for example, that the United Church of Christ's legal team, counseled by former FCC staff member Ann Aldrich, included a complaint of overcommercialization in their petition to deny relicensing of WLBT. Such a complaint, seemingly trivial in comparison to charges of racist programming, resonated with public and FCC concerns and fit comfortably within a preestablished category of legitimate consumer concern. In fact, even after the 1966 court decision ignored the overcommercialization charge, the UCC petitioned the FCC to revisit their complaint regarding too many ads.[68]

Beyond the contention that advertisements were too frequent and interruptive, anxieties regarding false or misleading ads were closely linked to notions of consumer protection. Applied to broadcasting, the

Consuming Civil Rights

logic of consumerism again focused on expenditure and the viewer's return from financial investment. "Consumer protection" was not so much protection from frustration or annoyance or more threatening systemic injustices as it was protection from uninformed, irrational, or unwise investment—in other words, protection from "not getting one's money's worth." This concern was evident, for example, in the 1960 *Consumer Reports* article, as it foregrounded public spending on television and radio purchases and spoke of "consumer use-value." This economic logic was also clear in the arguments employed by the UCC's legal team in this case, and it was adopted by the court in its 1966 opinion. The contention of the petitioners was that the public, through ownership of sets and "the appurtenances," had a large economic stake in broadcasting but had not received a fair return for their investment and therefore deserved legal standing as an economically aggrieved party.[69]

This formal argument, written in large part by Everett Parker, was a savvy strategic move. It also served as the very awkward formal equation through which the court defined local African American concerns as synonymous with those of the "American consumer." The judges gave considerable discussion to the specific history and practices of WLBT early in the opinion, focusing hard on the allegations of racial discrimination. However, as the court articulated its position regarding the issue of standing, considerations of this history dropped out of their writing in deference to formal constraints dictating that questions of standing be addressed before the merits of the case, and that standing be considered only in relation to specific persons, firms, or corporations, rather than social classes or groups.

These constraints were, and continue to be, the product of a philosophical framework that reproduces the artificial dichotomization of the individual and society, inconsistently privileging individual liberties over social responsibility. In writing and working within this tradition the court was formally limited to the address of specific economic grievances—individual material losses—rather than systemic discrimination. This was, and is, the purview of American administrative jurisprudence.

Thus, the court drew parallels between the consumers of margarine, coal, electricity, and broadcasting, arguing that consumers of these and other commodities had certain economic claims and in some cases had been granted temporary standing before administrative agencies such

Watching Jim Crow

as the Federal Trade Commission. By contending that television "consumers" and consumers of margarine needed similar administrative protections the court's opinion reflected a temporary and artificial, yet formally demanded, separation of social justice from individual consumer concerns.

The court's defense of individuated television consumers was summed up with a quotation from Edmond Cahn: "Some consumers need bread; others need Shakespeare; others need their rightful place in the national society — what they all need is processors of law who will consider the people's needs more significant than administrative convenience."[70] Employing such liberal proclamations, the court transposed middle-class assumptions onto other groups — in this case, predominately working and underclass African Americans in the nation's poorest state. By discussing which parties should be officially recognized rather than deemed legally invisible, the court effectively subordinated concrete cultural concerns regarding televised representations to the economic logic of consumer protection. Black Mississippians would be recognized, but only through the limiting lens of "consumer" investment.

The argument that viewers should principally be defined as consumers owning television sets, thus holding an economic stake in local broadcasting, had little resonance with many poor African Americans, even if accepted at face value. Such consumer protections assumed that the citizen was economically independent, when this was hardly the case for many black Mississippians. In 1969, for example, 71 percent of Mississippi's African American families had a total annual income of less than five thousand dollars, compared to the 71 percent of the state's white families who enjoyed annual incomes of more than five thousand dollars.[71] Truly independent consumer choices were a luxury afforded by relatively few African Americans in the state.

Further, although nationwide television purchases had boomed in the late fifties and early sixties, census data reveal that "nonwhite" households in Mississippi lagged well behind other populations in the acquisition of this technology, at least in the late fifties. Considerably less than half — approximately 40 percent of "nonwhite" households in Mississippi — reported having televisions as the decade began, compared with the 66 percent figure for "all occupied households in the state." In impoverished rural areas, even a smaller percentage of "nonwhite" households had a set at home.[72]

Thus, the court's discussion of standing via consumerism, while resonating with federal legislation prohibiting public discrimination against customers, effectively ignored important social histories and differences in its construction of the homogenized and individualized television viewer-consumer. Anxieties regarding state address of racial conflict were displaced by consumer and public interest discourses. Within the court's formal logic, viewer-consumers were legal subjects clearly marked by an individuality that black Mississippians lacked.

Such logic is commonplace within American court decisions fed by liberalism's paradoxical dichotomizations of public and private as well as individual and society. As critical legal and feminist scholars have argued, such "public and private interest" bifurcations are demonstrably incoherent, indeterminate, and hollow at their conceptual core, yet remain politically potent discourses within the practices of legal liberalism, and more specific to this case within American broadcast regulation, making neat separations of the individual from the social.[73]

What we see in the WLBT case is the matter of social agents recognized not as members of antagonistic classes (or races) but as individualized legal subjects. As Vincent Mosco has pointed out in his discussion of broadcast regulation, the state is responsible for controlling social antagonisms before they become systemic conflicts, thereby "presenting itself as the agent for solving the problems of individual juridical citizens."[74] In the WLBT case the state addressed a race-based threat to social and economic stability via an official legal discourse without directly appearing to offer such an address, and thus offered remedy only to the individual consumers of local television.

In Washington, the White House supported endeavors aimed at the furtherance of individual voting and consumer rights rather than rallies and large-scale public protests. By employing such strategies of accretion the administration took care not to trigger segregationist backlash.[75] As historian David Chalmers has noted, the national government was not willing to directly challenge the southern status quo much beyond the issue of voting rights, and as "the civil rights strategy of the early sixties increasingly became one of forcing the issue in the streets . . . the administration treated it as a problem of conflict containment."[76]

Members of the Jackson Movement frequently complained about the lack of federal support for their highly visible direct-action campaigns. In this case, the court's decision to deal with the petitioners as representatives of consumers worked to atomize or isolate the complainants as individual consumers of the televised programming. The court's employment of the issue stated in the quote by Cahn above foregrounded this atomization clearly with the message that "some consumers need this, others that." The court's alternative was more menacing — to recognize that the petitioners represented the concerns of a race or an aggregate threat to the status quo.

MEDIATING CONSUMERISM

In his 1965 address on the WLBT controversy, FCC chair William Henry declared that the issue at hand was "not civil rights," but "the integrity of the public interest standard and the Commission's renewal process."[77] This study puts the lie to such a claim, showing that the WLBT struggle was very much about civil rights as well as other social dynamics. The symbolic evacuation of racial struggle evident here in Henry's statement, if accepted uncritically, leads to a superficial understanding of an important moment in American social and legal history and reinforces the dichotomization of legal reasoning and social change. To contend that notions such as the "public interest" or formalistic legal and administrative process are the central issues in such a case is to grant them an undeserved and dangerous autonomy — one that denies their relationship to, and degree of dependence on, central social and political forces.

Situating the 1966 court of appeals decision (as well as the same court's 1969 opinion discussed later) within the sixties civil rights movement reveals how such rulings echoed the strategies and ambiguous legacy of the movement as a whole.[78] On the level of local and tactical politics, such decisions and the discourses they reproduced offered important resources for local activism and movement gains.

On another level, as the above analysis has shown, the limitations of legal liberalism and its abstract "rights" are also clear. And in this case, in terms of industrial and regulatory structures or existing patterns of power, the station challenge and 1966 court decision did little more than ratify the status quo by suggesting that the regulatory scheme was corrective — that it indeed "worked." The definition of television and radio as primarily and "naturally" commercial enterprises with the attendant consumer concerns was never challenged but rather rearticulated and reinforced within official discourses.[79] While the 1966 ruling regarding legal standing for WLBT viewers energized and facilitated the late sixties and early seventies broadcast reform movement, thus forcing some local stations to change programming and employment practices, by the late 1970s further bureaucratic retrenchment effectively diminished the power of this legal precedent and the ensuing activism even before deregulation under the Reagan administration.[80]

Even as American legal institutions proclaim their lack of political interest and distance from popular concerns, we can see in specific instances how social concerns and pressures force "breaks" in legal reasoning — disjunctures that are inadequately explained by institutional justifications. And what this analysis suggests is that in the examination of these "breaks" attention should be paid to the struggles surrounding official and popular discourses — such as those of consumerism — and their intersection with law. In the sixties, consumerism was invoked both by civil rights activists and federal institutions in the context of established new law or policy. For those in Jackson and in the freedom movement consumer concerns called for the recognition of social differences and a response to the historic, long-term neglect of the "free market." From Washington, the discourses of consumerism effaced social differences and tensions, reproducing the model of the individuated American consumer and the vision of an essentially fair, consumer-producer balanced society.

In the rhetoric of the court of appeals and institutions of law we see the uncomfortable mediation of these conflicting consumerisms, as well as an attempt to address racial tensions accompanied by a simultaneous displacement and recoding of these concerns. We see a particular, at times strategically rewarding, way of thinking and knowing about African American complaint in tension with the histories offered by local black voices.

In their distrust of the narrowly focused and ponderous federal address of their petitions many local freedom fighters were fighting outside the court and corridors of officialdom. As the next chapter details, popular television and entertainment were a primary flashpoint and locus for civil rights struggles. A rearticulation of middle-class consumerism was evident not only in the official opinion of federal courts but in the interventions of young college students convinced not only of popular entertainment's social significance but of their invisibility within existing consumerist discourses.

Watching Jim Crow

CHAPTER 3

Trouble around the Ponderosa

While benevolent federal courts recoded black voices and concerns as those of abstract consumers, a supremacist ventriloquism in and around Jackson spoke of African American contentment with the status quo — the notion of the happy satisfaction grounded in a lack of desire or appreciation on the part of blacks for the cultural, economic, and educational opportunities afforded whites. Speaking for African Americans, Jackson's dominant press and broadcast media worked daily to naturalize this myth. Black voices contradicting such beliefs were deemed too dangerous to be recognized or directly heard — instead, observers or leaders outside the black community would speak for them. The radical potentials accompanying black recognition were exactly what prohibited it. Thus Jackson's daily newspapers and broadcast outlets carefully avoided the reproduction of integrationist or African American voices regarding segregation, except in instances where such voices spoke out against change. As former Tougaloo College president A. D. Beittel testified before a federal panel, "the most controversial issue in Jackson . . . was the matter of the Negro group trying to get some recognition."[1]

Even within black districts and neighborhoods, to speak publicly of segregation's corruptions or to demonstrate knowledge of broader national and international perspectives on racial struggle were practices subject to surveillance and fraught with risk. In 1993, Jackson resident Reverend Willie Lewis spoke of these limitations as he told me about growing up in rural Mississippi "cut off" from the rest of the world, and about the danger of even being seen with a newspaper of any sort by white townspeople. He still remembers a man who read a variety of newspapers and who would "come in and let you know what was going on all over the world," and he remembers that the man was killed. Regarding the Jackson dailies, Lewis recalled: "[Those] papers wouldn't pay attention to us. They knew better than that. That's too much information. Once folks get all that information, that'll make more people get involved. We couldn't even stand . . . in a big crowd out there — they'd come and they'd want to break that up."[2]

Similarly, Sam Bailey, one of Medgar Ever's closest associates and friends, talked with me about the frightening oppression of the time and how people knew what they knew: "A whole lot knew [about movement activities] but they were scared to say anything. Now, they'd read *Jet* magazine out of Chicago. The [*Chicago*] *Defender* — papers from out of town. But their local newspaper was so prejudiced . . . at the time, they weren't going to print nothing unless you were accused of raping a white woman or killing a white. Then they would put you on the front page."[3]

In this environment activists worked, often in very discreet ways, to make African American discontent visible and to publish or "broadcast" this dissatisfaction with segregation as widely as possible. If the local dominant media ignored their voices, they would work through other means to be heard. In this chapter I examine some of these means. I first focus on the alternative press constructed by local rights activists — most notably, the short-lived but important *Mississippi Free Press*. Then I discuss in particular detail the surprisingly powerful activities of the "non-violent cultural and artistic agitation campaign" launched by a very small group of Tougaloo College students and staff, and the effect of this campaign in the explicit repoliticizing of popular culture.

The attack on Jackson's segregationist entertainment occurred on many fronts owing to activist disagreement regarding the most effective, immediately necessary, or principled response to racial oppression. Some powerful NAACP leaders, for example, stood opposed to the direct-action tactics of the Jackson Movement. But many fighting against Jim Crow also recognized attacks on multiple terrains to be practical and necessary. As another former Tougaloo president, George Owens, put it, referencing Thurgood Marshall: "You do the best that you can with what you've got. And what we had, we used. . . . We were fighting everywhere every way we could and as effectively as we could."[4] The fight was, in the language of Gramscian critical theory, a "war of position" — one that relied on a steady erosion and subversion of supremacist practices on multiple fronts. It would not bring success quickly or completely, but it would realize important victories.[5]

While these activist initiatives received varied levels of support from members of Jackson's civil rights community, and are separated out here for purposes of clarity and analysis, all were unified in their goal of changing segregationist practices through exposure of the latter's corruption and coercion. Further, all were designed to spread the word that black Mississippians were not happy with Jim Crow but forcefully constrained within it.

As was the case in this historical instance, coercion — or nonconsensual domination — operating in a variety of forms often acts as reinforcement for a dominant-order consensus regarding race. But such consensus is only naturalized or deemed common sense because it denies its dialectical relationship to coercion. As Kimberlé Crenshaw observes, "hegemonic rule succeeds to the extent that the ruling world view establishes the appearance of a unity of interests between the dominant class and the dominated."[6] The "efficiency" of policing or regulatory activities is jeopardized as such activities lose their "naturalness" or invisibility. When coercions are exposed, consensus is threatened.

What I examine in this chapter, then, is how various activisms, even with limited goals and resources, exposed coercion, and in doing so, temporarily disabled the creation of consensus necessary to white segregationist power. Again, the discourses of consumption and consumerism are highlighted. As historian Grace Hale has written, long before the sixties an emerging national consumer culture had created spaces — including railroads, department stores, movie theaters, concert halls, and public fairs — in which African Americans could challenge segregation, both "implicitly and explicitly."[7] Early civil rights activists targeted just such spaces, as did the Jackson Movement of the early sixties. And, as I argued in the previous chapter, legal institutions, particularly federal courts and executive branch agencies, participated in constructing a language of "consumer rights" employed, with mixed success and implications, by local activists.

Responding to such activism, many southern whites redoubled their efforts during the fifties and sixties to reassert supremacist control over consumption. But, as we shall see, they often failed. These supremacist failures represent not only a historical story but give contemporary witness to the difficulty of policing or regulating cultural consumption. While the reception or consumption of any product may be deemed impolitic, unpatriotic, or immoral, this history provides another example of how officially sanctioned proclamations about the "dangers" of popular culture are often publicly acknowledged and even praised, yet privately ignored.

FREEDOM FROM THE [SEGREGATIONIST] PRESS

The Jackson *Daily News* and the Jackson *Clarion-Ledger* were widely known as the dominant journalistic voices of the state. Each paper was also known, as one southern journalist described the *Daily News*, "as a violence-fanner, race-baiter and polarizer — a flat-out foe of anyone and anything advocating social change."[8] But in Jackson, two small-circulation alternative newspapers did consistently argue for change — the *Eagle Eye* and the *Mississippi Free Press*.

During the 1950s, while only five black papers were published in the state, only one of the five was boldly unequivocal in its rejection of corrupt white supremacy and embrace of black rights — the *Eagle Eye* published by Arrington High.[9] The periodical was actually a short newsletter; typically in the format of a two-page mimeograph that High would distribute personally in places such as Jackson's Farish Street district. The paper, at times carrying the banner of "America's greatest newspaper, bombarding segregation and discrimination," blended blunt, provocative commentary and description and threw aside the mainstream conventions of "objective reporting," taking instead the form of an aggressive advocacy journalism.

High's publication consistently criticized both blacks and whites who compromised progress on civil rights. For example, when black teachers and administrators failed to support or discuss local activism, High responded with reproach: "How can you Negroes teach young Negroes how to become self-respecting when you yourselves are in the ditch through fear?"[10] In remarking on another black publisher/editor — Percy Greene of the segregation-supporting *Jackson Advocate* — High called Greene's paper a "filth sheet" and said that Greene "is the voice of the decaying Negro who within a few years will become an outcast as far as leadership among Negroes in Mississippi. . . . He is a dangerous character to your freedom, I mean the Negro."[11] Regarding

Watching Jim Crow

some prominent segregationist governors, High opined: "This government needs a federal firing squad. If this were legal, George C. Wallace, Ross R. Barnett and Paul B. Johnson, Jr., I would recommend be brought before it. Wallace is from Alabama, Barnett and Johnson from Mississippi, for not obeying Federal Court orders, ordering school integration in their representative states. I am for shooting those who refuse to obey court orders." [12]

High's blunt advocacy and explicit moral claims made him a dangerous character in the eyes not only of white conservatives but also many in Jackson's black community. Alliance with such an outspoken critic of segregation — whether High, Medgar Evers, or any known member of the NAACP — was dangerous. Jobs, reputations, and physical safety were at stake. Ineva May-Pittman remembered the risks involved as she spoke with me about the Farish Street newsstand and High's *Eagle Eye*:

> I think the black community wanted it, but they were afraid. You know, they were afraid to let folks know that they wanted that paper, because it was very, very strong. It was very, very strong. It dealt with the morality and hypocrisy of the white community overall in the black community and it was the high ups, you know, he would name names, you understand. There were people that were afraid, and if [High] were to be on one side of the street and they were on the same side, they would go across over to the other side because they did not want to be mistaken . . . for being in friendship with him, or anything like that. I don't think deep down in their heart that is the way they felt. But for their livelihood and so-called security, that's the way that they felt they should have to treat him, and he got that. [13]

Readers of such publications and acquaintances with such publishers had every reason to be cautious and frightened, as white Mississippi's surveillance system focused on black media outlets. In the early sixties, fearing for his life and diagnosed by state medical officials as suffering from paranoia, Arrington High went from Mississippi to Chicago, where he continued to publish the *Eagle Eye*.

Tom Armstrong, who owned the Farish Street newsstand and sold *Ebony*, *Jet*, the *Chicago Defender*, the *Pittsburgh Courier*, and other publications to citizens such as May-Pittman, was also targeted by Sovereignty Commission surveillance. A 1957 memo from agent Hal DeCell to commission director Ney M. Gore states that a commission investigator had checked into Armstrong's past and discerned that his newsstand "is a regular hangout of Arrington High and like radicals." DeCell goes on to write that Armstrong "refuses to carry moderate negro newspapers on his shelves such as the *Jackson Advocate*. All in all, he is the focal point of the most rabid agitation we have in this area. I recommend that we contact Allen Thompson and give him the details and background, and see if something can be done to revoke the license given him by the city to operate the newsstand." [14]

In characterizing the small Farish Street newsstand as "the focal point of agitation in the area," DeCell articulated and exemplified the Sovereignty Commission's strong fear of black activism and anxieties regarding the regulation of popular media. African American access to popular media, in terms of production *or* consumption, was deemed inherently dangerous to the status quo. Years before national media outlets extensively visualized, reproduced — and thus exposed — the dramatic violence propping up Jim Crow, Mississippi's government had anticipated the power of such representations and worked daily to control them. Sovereignty Commission records show that the spy organization paid close attention to black press agents and initiatives such as Tom Armstrong, the *Eagle Eye*, and later, the *Mississippi Free Press*.

Recognizing the potential power of the black press, the commission also enlisted the services of African American journalist Percy Greene. Greene had a long prior history of publishing and advocacy. He began publishing the *Jackson Advocate* in 1938. In his early years as a civic personality Greene led an effort with the NAACP to increase the number of black voters in Mississippi. Greene voiced strong support for the Truman presidential campaign and African American rights during the Truman years. He was a strong voice speaking out for black interests when few such voices were heard. However, Greene was greatly influenced by the accomodationist philosophy of Booker T. Washington, and in the wake of the 1954 *Brown* decision and new desegregation initiatives, found increasing alliance with Jackson's white segregationist leaders. By the end of the fifties, the *Advocate* was widely viewed as a prosegregationist organ and was attacked by the NAACP and others for its extensive reliance on white business and advertising. [15] In subsequent years, several Jackson residents told me, stacks of bundled *Advocate* issues were left on the street, completely untouched by the citizens of predominately black west Jackson.

Frustrated by the almost complete dominance of repressive media outlets, R. L. T. Smith, Evers, and white attorney William Higgs initiated the publication of a short-lived self-defined "civil rights" periodical in 1961 — the *Mississippi Free Press*. Predictably, the publication of the *Press* drew immediate excitement from both national civil rights activists and Sovereignty Commission surveillance. In coordination with the Citizens' Councils of the state, the paper's newsboys, staff, and printer were scrutinized and harassed. The periodical's office was watched and photographed.

A key impulse for publication of the paper, and a recurring theme within it, was segregationist censorship and omission. In the *Press*'s inaugural December 16 edition a story based on frank comments by WLBT-WJDX news director Dick Sanders took up the problem of news censorship at the stations, noting in bold type that "for the most part the news media have refrained from reporting [a local NAACP boycott]."[16] In a 1962 column, Tougaloo professor and activist John R. Salter Jr. wrote at some length about censorship and popular representation as the motivating force behind the *Press*'s creation:

> The sorry nature of most of Mississippi's white newspapers — or what pass for newspapers — is not unknown by any means to the Negro residents of the state, although one is tempted to feel that, without question, nearly all of the white population has been so thoroughly brainwashed on this and other subjects that their minds are far from clear. Not only do the greatest majority of the state's papers avoid printing any news which would reflect unfavorably upon white-held attitudes of prejudice and white-initiated acts of discrimination against Negroes — but every technique of censorship, playing-down, and often outright exclusion is utilized to avoid printing anything that would reflect favorably upon the Negro people. And certainly, nearly all of these white Mississippi papers carry — some in a comparatively sophisticated way and most in a crude and primitive fashion — direct and overt campaigns against the Negro. . . . And the other white-owned and operated mass media — radio stations and TV — although occasionally not quite so rabid as the press, follow essentially the same basic pattern.
>
> It is precisely because of this racist throttle hold on the mass media of Mississippi — particularly in the newspaper realm — that Negro leaders in the state and a few liberal whites as well, combined forces . . . to launch the *Mississippi Free Press*: the first liberal Negro social action newspaper, in the history of this unhappy state.[17]

Two years later a 1963 editorial echoed this same theme, stating that "the dailies here in Jackson have no competition. They are responsible to the same ownership [the Hederman family]. They are both subject to the same controls. . . . An evaluation of a newspaper must consider not only what *is* printed, but what *is not*. The greatest fault of the Mississippi daily press is what it *fails* to say about what is wrong and what needs to be changed."[18] Subscription promotions appearing run in the paper stated: "Don't blow your stack at the situation and the way other newspapers report it (or don't report it). Subscribe to the *Free Press* and learn how to do something about the situation."

Filling an important void in local journalism, the earliest editions of the *Mississippi Free Press*, under the editorial guidance of Paul E. Brooks, gave generous attention to direct-action campaigns against segregation, as well as violence against local blacks and the congressional candidacy of R. L. T. Smith. With the appointment of a new editor, Charles Butts, in June 1962, the paper placed more emphasis on labor and poverty. So, for example, when a local bakery's employees went on strike, the dominant dailies gave the multiweek standoff virtually no coverage, while the *Free Press* both covered and supported the work action.

The resources of the *Free Press* were relatively small. Still, a press historian claims that circulation for the paper ranged from two to three thousand at various points in time.[19] Local black merchants, several on Farish Street, provided advertising money; for example, Farish Street's Alamo Theater ran regular movie ads. R. L. T. Smith provided office space and other support, and newspaper materials make it clear that considerable financial help came from out of state. The paper's size and publication frequency were always very limited, meaning that uncomfortable decisions about the inclusion and exclusion of stories and representation would also arise within the activist community. With the Butts editorship, the paper shifted from its previously close alignment with NAACP agendas, causing friction between the organization and the paper. Late in 1962, after wishing the periodical "godspeed," Medgar Evers resigned from the *Free Press* board of directors, fearing the paper had lost its focus on racial justice.[20]

Evers's fears notwithstanding, the *Free Press* continued to provide its readers with discussions of what they were *not* seeing and reading elsewhere. Several editorials or news articles in 1962 and 1963 spoke of specific censoring or racist programming incidents involving local

Watching Jim Crow

broadcast stations. In 1964, the official challenges to the licensing of WLBT and WJTV received much different coverage than that offered in other local media.²¹ And, as I will show, direct-action campaigns, including those aimed at local entertainment, received early and substantial discussion in the *Press*.

CONSUMING DIFFERENTLY

In addition to these publications more "low-tech" and covert forms of communication in and around Jackson were necessary. Neighborhood conversations, telephone calls, pamphlets, and regular mass meetings were employed to counter the narratives of dominant media institutions and circulate meanings and messages ignored by the "mainstream" press. Informal networks were established and mobilized on short notice, most often via phone calls and hastily arranged church meetings. Although white supremacy enjoyed "a racist throttle hold on the mass media of Mississippi," these inexpensive, less easily surveilled modes of communication could never be entirely thwarted. Indeed, they were vital to the existence and success of the Jackson Movement as it pursued goals of greater employment, respect for black consumers, the desegregation of public facilities, and increased representation in city policy making.

In 1961 direct-action interventions were aimed at Jackson's public institutions. As the Jackson Movement planned and organized in March of that year, nine Tougaloo College students walked into the Jackson Public Library and, after refusing to move on to "the colored library," were arrested by police. In June, Jackson was the focal point of the freedom ride campaign during which some three hundred black and white freedom riders, many young students, were arrested for refusing to abide by local segregation laws and customs.²²

In response to the jailing of the riders, Clarie Collins Harvey, manager of Collins Funeral Home, along with other Jackson women organized the group Womanpower Unlimited to provide clothing, bedding, bail bond support, and other services for the riders. Womanpower Unlimited continued supporting local activism even after the riders had left, participating in voter education and registration efforts. And in 1961 and 1962 it joined forces with students to circulate up-to-date information regarding boycotts or "selective-buying" campaigns targeting downtown Jackson. Independent of larger, male-led civil rights groups and their agendas, Harvey, Jesse Mosely, A. M. E. Logan, Aurelia Young, and other black Mississippians, working alongside an interracial network of women both in and out of state, made valuable contributions to the struggle for improved civil rights.

Tensions grew in Jackson during the winter and spring of 1963 as the movement's boycott exerted increasing economic pressure and more direct action protests began, including picketing, lunch-counter sit-ins, and mass student marches. Encouraged by the movement's increasing impact and by NAACP support, John Salter, Medgar Evers, and Youth Council leader Doris Allison composed a letter both to the governor and to Jackson's mayor promising to broaden the boycott campaign and use further direct-action tactics unless an end to segregationist practices in Jackson stores, schools, parks, and public facilities could be negotiated. Mayor Allen Thompson took his reply to local television. On May 13, 1963, appearing on WJDX radio and WLBT-TV, he announced: "There is no change in our policy whatsoever . . . there will be no meeting with the NAACP or with any such group."[23]

As mentioned earlier in this book, Evers requested and quickly received airtime for reply from WLBT, a station that by this time was sensing the watchful eye of federal regulators. On May 20 the NAACP field secretary for Mississippi spoke, uncensored and on television, to his fellow Mississippians, black and white, for the first and only time. His message was clear: "What does the Negro want? He wants to get rid of racial segregation in Mississippi because he knows it has not been good for him nor for the state. . . . But whether Jackson and the state choose change or not, the years of change are upon us."[24]

As Evers spoke some movement workers close to him felt uneasy with his presence on television.[25] As journalist Maryanne Vollers has written, some felt that "before this moment, Medgar Evers had just been a name in the newspapers. Very few white people could even recognize him. The televised reply put Medgar too out front."[26] Within a month of the Evers address the Jackson Movement would experience considerable excitement, organizational change, and discouragement, largely as a result of forces external to the movement. And Medgar Evers would be lost.

The assassination of NAACP field secretary Medgar Evers during the early hours of June 12, 1963 delivered a severe blow to the Jackson Movement. In the days following the murder and Evers's funeral, "go slow" forces within the NAACP and the Kennedy administration employed successful strategies to curtail the movement's sustained confrontation campaigns. Still, the deeply felt dissatisfaction of black Mississippians regarding segregation and its implications could not be quickly or strategically removed. And in the months following Evers's death, African American frustration with the segregationist status quo motivated further direct-action attacks on the terrain of consumerism, popular culture, and entertainment in the Jackson area.

Dissatisfied with the partial recognition and gradualist remedies offered by official institutions, a small number of Tougaloo students and staff walked uninvited into the spaces of segregationist leisure and recreation. Formally recognized strategies favored by the NAACP and conservative black Jacksonians were bypassed, and a persistent insistence made that black citizens be more directly recognized. The frustration with being excluded from various forms of cultural performance fueled the campaign of this small group, which lacked funding and significant organizational support. They would force the issue of their exclusion into the places of white middle-class entertainment, exposing as myth the assumptions that entertainment and its consumption were unentangled in the politics of race. As former Tougaloo president Owens stated, it was not coincidental that students from Tougaloo chose the public library as the site for their 1961 sit-in or that a few years later they targeted concert halls and places of performance—both resonated with concerns regarding access to public institutions of culture.[27]

In the balance of this chapter I describe and analyze what was called the "cultural and artistic agitation" campaign carried out by student activists in Jackson during winter 1963–1964, including their actions and segregationist reactions involving the popular television programs *Original Hootenanny*, *USA* and *Bonanza*. Although the student campaign was not directly aimed at Jackson televison it did engage television programs, television personalities, and audience practices. It was also part of the protest and activism against the status quo that threw the cultural practices of white supremacy, including those of local broadcasters, into question and under wider scrutiny.

In Jackson, televised entertainment and fiction (as opposed to news and nonfiction), then as now, was often dismissed as at best peripheral to the prominent issues and politics of the day. However, during the early sixties many area residents regarded the viewing of certain television shows and patronage of program sponsors as important social markers. For example, the question of whether or not one watched *Bonanza*, or patronized the advertisers of products during the program, was deemed significant as a point of political identification in the struggle over segregation. An examination of the activism surrounding *Bonanza* as well as other televised and local entertainment reveals how the student agitators, employing tactics and maneuvers often invisible to those in power, disrupted the hegemonic dynamics of coercion and consent necessary to continue such practices.

"LIL' JOE WON'T GO, BIG AL WON'T BLOW" [28]

A sense of glee, if not gloating, permeated the February 1, 1964 issue of the *Mississippi Free Press*. The periodical described trumpeter Al Hirt's last minute cancellation of a local concert as yet another blow to Mississippi's segregationist status quo. The two-inch headline announced: "Nobody's Coming: No Horn for 4000 — Too White." The *Free Press* described the Hirt cancellation as part of several recent attacks on segregated entertainment initiated by Tougaloo College students and staff devoted to "cultural and artistic agitation." [29] Over the course of approximately six months, the small but dedicated Tougaloo Culture and Arts Committee had prompted cancellations of scheduled visits to Jackson by cast members of popular television shows, world-class musicians, and other prominent personalities. About a half dozen activists, primarily college undergraduates, had severely disrupted the cultural and popular entertainment calendar for a large number of white residents in the Jackson area. In response, an infuriated mayor of Jackson and thousands of Mississippians called for white reciprocation. The seemingly solid walls of segregated entertainment had been exposed as vulnerable and would become a site of pitched battle.

The intensity of white backlash to these cancellations was surprising, even to the most enthusiastic activists. Public responses by Jackson mayor Allen Thompson and other segregationists manifested deeply held convictions regarding the power and importance of popular entertainment in the maintenance of particular social formations. In fact, the mayor went so far as to define the segregationist response to this agitation campaign as "one of the most important efforts" to date. Alongside the mayor, those defending the traditional yet fragile racial barriers of

Watching Jim Crow

A page from the *Mississippi Free Press*.

segregation included the vast majority of Mississippi's political, cultural, and economic institutions. Yet, even while enjoying this dominance, many white Mississippians were inconvenienced and deprived of long-anticipated cultural events by a small number of activists. The cancellations came unexpectedly because most white Mississippians, as well as some black citizens, believed the strict segregation of entertainment to be necessary and natural.

For Austin C. Moore III, a student from Chicago newly arrived to Jackson, such segregation seemed anything but necessary and natural. In Chicago, where segregationist practices were pervasive, racial integration was more common in a limited number of social settings. And as Moore traveled to Tougaloo from Illinois in autumn 1962 he was immediately overwhelmed by the oppression of southern segregation. Dingy, poorly maintained "Negro" waiting rooms along the railway had welcomed him to Mississippi. As he was driven into Jackson, his aunt pointed to a prominent downtown movie theater and remarked, "that's a white theater — I'll never be able to go in." Because Moore had worked as an usher at an integrated Chicago theater, he was surprised by his aunt's statement and silently pledged to change things in Jackson.[30]

Approximately a year later, Moore had become the coordinator of "cultural and artistic agitation" within the small group of Tougaloo staff and students calling themselves the Nonviolent Agitation Association of College Pupils. The group received considerable support and leadership from the college's white chaplain, Reverend Ed King, and his wife Jeanette.[31] At a November 1963 meeting in the campus home of the Kings, the association decided to "work intensively to open entertainment in Jackson." With regard to segregated events and venues, the group resolved that "if we can't go . . . nobody should be able to attend."[32]

The most recent catalyst for this meeting was the early November arrest of Tougaloo student Robert Honeysucker, along with visiting Cambridge graduate Nicolas Bosanquet, as they attempted, with tickets in hand, to attend a concert of London's Royal Philharmonic Orchestra in downtown Jackson.[33] Eventually the city police dropped all charges, aware of their precarious legal position yet unaware that their racial zealotry would have widespread consequences. Meanwhile, on the campus at Tougaloo the "cultural and artistic agitators" began correspondence with major motion picture distributors and with NBC, specifically asking the television network to cancel the Jackson appearances of the *Bonanza* stars scheduled for early February.[34]

Of more immediate concern to the student group was the appearance of the cast of ABC-TV's *Original Hootenanny, USA* at the Jackson City Auditorium on November 15. The network television show, hosted by Jack Linkletter, took the form of "a travelling musical jamboree" and was taped at a variety of college campuses. Pop-folk musicians such as the Limeliters, the Chad Mitchell trio, and the Smothers Brothers were featured on the program, while the producers routinely "blacklisted" artists thought to be too leftist, such as Pete Seeger and the Weavers. In response to these reactionary policies, some prominent musicians refused to appear on the show.[35]

Nevertheless, the *Hootenanny* cast set to appear in Jackson was comprised of folk performers riding a wave of popularity — including Glenn Yarbrough of the Limeliters, the Journeymen, and Jo Mapes. In Mississippi, *Hootenanny* fever had been spreading, especially among local youths and young adults. Shopping malls held "Hoot-teen-nany" promotionals to attract adolescent shoppers, and the town's drive-ins offered films such as *Hootenanny Hoot.*

While the preconcert excitement mounted, the Tougaloo students telephoned the *Hootenanny* cast at their Memphis hotel and arranged an informal meeting at the Jackson airport on the day of the concert. Three Tougaloo undergraduates — Austin Moore, Calvin Brown, and Steven Rutledge — met the entertainers on their arrival at Jackson to explain their position as well as their intention to force a confrontation, if necessary, by attempting to seat Tougaloo students at the *Hootenanny* concert. After an initial reluctance to cancel and intense negotiations involving talent agents and long-distance phone calls, the group canceled the downtown show just three hours before curtain time. The cast relinquished their appearance fee and volunteered a free and integrated concert that same evening on the campus of Tougaloo. The downtown auditorium box office provided refunds for fifteen hundred ticket-holders, many of whom were already dressed for the event.

Yarbrough, speaking for the folk singers, told the *Clarion-Ledger*, "We're not here to raise moral issues. We didn't want it to happen ourselves, but it was a decision we had to reach."[36] Given the reactionary history of the *Hootenanny* program, it was an especially surprising decision that testified to the persistence and power of the Tougaloo student tactics. A few days after the incident, Steven Rutledge, who also served as president of Tougaloo's student government, sent the *Hootenanny* cast a letter of appreciation for their "courageous and difficult sacrifice," adding that "our evening together with laughter and song did much to reinforce our conviction that we are not alone in the great struggle for human dignity and high principle."[37]

The white residents and officials of Jackson were embarrassed by the *Hootenanny* debacle, but said little publicly in the hope that a calm and measured response might be the best strategy. This tactic changed three months later, however, when similar pressure was mobilized regarding an upcoming visit by the stars of *Bonanza*, one of television's most popular shows, followed by a performance from trumpeter Al Hirt.

Advertisements for the Mississippi Commerce and Industry Exposition promised "five big shows" by the "three great stars of Bonanza — Little Joe, Ben Cartwright, and Hoss," to be held at the state fairgrounds in Jackson during the first two days of February. What the local show promoters did not know was that the agitation committee had written letters to NBC as well as to each of the *Bonanza* stars regarding the scheduled appearances. As Moore stated in his appeal to the network:

We of Tougaloo Southern Christian College are vitally concerned with the effort to free the white southerner from the bars of racial prejudice. The American Negro is now struggling for . . . basic freedom. . . .

You can play a tremendously important part in this venture. We understand that NBC is sending a group from *Bonanza* to Jackson in February. Two weeks ago a promising young musician, Robert Honeysucker, a Tougaloo music major was arrested. He walked to the same door the white people of Jackson will be entering to see the *Bonanza* cast. . . .

We cannot risk another arrest — or possible violence. Therefore, we hope that the *Bonanza* cast will be willing to take their stand on the issue. We are asking that you refuse to perform before a segregated audience. . . . We'd like to attend your show. We can't in Jackson.

The *Bonanza* program is an excellent proponent of the American ideals in earlier times. It would be good if the program could further extend its influence.[38]

In response to the Tougaloo appeal, the *Bonanza* cast contacted NAACP field secretary Charles Evers in his Jackson office to discuss the local conditions of segregation and subsequently offer their statements of cancellation. Dan Blocker ("Hoss") sent a telegram that was reprinted in the *Jackson Daily News*: "I have long been in sympathy with the Negro struggle for total citizenship, therefore I would find an appearance of any sort before a segregated house completely incompatible with my moral concepts — indeed repugnant."[39] Later the same day, January 22, Lorne Greene ("Ben Cartwright") and Michael Landon ("Little Joe") joined Blocker in withdrawing from the appearance. As a last-minute replacement, promoters scrambled to arrange an appearance by Donna Douglas — "Ellie Mae" of *The Beverly Hillbillies* — only to have her state that she would be unable to perform. Ironically, as the *Bonanza* cast announced its disgust with the sanctioned practices of Jackson and the South, *The Beverly Hillbillies* and *Bonanza* were among the region's most popular TV programs. Many Mississippians came to feel that the television stars, influenced by a liberal Hollywood, had snubbed their most faithful fans.

The frustration and anger of white Jackson only intensified when Al Hirt cancelled a March of Dimes benefit concert three days later. Moore attempted to contact Hirt before his arrival in Jackson via a friendly columnist for the *Chicago Sun-Times*, Irv Kupcinet. In his column on January 22 Kupcinet wrote: "A long distance call from

Jackson, Mississippi, informed us that Al Hirt . . . is scheduled for a concert in the municipal auditorium down there. Audiences in the auditorium are segregated. And the caller wants us to so inform Hirt. Which we hereby do."[40] When the trumpeter still traveled to Jackson for the January 25 concert, Moore sent a telegram to him. It read in part: "Your performance this evening at the Mississippi Coliseum will serve the purpose of perpetuating the vicious system of segregation in Jackson. We speak in behalf of many Negro citizens who would like to attend your performance in dignity but are prevented from doing so by the city's racial policies. Other groups, including Hootenanny USA and Bonanza, have cancelled their scheduled performances for this reason. We urgently request you to cancel also."[41]

Approximately three hours prior to curtain time, Hirt asked to talk with Moore face to face. Accompanied by friends, Moore gained access to the musician's room at a whites-only motel by borrowing a jacket and disguising himself as a room service waiter. Hearing that African Americans would attempt to attend the concert and that violence and arrests might ensue, Hirt finally decided to cancel. It was now forty minutes after the scheduled performance was to start. Four thousand concertgoers sat in place as a sponsor reluctantly came onto the stage and read Moore's telegram to Hirt, adding that the program was cancelled. Before he had finished, shouting voices and obscenities drowned him out. The *Jackson Clarion-Ledger*, after contacting Hirt, claimed that the musician reneged out of concern for the safety of his crew and the audience. It went on to quote Hirt as telling Moore, "I think you're kind of using me, and so are the March of Dimes people."[42] Another local newspaper account stated Hirt's agent "had been worked on by Negro groups."[43]

However the incident was portrayed it was the talk of Jackson — a story told with considerable resentment and anger by many. Not only had all-white audiences been snubbed by Hollywood, but now they literally had been "stood up" by a white southerner of considerable fame. Further, the *Hootenanny*, Hirt, and *Bonanza* incidents had established a threatening precedent. A few days later, a top administrator of the National Aeronautics and Space Agency (NASA), James Webb, cancelled an appearance sponsored by the Jackson Chamber of Commerce, citing the problem of segregation. In February and April, pianist Gary Graffman and soprano Birgit Nilsson both refused to perform before all-white Jackson audiences. The musicians, both internationally renowned, had been contacted by Moore through the Culture and Arts Committee's efforts to target all visiting artists associated with the Jackson Music Association community concert series.

Reacting to these events, the *Mississippi Free Press* editorialized in a column titled, "Now It's Beginning to Hurt Both Ways": "It appears as though a precedent has been established that anybody that is anybody in the entertainment field does not perform in Jackson to segregated audiences. . . . So now, some of the white folks know what it is like to have the right to enjoy something kept from them. Under the circumstances, we bet that they do not like the system any better than we do. Let's get together and do something about it."[44]

The cancellations in Jackson also had implications outside the city, as they articulated a successful strategy for drawing national attention to the practices of various entertainers and southern communities. Prominent newspapers such as the *New York Times* began to carry articles highlighting the debates between performers, agents, and talent organizations regarding appearances before segregated audiences. During the winter months of 1964, the national SNCC leadership as well as the Congress of Racial Equality (CORE) and the NAACP joined in the protest against segregated entertainment in Mississippi. In March the NAACP appealed to approximately sixty prominent musicians to form a committee to help make cultural events accessible to both black and white citizens in southern cities, using musician boycotts when necessary.[45] These appeals paralleled other industrial and organizational actions addressing race, such as a 1963 nonbias declaration made by a coalition including the American Federation of Television and Radio Artists (AFTRA) union, as well as formal NAACP and CORE demands for increased employment of African Americans in all sectors of the entertainment industry.[46]

Although the NAACP, CORE, and other civil rights groups had made progressive strides through legislation, law, and direct negotiation with various industries, the tactics of Tougaloo's Culture and Arts Committee were noticeable for their relative informality, immediacy, and lack of official sanction. The student committee and the Jackson Movement chose to engage in direct-action strategies that were outside the purview and control of the larger official institutions. Rather than enter into processes of negotiation and compromise, when various performers such as Hirt and the *Hootenanny* cast initially resisted committee appeals to cancel local segregated appearances, the students countered by threatening to appear at performances, thereby risking violent confrontations with local patrons and police. These plans and tactics were agreed on without consultation from those outside campus or within the college administration, as students knew that while Tougaloo was a "safe haven" for black Mississippians, a majority of campus residents and employees, as well as many outside the college gates, were uncomfortable with or opposed to such activism.

So while the constituents of legitimated culture planned and promoted events, Moore and others quietly engaged a counterattack, using quasi-invisible practices — that is, actions that were visible only as they disrupted public activities and consumption.[47] Operating on the terrain of dominant culture, the student agitators looked for, and found, points of vulnerability in a superficially stable social practice. This was a tactical struggle in which the creativity of the subordinated was revealed, and artfully practiced in hostile territory.

The territory chosen by the students — spaces that were not easily policed — was crucial and required high levels of vigilance and coercion to maintain the "natural" social order. In entering into such spaces they immediately challenged dominant discourses of "the public." Was a segregated event or space truly "public"? What did it mean to hold a public event? Who was the public, and most important, who was excluded in its everyday material definitions?

While there was little the Tougaloo group could do in regard to the production of network television shows or popular music, it was able to intervene in the "foreign territory" where segregation was most pronounced and most vulnerable — the local conditions of performance and reception. These conditions represented a momentary window of opportunity for the students, and they were the point of productive struggle.

Given the size and resources of the Tougaloo group there were relatively few opportunities for such an effective public resistance to the status quo. And the student's activism served as more than a coping mechanism or "making do" within an oppressive social system as it reaffirmed other efforts to boycott or disrupt segregationist white commerce in Jackson and elsewhere and it effectively publicized the continuing African American fight to change racial segregation.

White Mississippians were nothing if not surprised by the exposed vulnerability and instability of the segregationist tradition. Most of the state's citizens had known nothing other than a segregated society. As

Ed King and other progressives told me, it was extraordinarily difficult for white Mississippians to even imagine a new social order in which they had never lived. Now, the routines and traditions of a familiar way of life were "under attack," as was the familiar and foundational myth of the happy Negro living in a world shut off from white experience and privilege. While the Evers murder, funeral, and ensuing mass marches publicized black dissatisfaction, the Tougaloo students demonstrated that this discontent was not anomalous or short-lived but enduring and deeply rooted.

BLACKING OUT BONANZA

Recognizing this as a moment that threatened segregation, some of Mississippi's dominant institutions responded with appeals to consolidate white power and further police popular tastes and practices. Leading the charge to rescue Jackson's "way of life" and cultural reputation was Mayor Allen Thompson, who initiated the segregationist counterattack with a lengthy speech to the city's department heads the day after *Bonanza* stayed away: "I would like to start off by saying that Jackson, and Mississippi, and the South, and maybe the whole nation, may have been insulted before; but this 'Bonanza' thing to my mind is one of the greatest insults to the intelligence and to the activities and the good works that the people of Jackson and Mississippi are doing that I have ever heard. . . . But let me tell you something. We want industries, we want business, we want people to come to Jackson *only* if they like what they see — only if they like what we are doing, and only if they see the potential booming future of this City."[48] The civic leader went on to read letters that Moore had sent him, outlining the Cultural and Artistic Committee's concerns and correspondence with NBC-TV regarding the *Bonanza* appearance. The mayor had underestimated the student activists and admitted as much, albeit with marked condescension: "Feature that — a student writing a letter like this and having more influence than all of the other conservative White people, good Colored people — one little pupil."[49]

Thompson concluded his attack on the Tougaloo students and *Bonanza* cast by calling for a countermovement that reemployed the selective buying strategy already used with great success by black Mississippians against white businesses. During the 1963 "Black Christmas" campaign, the Jackson Movement, including students and staff from Tougaloo, conducted a sustained, successful boycott of downtown merchants and discouraged the holiday purchase of decorations and gifts. The economic impact of the campaign was severe, and several white businesses eventually closed or moved. Still hurting from this experience, and with another embarrassment fresh on his mind, Thompson called for reciprocation, echoing a local newspaper columnist who suggested, "Why not fight them with their own weapon?"[50] Selective buying of goods advertised on television was to be accompanied by what he termed "selective looking" at television programming. Under such scrutiny, he was convinced that programs such as *Bonanza* would fade away: "Jackson, a typical Mississippi city, and Mississippi will be here a long time after 'Bonanza' is gone, a long time after 'Hoss' and the others have galloped away — because TV programs come, and they go. You look at some of the wonderful people who have been stars in the past. Look at the TV programs that you wouldn't have missed a year or so ago — you won't even sit down and look at them today. 'Bonanza' will be gone unless it is a great exception, and it seems to me the great exceptions are people who don't get to meddling with other people's local business."[51]

The daily newspapers of Jackson immediately picked up and retransmitted the mayor's remarks, as did the Jackson Citizens' Council's February newsletter. Thompson admitted that he had enjoyed *Bonanza* — in fact, had "thought it was a wonderful program" — but vowed that it would never come into his home again. A few days later, the Jackson *Daily News* pictured him sitting in front of a desk covered with "approximately 2,500 cards and letters . . . calling for a blackout of the *Bonanza* television show."[52] Heartened by this "favorable response," Mayor Thompson announced he would expand his efforts to destroy *Bonanza* across the state. In an accompanying article, the mayor was quoted as saying: "If there is in Mississippi this Sunday night — and forever — a complete blackout of the Bonanzas by the good white and colored people, we will be accomplishing these things. It will lead to the cancellation of the Bonanzas. . . . It will renew our courage to do what is right and necessary. Hundreds of thousands of people in at least several southern states will go along with us — and other millions all over the US will later on regret they did not. . . . But if we prevail in this — one of our most important efforts — your public officials in Mississippi and all over the South will be tremendously encouraged."[53]

The Jackson Citizens' Council used Thompson's statements as an opportunity to warn Mississippians against watching "TV programs which feature. . . . integrationist entertainers, or any other program which favors race-mixing." The council's newsletter also reiterated the mayor's selective buying scheme. These repeated calls for boycotts came as the state senate passed a law, aimed solely at integration groups, making it punishable by fine and imprisonment to "maliciously and willfully" print or distribute literature promoting such activities.[54]

Thus, a turn of events that some might have considered trivial or, at worst, slightly frustrating, had become very important at the point of white reaction. Concert cancellations and white boycott plans became regular front-page news in Jackson's *Daily News* and *Clarion-Ledger*. Going beyond expected statements of white denunciation, the mayor forced the issue: watch *Bonanza* and further imperil southern culture and traditions or "black out *Bonanza*" and bring honor to the state of Mississippi as well as to the segregationist fight. In bringing this battle to the fore, Thompson and institutions of dominant culture called attention to the centrality of coercion in racial crises. They had, perhaps unwittingly, recirculated the knowledge that at least some if not many African Americans both desired and were forcibly denied cultural opportunities. The racist myth of the happy, content Negro was being eroded. Rather than ignoring, trivializing, or downplaying the Tougaloo interventions, segregationist leaders marked them as a point of primary identification and opted for a response that only encouraged wider scrutiny and discussion of entertainment, popular culture, and their relationship to nonconsensual domination.

Letters to the editors of the Jackson dailies reflected some of the issues of identity and passion converging at this point in time. A majority of the letters printed in the *Clarion-Ledger* and *Daily News* repeated the mayor's call for a "*Bonanza* blackout" while asserting that such programs were unneeded and unwanted. One letter, written by a resident of Vicksburg, Mississippi, and reprinted in different forms by both Jackson papers, epitomized much of the published correspondence:

When the Hollywood stars of *Bonanza* refused to appear in Jackson recently, I immediately cut that show off my list. I am sure most of my fellow Mississippians feel as I do. Who gives a tinker's dam about Hollywood stars, or that rat race in Hollywood anyway, and who needs some Hollywood actor or actress in Mississippi to be happy, or to put over any show in Mississippi when we have Mississippi people with the best talent in the U.S.A., and our Mississippi girls are the most beautiful in the world.

I predict television won't last, just as the movies didn't. Some of the TV shows are terrible and the singing commercials and other stupid commercials get on an adult's nerves as well as children and sometimes they feel like busting the TV up, and it probably would be a good idea. . . .

If the actors from Hollywood do not want to come to our wonderful state, I say good riddance. Let Al Hirt blow his trumpet in the French Quarter in New Orleans or on Ed Sullivan's show.[55]

Along the same lines, a Jackson citizen wrote a letter combining the common "who needs them" theme with an inflection of Christianity that was also standard to segregationist arguments, juxtaposing the purity of white Bible belters with the heathens outside:

Like Mayor Allen Thompson I would like to express my view on these outside do-gooders who only want to do good for themselves and try to hurt the good people of the South.

Speaking of the Cartwright family of the Bonanza Chevrolet show, we got along fine before we ever heard of them, and we can get along fine without them or the products they advertise, as long as they feel the way they do.

They should stay away from Mississippi, or some good, kind, warm-hearted Christian may get to them and convert them to a real clean way of living and loving. I feel sorry for them because they need some teaching on God's Word, because they do not practice what they preach. I watch their show mainly because I haven't seen any Negroes on it. But from now on my TV set will be turned off during this and Ed Sullivan's shows — and neither will I buy their sponsor's products.[56]

Throughout the newspaper coverage and official comments on the cancellations, as well as letters to the editor, were condemnations of "promises broken" by the stars who failed to appear. As a woman from Jackson wrote:

In the first place if a person's word means nothing there can be no honor there. Why would we spend our time watching a hee-hawing hoss who slaps at our Mississippi beliefs and who's word means nothing. When in Mississippi do as the Mississippians do.

Secondly, it reflects on his lack of knowledge of history and current events if he doesn't know about our convictions and the strength behind them. There will be no more *Bonanza* in our house on Sunday night.[57]

In connection with the broken-promise theme, Hirt was the target of several letters claiming that he had abandoned sick children by failing to appear at the March of Dimes fundraiser. N. S. Brown of Jackson wrote: "It has been really amusing to watch the NAACP frighten the Ol Hoss mules and *Hootenanny* goats into tucking their tails and littering the air with heel dust. But the amusement was turned into 'Hirt' horror to find that there exists, anywhere in the civilized world, a group or any kind of being capable of striking such a low blow to little sick and helpless, crippled children, in need of medical aid, as Al Hirt did here. . . . Civilized people should not tolerate an entertainer with that kind of a heart."[58]

Throughout the letters, mayoral statements, and periodicals of the Citizens' Council were characterizations of Al Hirt, the *Bonanza* cast, and other artists as immoral, unethical, untrustworthy, un-Christian, and liberal or communistic. Virtually overnight tremendously popular personalities were transformed into dishonest, cowardly villains. As *Clarion-Ledger* columnist Tom Ethridge wrote with regard to *Bonanza*: "These famous 'Cartrights' portray he-men of courage and honor on television every Sunday night — heroes who brave all manner of dangers and threats in a routine manner. But now, they stampede when the NAACP whispers 'Boo' off camera. It is well known to all 'Bonanza' fans that the word of a 'Cartwright' is as good as his written bond. On the screen, that is. But in real life, it now develops that the 'Cartwright' word can't be trusted any further than a Ponderosa bull can be tossed by the tail."[59]

A few days later the *Clarion-Ledger* took the unusual step of publishing a response to Ethridge from Charles Evers, the state's NAACP field secretary after the death of Medgar Evers. Evers directly challenged the hero/villain theme advanced by Ethridge and others. Speaking of Dan Blocker, Lorne Greene, and Michael Landon, Evers argued "that these three men have indicated that they will not aid or abet 'age old customs in Mississippi' is not astonishing. It is astonishing, however, that the people of Mississippi continue to believe that they can expect to be treated with respect while they treat nearly 50 percent of their native Mississippians with disrespect. Sorry, Mr. Ethridge, any way you read this incident, Mississippi can't be made the hero."[60]

Watching Jim Crow

Although the published letters of support for the *"Bonanza* blackout" far outnumbered the correspondents critical or skeptical of the crusade, a few letters provided unusual perspectives on the cancellations. For example, after folksinger Joan Baez had a successful concert appearance at integrated Tougaloo College, a Biloxi resident concluded his letter with tongue firmly in cheek: "If many more renowned artists cancel Jackson performances, we may all have to go to Tougaloo for our cultural and aesthetic pleasures. But, of course we could always watch TV — or could we?" Weeks earlier, the same writer had penned:

> Another drab week has passed without *Bonanza*. Tell me again, now, just what is the difference between white and Negro boycotts? Of course, this dilemma would never have arisen if we pure white Christians had been attending our segregated worship services on Sunday evenings.
> P.S. Rumor has it that some Jackson citizens have lowered their shades and watched *Bonanza* anyway.[61]

Finally, after weeks of angry letters to the editor decrying the actions of Hirt, Hootenanny, and the Ponderosa gang, one reader said "enough": "Quit sending in those letters concerning 'fat old Hoss Cartwright.' Don't you realize that this is just what that communistic NAACP wants you to do? Nothing could make them happier than to see all you learned sociologists, politicians, and philosophers out there in prejudice land squirming. All this outraged uproar is just what Mr. [Medgar] Evers would have wanted — had he not been murdered in cold blood. If you had just ignored the whole situation and acted as if you didn't care, you would have defeated the NAACP."[62] This reader's assessment was largely correct. Although the Jackson movement and Tougaloo students would not have been stopped simply by white apathy and silence, white reaction of a public, aggressive sort called attention to the operations of white power and domination. These previously naturalized operations of power were put into public debate, discussed on the streets of Jackson, and detailed in popular media accounts both outside and within Mississippi.

Earlier Jackson activism such as the Tougaloo student sit-ins had received little if any local media attention, and the agitation group expected more of the same in the *Bonanza* incident — unofficial censorship and nonrecognition. In fact, nonrecognition had long been at the heart of segregationist strategy, in reaction to individual African

Americans as well as the larger black freedom fight. White supremacist violence against rights activists was certainly a constant threat and reality, but publicly both it and the voices of dissent were either ignored or explained away. The Jackson police had an informal agreement with the local broadcast media that any scenes of racial confrontation or violence were not to be aired in order to maintain "public safety." The local censorship of any broadcast materials deemed communist, integrationist, or otherwise unsettling to the status quo was commonly justified by the seemingly ambiguous, yet quite revealing, call to "maintain the public order." At local television stations the news policy was that controversial or confrontational news footage would not be broadcast, nor would any programs discussing issues of "segregation or integration."[63] Thus it was to the student's considerable delight that the mayor and local media loudly articulated the counterattack in the case of *Bonanza*, thereby confirming the importance of entertainment and the struggle for its control. What was usually dismissed as "just entertainment" now became a vital social concern.

While dozens of Mississippi residents spoke of their disinterest in *Bonanza*, Al Hirt, and others, they took the time and energy to write letters to publications for months after the initial incidents. The issue had incredible salience and resonance within the white community. For at least two years after the cancellations the newspapers received letters denouncing the performers and advising boycotts. Moore received letters from detractors outside Mississippi who obviously had heard of the agitation campaign and had taken the time to rebuke his "dangerous" activities. For all the language about not "giving a damn," it was clear that many people did care, and some announced that they were foregoing their favorite shows. Others said nothing, or perhaps publicly toed the segregationist line but kept the TV on and the shades down.

WATCHING OUT OF SIGHT

While claiming a dedication to segregation and a southern "way of life," many Jacksonians were loath to give up Sunday evenings with the Cartwrights. The popularity of *Bonanza* had grown with its move in 1961 to the nine o'clock Sunday evening slot. In fact, shortly before the cast canceled in Jackson, a local newspaper described the program as

Jackson's top-rated television show.[64] Even those most committed to killing integrationist efforts, such as the mayor, admitted that the program was a personal favorite.

And Jacksonians were not alone. Around the country, ratings pronounced *Bonanza* to be the nation's number-two show in 1963, and it was ranked number one from 1964 to 1966.[65] In modifying the widely used western genre, *Bonanza* placed its male heroes on a piece of private property, "the Ponderosa," which was integrally connected to their sense of identity and social power.[66] Subsequently, cultural critics have identified *Bonanza* as one of the popular "paternalistic property westerns" of the 1960s, alongside *The Virginian*, *High Chaparral*, and *The Big Valley*.[67] They note that within these programs not only were property owners usually deemed virtuous, and those without property encouraged to be content, but that the notion of "law and order" was routinely invoked as an intelligent, enlightened protection of, and for, property holders and dominant institutions — "a [thinly] veiled defense of the status quo."[68] Placed in the hands of the virtuous, the "wild West" could be transformed into the "not so wild, better ordered, West." Mixing these themes and characterizations with those of white patriarchal benevolence to nonwhites and social outcasts, *Bonanza* provided an entertaining, well-crafted comfort for many during a decade in which fears of social unrest and "lawlessness" ran high.

It is understandable then, that the rumors regarding the concealed viewing of *Bonanza* behind lowered shades had considerable substance. Despite the mayor's plea invoking all things good and southern, and despite, perhaps, feelings of guilt, the pleasures of the Ponderosa often privately won out. Watching the program was nothing to announce in church or to talk about with friends in restaurants but rather a pleasure to be enjoyed when outside the surveillance of institutionalized segregationism. Indeed, the show's local ratings remained strong in the midst of a publicly well-supported campaign against it.

A few months into the failed boycott, R. E. Dumas Milner, president of a local General Motors (GM) dealership, wrote to the Chevrolet Motor Division of GM, a national advertiser on *Bonanza*, referencing a March copy of *Jet* magazine and its cover photo of *Bonanza's* Lorne Greene with "a negro cow-girl." Milner wrote "this is really going to hurt us in this area. We have been advised by the local station (WLBT) that if this show is run, they will not carry it. I can say without reservation that this situation is hurting our business in this area and will obviously get worse. . . . I would appreciate it if you will look into this matter and see what can be done."[69] In turn, the Sovereignty Commission pressured the station, writing to manager Fred Beard that "all Mississippians concerned about Bonanza and the action of its stars will be mighty proud if your station can set the pace and start a chain reaction among other stations to remove the program from their schedule."[70] In Detroit, GM threatened to withdraw sponsorship of an episode with black characters, only to relent after confrontations with the network and the NAACP.[71] In Jackson, Beard explained to the Sovereignty Commission that the controversial episode would air, and he defended his decision by emphasizing that given increased FCC scrutiny he had no recourse.[72] In effect, the government made him do it.

What Beard did not highlight in his defense of airing the integrated program was the economic downside of canceling the station's number-one show, including implications for advertising revenues and the station's contractual relations with NBC. But certainly these were powerful, perhaps primary, considerations. Even as fallen segregationists watched in privacy behind drawn shades, WLBT-TV refused to disrupt airing the weekly program and local businesses continued to air advertising alongside the show. In this instance, WLBT, as well as thousands of viewers, had only a deaf ear for the mayor's appeal. The station's programming director, Hewett Griffin, recalled that the show continued to be a strong economic performer for the local broadcaster. In short, people continued to watch and businesses persisted in their pursuit of profit.

By repeating widespread calls for boycotts of *Bonanza* and network sponsors, Jackson's mayor and many white Mississippians hoped to "boycott the boycotters" — that is, to wound the civil rights movement with one of its own weapons. Hundreds if not thousands of Mississippians publicly vowed in newspapers and meetings to undercut integrationist interests through the power of white dollars. Published letters carried promises not to purchase Chevrolet cars or other products advertised on *Bonanza*. Writers argued that a unified white Mississippi would be a crushing economic force opposing civil rights activity. Typifying this argument was a letter to the editor of the *Clarion-Ledger* from a Jackson businessman: "A very small fraction of the 10 percent minority has used the [downtown Jackson merchants] boycott most successfully. You have only to watch television to see what I mean. Yet the country's 90 percent majority really controls the purse strings.

Watching Jim Crow

What if this 90 percent decided to boycott TV programs, products, etc., until things were changed to suit them? Unless a planned program is developed, and soon headed by a leader like Ross Barnett or George Wallace, the factional minority will continue to bully the great majority."[73] Columnist Tom Ethridge was among those reinforcing the mayor's call: "If the South would organize and fight back, there would be far less objectionable propaganda on radio and television network programs which depend on national advertising for their support. Nothing hurts anti-South propagandists like a hefty kick in the pocketbook. . . . The forces of 'social revolution' . . . are using the boycott weapon against us at every opportunity, but it is a two-edged sword that can cut both ways."[74]

However, despite the best efforts of Mayor Thompson and the supremacist pleas of the local press and prominent Jackson citizens, the white counterboycott never achieved its goal. In practice, the southern "way of life" was quite at odds with its romantic and politicized abstraction. The continued airing of *Bonanza* by WLBT-TV, decisions to continue advertising by local sponsors, and the choice of thousands of Mississippians to remain at least privately loyal to a publicly discredited practice, worked together to effectively split the white-resistance campaign and unsettle historical alliances of white power and domination. As time progressed, the Jackson Citizens' Council grew more resentful of what it called the "surrender" by prominent businesses represented on the Chamber of Commerce.[75] Segregationist voices in the Jackson newspapers spoke out against those who failed to fully support Thompson's boycott call. As the various factions of Mississippi's white establishment argued among themselves and failed to form strategic alliances, the fissures in racial segregation grew large and more vulnerable to attack.

In terms of economic interests, Jackson's commerce and industry followed a pattern common throughout the South. Businesses at first reacted to local activism with shock and resentment, then went through a period of silence (allowing extremists to fill the vacuum), and finally took back a degree of civic leadership through opposition to the extremist activities that threatened economic progress.[76] As one historian has argued, while southern businesses previously believed that economic progress and southern racial practices could simultaneously be supported, civil rights activism forced a choice, and in the "new ordering of their values and priorities" economic imperatives were placed above those of race.[77] In Jackson, for example, the Chamber of Commerce publicly urged compliance with the 1964 Civil Rights Act following its congressional codification. And even while Mayor Thompson urged wide-scale boycotting of *Bonanza* and its sponsors, many conservative state politicians remained mum. Behind such action, or inaction, was an abiding fear that in the absence of legal obedience and order, new investments would be discouraged and/or economic stability and progress would be imperiled. As civil rights unrest grew, Jackson businesses were increasingly sensitive to how "Jackson" would be understood outside of the state. As consumer culture and business expanded nationally, segregationists faced the tension of buying and selling within the region versus buying and selling the region itself.[78]

As was the case throughout the history of southern segregation, the contradictions "between market incentives and the desire to encode white racial supremacy" were pronounced and constantly evolving.[79] In this instance the contradictory impulses of capitalism, although fraught with their own histories of racism and oppression, prompted Mississippi business interests to prioritize the pursuit of profit over adherence to a particular white supremacist agenda. To pursue a hard segregationist line was to risk the appearance of political and racial extremism, thereby jeopardizing cooperative efforts with interests outside the state as well as long-term development and growth. Eventually, southern business people began further to acknowledge and appreciate the economic power of African American patronage, and gradually a desire to gain a larger share in the economic prosperity of the fifties and sixties diluted southern segregationist zeal.[80]

EXPOSING COERCION

When considered within the larger context of the sixties civil rights movement, the Tougaloo students' "cultural and artistic agitation" efforts bear similarities to integrationist campaigns waged elsewhere. As in other parts of the South, the majority of black Jacksonians who agitated for change and risked segregationist retaliation were, with some notable exceptions, youths and college students who had grown impatient with gradualist agendas that looked to law and official governmental institutions. In Mississippi and elsewhere these direct-action

Watching Jim Crow

and confrontation campaigns signalled the rise of the SNCC and altered the course of the black freedom fight.

The Tougaloo committee was a small, racially integrated group of young adults from Mississippi and outside the state. And although the students from Mississippi needed no additional inspiration to fight segregation, black middle-class "outsiders" such as Austin Moore brought a vision and sense of immediacy to the South and to Tougaloo that further empowered those agitating for change. The student attacks on oppressive practices, in Jackson and elsewhere, occasionally yielded clear-cut victories but more often temporary gains that, although tenuous were nevertheless important.

Gradually — too gradually — the ideas and beliefs that undergird racial oppression were, and continued to be, more fully revealed and challenged. Key to this social change was the public denunciation of white narratives announcing black consent with the status quo. And as one "outside agitator" has written, "the Jackson movement destroyed forever the self-serving segregationist myth of Mississippi black satisfaction."[81]

Although Austin Moore left Tougaloo College and Jackson after the eventful winter of 1963–1964, he claimed a personal victory as his Aunt Sugar was eventually admitted to the previously segregated movie theaters in downtown Jackson. Moore and the Tougaloo students did not suddenly break the tradition of southern segregation nor did they change any official policies during their months of protest and activism. The practice of segregating audiences in entertainment venues was tenaciously and violently defended for years after Moore left town and the student committee had disbanded. But the students had forced the citizens of Mississippi, both black and white, to confront again the importance of popular entertainment and its relationship to coercion and race. Black activists such as Moore and Medgar Evers had targeted and defined popular culture as a space for serious social struggle. And, as shown elsewhere in this volume, this struggle intensified as local black concerns were aligned with those of national consumerism.

Within the longer story of African American struggle this moment provided an example of an oppressed alliance using disruptive tactics on the terrain of the dominant in hopes of social change. Civil rights supporters secretively entered a public stage they neither owned nor permanently controlled. *Hootenanny, Bonanza,* and Al Hirt, as products of popular culture, were both sites of, and resources for, racial struggle, appreciated and employed by both oppressor and oppressed. The activism and reactionism in Jackson disproved the notion that popular culture and its productions or pleasures could be perfectly disciplined or policed.

Somewhat ironically, it was the voice and communicative power of white Mississippians that aided in this momentary disruption of the dominant social order. As the letter writer to the *Clarion-Ledger* noted, white reaction worked to the advantage of the activists, calling wider attention both to the segregationist position and the reality of coercion. In doing so it forced a veiled contradiction into public view. Contrary to the fundamental tenets of segregationism and the southern "way of life," African Americans were not satisfied with limited cultural opportunities and resources but rather were forced to adapt under the threats of white domination and oppression.

As this knowledge gained circulation, white consent and cooperation with segregation began to fragment. Various performers, public personalities, artistic agencies, and business interests began to distance themselves, physically and symbolically, from Jackson's segregationist institutions.

In Jackson, consent was enabled through the coerced segregation of popular entertainment and the arts. This coercion took many different forms — some overtly violent, others less so — and enjoyed the sanction of the state. It operated most powerfully and encouraged consent most efficiently when its operations were silent and unseen — naturalized or hidden by dominant alliances and institutions. Certainly this was an insight not lost on the leaders of segregation or on the managers of southern media outlets, as they often stopped broadcasts of white-on-black violence or censored representations of racial struggle. And, as the following chapter details, these media workers labored diligently, employing the resources offered by legal bureaucracies, to recode and "naturalize" their strategic maneuvers. They knew that at the moment coercion was articulated, and its implications revealed, it became vulnerable to attack.

Watching Jim Crow

CHAPTER 4

Programming/Regulating Whiteness

Although more than thirty years have passed, residents of the predominantly black neighborhoods of west Jackson still recall the popular "in-house" jokes of the fifties and sixties that circulated whenever local stations aired "cable trouble" or "technical difficulty" signs. In these households knowing quips would be exchanged, such as: "It must have been something about black people, because they're messing up the TV."[1] In Jackson and elsewhere, appearances by African Americans on local television screens were exceedingly rare, limited to occasional glimpses of popular performers on the Ed Sullivan show, or more painfully, representations of blacks linked to ignorance and crime.

Still, considered within the context of southern network affiliate practices, the programming of WLBT and WJTV were in many ways unexceptional. The stations regularly aired network fare during the day and prime-time viewing hours, including such popular shows as *Dragnet*, *Gunsmoke*, *Wagon Train*, *Life Is Worth Living* with Bishop Fulton Sheen, and the *Milton Berle Show* during the late fifties; and *The Beverly Hillbillies*, *Bonanza*, *Candid Camera*, and *The Donna Reed Show* in the early sixties. While WJTV enjoyed affiliation with CBS, the network that carried a majority of the top-rated programs during the early sixties, WLBT carried a primary affiliation with NBC and secondary affiliation with ABC, using programming in prime time from both. Both stations frequently used syndicated offerings. Although WLBT's primary economic agreement was with NBC, on the whole the station's programming reflected about a fifty-fifty split of programming from the two networks. Hewitt Griffin, the station's programming director during the mid-sixties, remembers that during that decade network affiliates in Mississippi enjoyed an industrial climate where networks were eager to please and local stations had a variety of programming options. Network representatives visited station decision makers almost weekly. As Griffin put it, NBC and ABC "were anxious to have our good will."[2]

A perusal of published prime-time program schedules during the fifties and early sixties reveals that, similar to other affiliates in the region, the stations consistently presented prime-time schedules heavy with network offerings, but often delayed or changed air times for a variety of network fare. And, at least until the mid-1960s, with several programming options at hand, station staffs were careful not only regarding what to include but also what to exclude from the schedule — most notably programming that showcased articulate, accomplished African Americans. For example, when NBC offered the *Nat King Cole Show* during the 1956 and 1957 seasons, affiliate WLBT did not air the program, instead broadcasting ABC offerings in its place or syndicated fare such as *The Whirlybirds*, a helicopter adventure show. This prime-time practice was modified in the years subsequent to the 1964 petition, as programs such as the *Sammy Davis Jr. Show* and *I Spy* were being aired by 1966.

Public affairs and news programs were the most scrutinized and censored of all broadcast materials. On WLBT, of the seven regularly scheduled NBC network "public affairs" programs that occasionally discussed racial integration and were offered to affiliates during approximately fourteen months between 1962 and 1963, the station chose to regularly air only the *Today Show*, and even then allegedly omitted "pro-integrationist" portions of that program.[3] Of twelve network special programs listed by NBC as dealing with integration and available to affiliates in 1962 and 1963, four were carried by WLBT. The weekly program *David Brinkley's Journal* was never aired. *Chet Huntley Reporting* was not used, ostensibly because management feared it would "promote violence." WJTV stayed away from airing the award-winning *CBS Reports*. WLBT would also air advisories before chosen *Today Show* segments stating "the following news is network news and represents the view of the northern press. Stay tuned for the local news, which follows immediately."[4] In 1964 such local station programming inserts were so frequent, particularly during the *Today* program, that even an editor for the *Jackson Daily News* noted "more and more" people complaining about the interruptions and commented, "I've not seen anything on one of them which interested me nearly as much as what I am missing on the network show."[5]

Watching Jim Crow

In regard to the noncarriage of network programming, the Jackson stations were also not entirely exceptional, because national and regional broadcast program sponsors were often reluctant to support programming featuring African American hosts or with a focus on southern race relations, for fear of offending southern advertisers and audiences. For this, as well as other well-documented reasons, early network prime-time productions could be characterized as offering very little in terms of African American voices, images, or perspectives.[6] As one audience member remarked in a letter to NBC regarding the prime-time offerings of the fifties: "Take, for example, Dragnet . . . its writers believe Los Angeles [has] no Negro policemen, no Negro criminals, no Negro citizens who are victims of crime or witnesses or innocent bystanders. When it comes to dramatic shows or situation comedies, TV writers never heard of Negroes."[7]

As broadcast historian William Boddy has detailed, networks grew increasingly sensitive to controversial materials in the second half of the fifties and into the early sixties.[8] Conditioned by overweening sponsor censorship and creative control during the fifties, the television writers of the early sixties practiced self-censorship. An Office of Network Study report summarizing the testimony of television advertisers in 1959 and 1960 concluded that "as a general proposition, sponsor aversion to controversy, thought-provoking material, 'downbeat' material, etc. permeates and shapes the production of 'formula type' program series [such as the ever-present westerns of the early sixties] from start to finish."[9] And certainly "the race issue" and integration were toward the top of the "controversy" and "to be avoided" lists.

Still, not all Mississippi stations mimicked the powerful Jackson outlets in this regard. During the early sixties there were at least ten television licensees (including the Jackson stations) within the state or with interstate coverage from New Orleans (WDSU) or Memphis (WMCT and WREC). Outside of the capital, local stations offered television in Columbus (WCBI), Biloxi (WLOX), Meridian (WTOK), Greenwood (WABG), Tupelo (WTWV), and Hattiesburg (WDAM). Published broadcast schedules show that some of these affiliates ran network programming rejected in Jackson. For example, WDAM broadcast the *Nat King Cole Show*, at least briefly, and *David Brinkley's Journal*. WTOK aired *CBS Reports*. Mississippi broadcasters were not unified in the belief that an absence of network public affairs programming was necessary or positive. While the Jackson stations often defended their network noncarriage as based on public safety, ratings, or economic considerations, affiliates outside of the capital chose otherwise — offering their viewers a different journalistic view of contemporary events.

This is not to say that documentary series such as CBS *Reports* were giving national audiences abundant discussion of domestic racial or civil rights struggles — at least, during the early sixties they were not. As Michael Curtin shows in *Redeeming the Wasteland* (1995), the "flagship" documentary series for all three networks were instead preoccupied with the drama of superpower struggle and "Communist threat to the Free World." Between 1959 and 1964 the NBC *White Paper* series, CBS *Reports*, and *Bell and Howell Close-Up!* broadcast a combined 11 programs focused on civil rights, which was a small fraction of the 167 episodes aired during this period.[10] Within such a context it stands as even more impressive that such series, with their consistent reiterations of American capitalist superiority in the midst of cold war tensions, were still considered sufficiently dangerous or volatile to be censored by Jackson managers.

Instead, WLBT offered a heavy diet of patriotism differently defined. The station's petitioners took special note of these programs as well as the NBC affiliate's local "news" and "commentary" segments, which seemed particularly unresponsive to "fairness" concerns. Under the banner of "patriotic" offerings the station aired syndicated programs such as *Lifeline, Dan Smoot,* and *Freedom University of the Air* — all reactionary, McCarthyesque productions obsessed with combating the imminent dangers of communism and its perceived partner, the black civil rights movement.[11] Typical of specials offered within this narrow range of programming was *Hollywood's Answer to Communism,* a program describing a 1961 Hollywood Bowl rally organized by the Christian Anti-Communism Crusade and focused on "combating Communist influence in government and public institutions."[12] Many of the personalities featured on these programs fit Stephen Whitfield's description, in *The Culture of the Cold War,* of those who had "inferred from the evidence that Communism was loathsome the conclusion that anything loathsome was Communism."[13] In the midst of cold war fears any actions or beliefs that did not conform to dominant white segregationist practice, whether pertaining to economics, politics, or race, were immediately suspect as communistic and condemned by the mediated guardians of "the American way." This conflation of racial integration with communism was a hallmark of Jackson's patriotic broadcast programming.

WLBT was also exceptional in that its physical plant facilities served not only as a broadcast center but also as an outlet for anticommunist, anti-integrationist literature. The "pro-American" shows aired on the station frequently promoted the conservative books and pamphlets available at WLBT's Freedom Bookstore, which originally was located within the station's main buildings. Monographs promoted by television spokespersons, such as Dan Smoot and *Freedom University*'s W. Cleon Skouson, included *The Naked Communist* authored by Skouson; *Black Monday*, a jeremiad aimed at the 1954 Supreme Court *Brown* decision; and *The Bondage of the Free*, which argued among other things that "Americans have not yet learned to wage a political offense against a collectivist [communist] scheme which holds the onus of color over their heads as a psycho-social guilt factor. Trying to avoid the accusation of 'racial prejudice,' white Americans are abandoning an entire social system and way of life — the consummation of centuries."[14]

But perhaps the best known and most remembered segregationist program on WLBT's weekly schedule was *Citizens' Council Forum*, a syndicated fifteen-minute program that had its organizational roots in Jackson and usually aired locally on Sunday mornings or afternoons. As mentioned in chapter 1, the council claimed that *Forum* was also shown or heard (in radio formats) on more than three hundred stations nationwide. However accurate or exaggerated this claim was, it was most likely that a majority of the broadcasters running the program were conservative radio stations. In Jackson, for example, WJTV did not televise the *Forum*, but ran the audio program on its sister station, WSLI radio. The program offered a frequent critical focus on northern or federal "threats," as well as the problem of northern "news management."

"News management" was indeed an area of primary complaint, not only for segregationist leaders but also for local African Americans and civil rights activists. In the South it was not unusual for television stations to simply suppress images or narratives of white-on-black violence and police brutality while citing a concern for public safety and fear of increasing racial tensions.[15] And in news programming as well as entertainment, before the crises prompted by student sit-ins, boycotts, and freedom riders, many local television news directors paid little attention to African Americans or the issues that they faced. As a former television news director summarized at a 1965 conference titled "The Racial Crisis and News Media," although television was the "chosen instrument of revolution" during the sixties, during the fifties "with few exceptions, southern newspapers and southern radio and TV stations carried very little news about Negroes and paid almost no attention to news involving racial issues."[16] In Jackson this omission of African American images and perspectives was nearly complete, at least in "mainstream" print and electronic media, and extended well into the sixties. Certainly, attention was paid to racial issues, but African American voices were most often excluded and direct address of racial struggle was deflected through the use of code terms such as "states' rights" and "patriotism." However well this veneer of broadcast codes covered supremacist agendas, at times undisciplined bigotry exposed racism in more raw forms. For example, two of Jackson's best-known news personalities and on-air spokesmen, Alon Bee of WLBT and Bob Neblett of WJTV, were identified as offensive based on their news/weather presentations which often carried a tone of smug mockery and ugly language. The station petitioners identified Jackson's on-air personalities as making slurred references to "negras" and "niggers," accompanied by insulting facial and hand gestures or derogatory quips in reports on civil rights demonstrations.[17]

Longtime Jackson residents remember these insults, as well as the station's disproportionate emphasis on African American crime. In a 1992 conversation, Ruth Owens, a former director of public relations at Tougaloo College, vividly recalled newscaster Bee using a newsreel shot of African American students and remarking with disgust, "look at all that black." As she talked about such past newscasts, the power and emotion of these memories were very acute. Owens told me, "I'm just as American as he was . . . this is home for me too. . . . It just hurts to see somebody on the screen saying something like that."[18] But for the official record these electronically transient performances of vulgar racism were not made manifest through a scrutiny of official station logs or records as the station came under formal review.

High on the notoriety scale for offensive programming, on par with the *Citizens' Council Forum*, was the local station's *Comment* series — a five-minute opinion and editorial piece that aired weekdays on an irregular basis, usually alongside the local evening news, weather, and sports. While a variety of guest commentators, including a few "moderates," were invited to make observations regarding current events or news stories, the station again shut out any African American or activist perspectives that might forcefully challenge the white status quo. Although the station defended the series as reflecting a broad political spectrum, the management clearly had its "favorite" commentators, including Tom Q. Ellis who alone made more than 150 appearances between 1951 and 1963.[19] And before the series was curtailed by the station, audiences had heard station manager Beard pronounce "never" in response to the integration efforts of James Meredith at the University of Mississippi, as well as Ellis refer to black Mississippians as "nigras" and "niggers" and repeatedly link racial integration efforts with communism.[20] Again in many of these cases the commentator's insulting interpretations, gestures, or departures from an official script were formally transient and informally enduring — "lost" after broadcast but very much remembered.

In the balance of this chapter I deal with memory — ways of "recording" and establishing the past — and with legal decision making. I examine how the FCC evaluated the WLBT programming described above in formal reviews, public hearings, and published statements dating between 1964 and 1969. I join these commission actions and statements to the testimony, complaints, and memories of the petitioners, and in doing so, I focus on the processes of state policy and law, showing how local activist and African American testimony was formally delegitimated by commission actions defended as procedurally necessary. In a manner analogous to the contemporary practices of white supremacy, regulators asserted that serious racial discrimination was not proven while marginalizing black testimony articulating its existence. Voices were dismissed as they announced the omission of similar voices from the television screen.[21]

CHALLENGING INSTITUTIONS

As I discussed in the first chapter, Medgar Evers and the NAACP had established a record of black complaint regarding the programming practices of Jackson's television outlets long before the complicated legal wrangling over Jackson television took form in the mid-sixties. In 1955 and 1957 the FCC received complaints centering on the omission of African American voices on WLBT and its refusals to grant airtime to integration proponents. In both instances, the commission considered the complaints and solicited station comment, but defined the local programming incidents as exceptional, opting to take no further action.

When the NAACP first brought complaints based on accounts of the 1955 "cable trouble" incident, it requested that an examination be made of the station's official logs, seeking clarification as to how and why network programming was deleted. In rejecting the request, the commission reasoned that the logs were "not required to show why a particular program or portion thereof was not carried, and therefore no purpose would be gained by examining them." Rather, the commission assured the organization that such complaints would be considered when the station filed for its license.[22]

However, even as the commission granted the station a license renewal in 1959 it recognized its limited knowledge regarding transitory station practices. The station logs, usually considered to be the official and permanent record of "what had occurred" — before the age of VCRs and cheap videotape — were, by the commission's own admission, limited and incomplete. And as the commission itself had argued, stations were not required to record justifications for even the most peculiar programming practices. Thus, over the course of investigations into station practices during the fifties the commission acknowledged, at least internally, that judgments were made with lingering uncertainties as to what had actually taken place.[23] Finding little that it could satisfactorily document, the commission downplayed focal incidents as "isolated."

However, the 1955 "cable trouble" incident, as well as other controversies that followed, exposed a central problem for the agency — satisfying the knowledge requirements and standards of proof in official legal and regulatory processes. In working with unreliable station records, absent video recordings, or independent monitoring efforts, the commission frequently struggled to find grounds for authoritative judgment. An absence of satisfactory documentation — legitimated knowledges that would provide official truths and justify federal action — was a recurring theme rehearsed by FCC examiners during the long legal fight over the station's license, and on one level it explained the commission's reluctance to significantly change the status quo.

With the 1964 petition, voices deemed dangerous to the status quo gained legal force, building on the important historical record and precedents established by Evers, Smith, and other station petitioners. At the time of the challenge, there was little doubt regarding which interests dominated the racist, broadcast construction of local history, or the resistance that contrary voices would face. Still, the United Church of Christ Office of Communications set out to gather local African American perspectives regarding the station and its programming practices. And black Mississippians spoke in response to a request from a civil rights ally, circulating alternative versions of the present and past.

The number of African Americans who testified or filed testimony for the petitioners was not large. Few Mississippians, black or white, were willing to speak out publicly given the attendant risks. Those who chose to do so confronted the difficulty of translating historically marginalized concerns into a form acceptable to the regulators, and perhaps more ominously, faced the response of those who assumed the guardianship for white supremacist histories. The segregationist response to activist challenges aimed at prominent institutions had grown increasingly violent in the early sixties, and the local television stations had established themselves as cultural giants — powerful political and economic institutions with close ties to big business and government.

In New York, Everett Parker had a difficult time finding a lawyer who thought the case could be won, given the conservative, proindustry disposition of the FCC, and in Mississippi many blacks doubted that such a powerful local institution could be significantly changed.[24] R. L. T. Smith, one of the official petitioners, explained to the FCC that it would be difficult for the UCC to gather public complaints against the station within the black community: "It is extremely difficult to get statements that speak out against the status quo from the victims of an oppressive society. I believe that it will be next to impossible to get statements about the unfair behavior of WLBT from any Negro employees of the state or any subdivision thereof. Making such a statement would almost certainly result in the loss of his job by such a person."[25] Smith's own experience added weight to his comments regarding the risk of public activism. His home and grocery store, both centers for local movement organization, were targets of terrorism. Over a period of five years the minister's home had been the target of gunfire and his business had been bombed three or four times.[26]

As discussed earlier, Smith had interactions with WLBT in attempts to buy airtime for his 1962 congressional campaign. At WLBT his requests met acrimonious denials and threats in personal conversations, which later were followed by more restrained and formal written rejections. When Smith reported the station's threats and hostility during the course of the commission hearings, WLBT programming director Maurice Thompson offered the commission a very different version of Smith's interaction with the station and proceeded to attack the black minister and the credibility of his account. He wrote: "The action of Rev. Smith in distorting the oral statements of WLBT personnel demonstrates the difficulty encountered by WLBT on occasions when it has endeavored to maintain channels of direct, oral communication with individuals engaged in militant racial activities and emphasized the necessity of limiting exchanges with such persons to written communication which form part of a permanent record and are less subject to misinterpretation."[27]

Throughout the process of FCC hearings regarding the station's practices, it was such "written communication" or "permanent records" — that is, the papers and files of the station — that a majority of FCC commissioners and the station's defenders held as most informative, objective, and reliable. This record was the standard against which the lived experiences and testimony of local African Americans were judged. In the events involving Reverend Smith and others, black memories of discriminatory or threatening behavior were subordinated to the claims of carefully worded written correspondence.

Early in the challenge process black Mississippians anticipated these bureaucratic limitations and recognized the problem of translating their concerns into arguments that distant federal officials would find credible or convincing. Doris Allison, a young student leader in the Jackson Movement and president of the Jackson branch of the NAACP, put it this way as she concluded a detailed list of complaints regarding WLBT programming: "You have to understand that I must be very exact about what I say because the Federal Communications Commission is in Washington and I am here in Jackson, Mississippi. After all, it has become a grinding effort just to be a Negro in Mississippi. The only time the Negro community is given free consideration on television is when the station wishes to make known that a Negro has raped a white woman or when it brings into focus all the weapons at the white community's command in its attempt to keep the Negro at the bottom of the perpetually shifting and bewildered populace."[28]

As local media operations and regulatory mechanisms surrounding them contributed to the alienation and disempowerment of many black Mississippians, few stepped forward to challenge the station, ask for on-air rebuttals, or criticize its practices. As Hartman Turnbow, a black farmer from Holmes County, Mississippi, put it: "I can't rember having ever seen a local Negro [on TV] allowed to speak in favor of civil rights. If there had been such a local Negro, I would have tried to get on and talk some too. I would want to get on because I want the white people to know we don't want to take the courts over, but rather to help them with the courts because we feel they need help there. I haven't tried, however, 'cause I've never seen any local people on, and I figured there are some local Negroes shrewder than me, and if they can't get on, I haven't got a chance to get on either."[29]

TESTIFYING IN THE SIXTIES

Hartman Turnbow was one of several African American witnesses who responded to the formal invitation to testify against WLBT. The complaints brought forward by these witnesses may have been shaped and guided by outside legal counsel and may or may not have been representative of black Mississippians across the state, although it is clear that most of the witnesses assumed the responsibility of representing the many voices that historically had been silenced. Certainly those who volunteered for this role were exceptional in their courage.

The testimony of Turnbow and others discussed in this chapter comes primarily from the transcribed testimony of African Americans placed in the official dockets of the FCC. Clearly these "official" histories and recollections may be significantly different from other "unauthorized" and previously unrecorded memories: very different audiences and dialogue dynamics are among the variables involved. However, in using these government materials I want to draw out observations and insights that resonate with the "unofficial" — that is, with histories and popular memories I found outside of the records of the government and court. In doing so I offer a triangulation of materials foregrounding perspectives marginalized, if sometimes recorded, via processes of state regulation and law, while looking for common themes. Rather than attempting to theorize or fully define the nature of the "official" sphere, my more modest goal is that of showing how notions of "officialness" have been mobilized to support a racial status quo. The examination of "official" testimony, its definition and its handling, in this instance reveals the inevitable interaction of the official and unofficial as well as the hierarchies of legitimacy and authorization rooted in particular, "legal," ways of knowing.

Such hierarchies are present not only in negotiations defining the official and unofficial but also within the realm of the official itself because not all official texts are accepted as equally legitimate or authoritative. In evaluating Chicano activism during the sixties and subsequent decades, Chon Noriega has argued generally that a lesson learned by media activists was that entrance into the official institutions of industry and state does not equal acceptance. He further elaborates that "acceptance itself is a problematic concept insofar as it requires an authority — that is, someone or something that can confer acceptance upon the supplicant."[30] Noriega describes how Chicano testimony before the federal agencies such as the Equal Employment Opportunities Commission "fell outside the interpretative framework of the various agencies that were approached or confronted. Chicano media activists understood neither the style nor the substance or the 'appropriately neutral and expert policy language' for mass media. After all, they were *not* policy experts, nor were they professionals within the industry; they were outsiders demanding to be let inside."[31]

The petitioners who testified before the FCC and submitted statements opposing WLBT relicensing most likely did not even consider themselves media activists, much less media policy experts or professionals. They most often simply self-identified as viewers and concerned citizens. Their focus was on attacking Jim Crow segregation and promoting civil rights change, and they recognized local television as a strategic site of struggle and potential resource. Thus for all the problems gaining "official" access posed and continues to pose, they did demand to be "let inside" the regulatory processes of the state.

The complaints that antilicensing witnesses officially submitted to the commission were quite specific and included the use of offensive gestures, language, and pronunciations, as well as the lack of use of courtesy titles such as Mr. and Mrs.; news programming and personalities that portrayed local African Americans as essentially criminal and inferior to whites; and the interruption, omission, or blacking out of programming that discussed integration or African American affairs in a positive manner. It was this last complaint — the problem of omission and blackouts — that drew repeated mention and substantial commission attention. Hartman Turnbow, for example, expressed several of these complaints:

> As a farmer good television service would be helpful because I like to keep up with the news. It means a lot to me. I've noticed the national news programs are often cut off. Huntley-Brinkley is often cut in on. I've known this to happen quite often. When they cut in I usually cut out because I'm interested in the news and not the other things they show.
>
> When any incident of any kind happens so that they have to use colored peoples' names, they called the colored person by his name only or use the title "Negro" instead of Mr. or Mrs. They generally use the title Mr. or Mrs. for white people in similar circumstances. This is true of both television stations.
>
> Very rarely do we see Negroes on shows originating locally. We see them on national network programs, but very rarely on shows originating locally. Of course I don't watch television twenty-four hours a day, but it happens so seldom that I can't remember when I last saw one. When one appears my wife and daughter call me to the TV to see the Negro. They know I like to see Negroes so they always call me if one appears.[32]

Witness Doris Allison also made remarks along these lines:

> The general practice of WLBT is to just serve some of the people, and not the community as a whole. And when they do carry an announcement as a service to the Negro community, it is so distorted that even the person who made it cannot recognize it. And when a person speaks out against the oppression of the Negro in Mississippi, he is often very conveniently interrupted. If such a presentation is not cancelled, there are so many interruptions during it that one is forced to guess what the presentation was about. One sees enough of the presentation to know what it probably means, but often one cannot be sure because of the interruptions. This practice was often observed on the *Today Show*.
>
> Mr. Alon Bee is an announcer who is particularly obnoxious whenever he refers to Negroes. When Sidney Poitier won the Academy Award, he said he was sure that no one agreed with the decision that selected Sidney Poitier as the outstanding actor. When he has to report something good about a Negro, he carefully makes sure that everyone sees all his venom and hate. When Dave Garroway's wife committed suicide, Alon Bee commented that even she could not stand to continue to live with Dave Garroway. This was clearly because of Dave Garroway's sympathy for the civil rights struggle.[33]

The prominent clergyman Reverend Wendell P. Taylor, pastor of the largest African American Methodist Church in Jackson, also testified. He commented that while living south of Jackson in the Laurel-Hattiesburg area he found local station WDAM to be "fairer" and more cooperative with local African Americans than the Jackson broadcasters. Taylor reiterated the complaints so common among those who submitted testimony:

> Since I have been in Jackson I have been concerned about the type and quality of television programs over the local stations. The station WLBT (which I have viewed more regularly) has been of more serious concern because of the following things I have observed in its telecasting:
> 1) Up until recent months there seems to have been a policy of blacking out most programs that dealt with Negroes in their struggle for civil rights.
> 2) Network programs such as *Today* which attempt to present controversial issues unbiasedly are often interrupted in their items with reference to Negroes[,] or when Negro guests appear on the program[,] with trivial news of local interest which is slanted toward the white community. Its local news programs are always slanted in dealing with Negroes or issues involving Negroes.
> 3) Alon Bee, the newscaster on *Today in Jackson*, a program that can be seen at 7:25 and 8:25 A.M. is probably the worst offender in slanting the news with reference to Negroes.
> 4) Another objectionable feature of the news broadcast of this station is its editorial *Comment*. This feature is supposed to deal with controversial issues but only persons with fixed ideas and who support the status quo ever appear on the initial invitation.[34]

Stella Harrington, a woman active in local voter registration and freedom rider support efforts, also touched on these themes, including problems with the station's entertainment programming:

> The first thing I watch in the morning is the *Today Show*. I find that they use anything that can be put in to cut off the show. For instance, on Tuesdays and Thursdays John Stennis appeared for fifteen minutes to interrupt the *Today Show*. . . . Last summer when the *Today Show* was bringing in a lot of national news, any program was used to interrupt it. Some days one could only see an hour and a half of the two-hour program. . . .
> Two or three years ago the program *The Rifleman* advertised that

Sammy Davis, Jr. was to appear as a guest star. When the time for the program came they did not show it, but instead ran a film of *The Loretta Young Show*. This is typical of what seems to be a general policy of keeping out appearances of Negroes when possible.[35]

Finally, Mrs. Arthur Mitchell of Jackson also testified that not only news but entertainment fare had been omitted from WLBT broadcasts:

> There is a general reluctance to show Negroes in starring positions, even on national programs, for instance. Sunday, April 19, 1964, the preview for the program, *Bonanza*, was not shown, instead we saw commercials. Every week before the preview had been shown, and every week since the 19th the preview has been shown. Only in this case where a preview of a Negro star was going to be presented did they fail to show the preview. . . .
>
> I'd like to have accurate, objective news reports. I would like to have the station's employees use courtesy titles for all people. I would like to see Negroes freely participate in all the television activities that white people participate in. I would like to have our activities and programs announced by the station. In short, I would like to see the station begin to operate really in the public interest. . . .
>
> The television stations follow the established state policy of discrimination and segregation. This kind of policy is not fair to us. They only seek to show Negroes in a derogatory fashion, if they cannot avoid showing them altogether.[36]

As news of the challenge to WLBT's license spread throughout Jackson, form letters and local petitions were circulated, both supporting and opposing the station's license renewal. Petitions and form letters were placed at locations in black neighborhoods and businesses such as R. L. T. Smith's grocery store and brought to the attention of Jackson Movement participants at NAACP and church meetings. Even in an environment threatening severe reprisals to antilicensing petitioners, during April and May 1964 the commission received more than 250 signatures on form letters addressed to the FCC chair, E. William Henry, articulating local concerns regarding the dignity and prestige of African American representations: "Dear Mr. Henry: The Federal Communications Commission is urged to investigate programming policies of television station WLBT-TV and its affiliate radio station WJDX before a new permit to operate is granted. It is my firm belief that these stations avoid programs which give prestige parts to Negroes. I am also convinced that the news is stated in a manner prejudiced to the best interest of Negroes. Respectfully yours."[37] A barely legible handwritten letter received at the FCC chairman's office made the simple, one-sentence appeal: "I am asking you please do not renew the license of WLBT on channel 3 here in Mississippi, for the Negro is absolutely ignored."[38]

In the testimony and correspondence of black Mississippians there was considerable reiteration of these issues. Almost all of the witnesses testified that network programming had been blacked out or replaced by locally inserted programming, continuing the very common complaint regarding the omission of black voices and perspectives. Several witnesses told the same stories regarding specific events and newscasters, notably the offensive language and pronunciations of "Negro" as well as the attacks on celebrities such as Sidney Poitier and Dave Garroway. Many spoke also of the all-white programming for children and teens. Implicit, or sometimes explicit, within the letters and testimony was an appeal for representational respect and dignity — a central theme within the larger scope of the local civil rights movement.

Within the testimony offered by citizens such as Hartman Turnbow were references to the excitement and joy experienced by local African Americans as they viewed rare images of black personalities. Appearances by black actors, actresses, professionals, leaders, and entertainers were exceptional moments, prompting families to call others to gather around the TV set. As the duplicated letters to the FCC chair emphasized, such entertainers in "prestige parts" were noticeably absent from local television.

Several witnesses provided detailed accounts of station practices. Some offered precise records of times, dates, and program titles, thereby corroborating more general observations offered by other viewers. As one of the station's challengers put it, after surveying the very specific, concrete recollections of local witnesses: "I note that in their attached statements, witnesses have to go back into history — two years ago, three years ago. If these channels had used Negro news as it came along, who would have such an accurate memory?"[39] The general absence of black representations made the exceptions all the more memorable, especially within the context of the struggles for integration.

The same woman making this observation offered her own vivid memories, including incidents involving Alon Bee of WLBT and Bob Neblett of WJTV. She wrote: "The latter actually has said 'nigger' on

Watching Jim Crow

his program, not 'nigra.' Lately, he has been carefully saying "Neee-gro,' drawing the syllable out. The time I heard him do it, I also heard him laugh. As for courtesy titles, most announcers use none at all for Negroes; they simply give the name in full the first time, and then, for subsequent references, they say 'the woman,' 'the Negro man,' 'the Smith woman,' or 'she.' "[40] While the call for human dignity and courtesy figured prominently throughout both the larger civil rights campaign and the local Jackson Movement, it came as no surprise to African Americans that this demand, which had been largely ignored by Mississippi's most powerful politicians, business, and religious leaders, was also snubbed by local broadcasters. Such disregard rearticulated the problem of having African American complaints held subordinate to the narratives established by powerful segregationist institutions.

Many local black complaints could not be documented via station records any more than could Beard's alleged posting of a fraudulent cable trouble sign in 1955. The same interests managing daily broadcast programming also managed the technologies of official record—station tapes, correspondence, and logs. Thus, one thin hope of the station's challengers in 1964 was that the FCC would grant a full investigation and hearing into the practices of WLBT, in order that any paper trails could be further investigated and black voices invited into the official record.

Of course, the commission also received letters supporting the stations and their renewal applications. A common theme among these letters was one of genuine shock and surprise that the Jackson stations were found offensive by anyone. A common reiterated phrase was "I cannot understand [how or why the station is being challenged]." These writers were convinced that WLBT and WJTV were engaging their community in a fair and sensitive fashion. Complaints against the stations, much less formal license denial petitions, were sincerely confusing. For example, a former FBI agent living in Jackson wrote that it was "inconceivable . . . that anyone could have an honest and sincere complaint against either or both of these broadcasting companies. . . . It would be nothing short of tragic if their licenses were not renewed, and I cannot conceive of our Government having any question whatsoever as to licensing them."[41] Another Jackson resident wrote: "I am quite surprised that anyone would wish to deny the license. However I do feel the so-called church group is applying pressure in a manner which has little to do with the quality of the TV station."[42]

Other letters in this camp were marked not only by anger but also by fears regarding the loss of an important, cherished cultural institution, along with a corresponding shift in racial power. Resentment was expressed regarding black gains in popular representation and politics, as well as the interventions of northern church-affiliated "outsiders." It is also striking how many Jackson residents were concerned that television would, in some sense, be "lost" — either completely taken away from Jackson by federal bureaucrats, or given away to some undeserving group. Exemplifying these fears, one writer wrote at some length:

> This week we learned on the news that the NAACP is seeking to have our two local TV stations' licenses revoked. That is the most ridiculous thing I've ever heard of. . . . We still see *Bonanza* (even though the three members cancelled their contract to come here because of segregated seating). We still see Lawrence Welk since he has added a negro tap dancer as a regular to this show; Ed Sullivan has always had them; They are often seen on *Password, Nurses, Concentration*, etc. We saw the Academy Award presentation with Sammy Davis, Jr. and Sidney Poitier.
>
> I haven't heard of any other TV station licenses being questioned and I'm tired of it. There are more color TVs in homes of niggers in Jackson than whites. Are they complaining?
>
> Jackson doesn't want trouble and bloodshed — we just want to be left alone to live in peace as we used to. . . .
>
> I have 29 fourth and fifth grade Girl Scouts and this past Christmas we spent $20 of our dues giving Christmas dinner, new toys and many good used clothes to a very nice needy negro couple with six children. . . . The color of their skin didn't matter to us! Others have done the same. Please don't black out TV's in Jackson.[43]

Such letters reiterated the white segregationist vision of the person of color that was quiet and compliant with white control and patronage. For such "Negroes," skin color "didn't matter." Within this imagination large numbers of blacks were well off due to white generosity and concern, and had no reason to complain. In fact, what was startling and offensive, and remains offensive to white privilege today, is the very existence of black complaint — particularly black complaint aimed at established cultural institutions.

Among those writing in support of WLBT and WJTV were also some very prominent black leaders. Jackson, like other southern cities, had a significant number of accomplished African American professionals — such as Percy Greene, discussed in chapter 3 — who had achieved roles of leadership while routinely endorsing segregationist policies for a variety of reasons, including the sincere conviction that integration would harm local black concerns. This group included established educational and religious leaders; for example, two black college executives, including Jackson State University president Jacob Reddix, signed letters of station support. A primary difference setting these professionals apart from others in the black community arguing against station licensing was the former's alignment with institutionalized power. In most cases, those writing against the station not only did not enjoy such power but also were using their resources at considerable risk in the hope of building alternative alliances with more power.

THE MAJORITY RULES

For more than a year the FCC held both Jackson stations on temporary permits while reviewing their relicensing applications. On 19 May 1965 the FCC voted five to one to renew the license of WJTV and its companion radio station WSLI for a full three-year period. The commission reasoned that subsequent to the petition the station had demonstrated a pattern of operation "designed to ascertain and serve the needs and interests of the entire service area during the next license period."[44] The commission warned WJTV not to discriminate against blacks in the future, and to consult with black community leaders and more consciously apply broadcasting's fairness doctrine.

The commission's address of WLBT was considerably more complicated. In a relatively brief statement, a majority of the commissioners reviewed the allegations against the station and admitted that serious questions existed regarding "whether the licensee's operations have fully met the public interest standard."[45] Nevertheless, the majority, by a vote of four to two, decided to grant a probational short-term license renewal to the station, offering the following, rather curt, justification: "In making its judgment, the Commission has taken into account that this particular area is entering a critical period in race relations, and that the broadcast stations, such as here involved, can make a most worthwhile contribution to the resolution of problems arising in this respect.

That contribution is needed now — and should not be put off for the future. . . . We are granting a renewal of license, so that the licensee can demonstrate and carry out its stated willingness to serve fully and fairly the needs and interests of its entire area — so that it can, in short, meet and resolve the questions raised."[46]

Faced with the complaints that created what FCC general counsel Henry Geller characterized as the clearest call for an evidentiary hearing that he had ever seen, the commission majority overruled staff recommendations for a hearing due to, at least within their formal rationale, the urgency of local race relations. Given the "sensitivity" of these relations, they reasoned, the federal intervention and disruption attendant with hearings would be contrary to the public interest. Supplementing this rationale, a stark footnote announced the commission's position regarding the legal standing of the petitioners and the FCC definition of the "public" in "public interest."[47] The commissioners wrote that the station's challengers, "as members of a minority group," could "assert no greater interest or claim of injury than members of the general public."[48] This comment stood in marked contrast with the body of the commission's decision. For pages it discussed whether or not a minority group had been treated or represented fairly compared to other members of the viewing public. The regulators all but explicitly stated that African Americans had been distinctly "injured," while at the same time arguing that the black petitioners could assert no different claim of injury than those inflicting the injury. While such language espoused a peculiar legal logic, it also enacted a marginalization of lived racial oppression. The commission ended its formal decision admonishing the station "to immediately cease discriminatory programming patterns," and to establish programming changes as a contingency for relicensing.[49]

Certainly this tortured opinion and justification reflected the proindustry position of the FCC. Particularly large, powerful broadcasters such as those established in Mississippi's capital were routinely protected by commission actions. However, this decision made it equally apparent that the commission's investment in the status quo operated along multiple axes. The commission majority's arguments were an explicit attempt to shield commercial broadcasters from minority activism. Fearing a flood of "minority" petitions disrupting the coeffi-cencies of industry and regulation, the commission articulated an en-

Watching Jim Crow

during strategy for the address of contemporary racial struggle. This strategy entailed foregrounding racial tensions as a justification for caution and conservatism while at the same time evacuating any notions of racial or social difference — in this case noting the "sensitivity" of conflicting racial interests while simultaneously denying that black Mississippians could assert different interests or claims than white Mississippians — all within a segregationist society that had produced divisions precisely around questions of race. By placing faith in "broadcast stations [to] make a contribution to the resolution of [racial] problems,"[50] the commission effectively surrendered address of racial tensions to the very institutions that African Americans had targeted as problematic.

Charged with discovery of "the facts" in this station's history, the commission responded with a decision explicitly grounded less in factual discovery than in the conflicting social practices of the time. Understanding itself as an institution intertwined with contemporary civil rights struggles, the commission majority envisioned themselves as a benevolent power offering help to the black citizen.

The 1965 majority decision was also notable for its complete neglect of petitioner complaints not directly aligned with the fairness doctrine. This focus was predictable, as the petition included fairness allegations and the commission had taken the extraordinary step of issuing a "clarification" of doctrine requirements in 1963 — largely in response to southern broadcaster handling, or more precisely neglect, of the integration-segregation debate. Still, while fairness considerations were central to station challengers and defenders, they were not the exclusive grounds for complaint, and arguably were not even the most dangerous accusations aimed at the license. Historically the FCC had dealt severely with stations involved in misrepresentation or misinformation, and as the minority dissent in this case noted, these were exactly the types of issues that begged further investigation. At several points the petitioners' testimony starkly contradicted station claims and representations. But instances of station misrepresentation received no consideration in the formal majority decision, as the commissioners concentrated on questions of fairness, finally defining the problematic fairness incidents as isolated or related to previous renewal periods.[51]

Commission concentration on narrowly defined fairness doctrine concerns meant a nearly complete dismissal of African American testimony speaking to the problem of omissions and blackouts in important programming. As noted earlier, a central thread in the testimony gathered from black Mississippians was frustration regarding omissions, blackouts, and interruptions. Yet these station practices, taken alone, were not a fairness doctrine violation per se and could be defended as the legally protected First Amendment right of any local broadcaster. The station's formal fairness obligation was only to address "controversial issues of public importance" while offering "reasonable" opportunities for all sides to be heard — all within the context of reconciling overall programming with "the public interest."

Thus the complaints of African Americans would be accorded no more force or recognition than citizens protesting loud commercials or teenage rock and roll. The public interest criteria had been circumscribed by the commission definition of the public as an essentially homogenized group — in which African Americans would have no legally recognized interests distinct from those that supported an oppressive status quo. By reiterating dominant racial discourses, the commissioners in the majority claimed to aid a historically oppressed group by treating them no differently than their oppressors. Perhaps this was one reason the dissenting commissioners, while raising the problem of programming omissions in their response, placed more emphasis on conducting fuller investigations and hearings rather than marshaling African American voices.

The dissenting commissioners hoped to further examine some dramatic discrepancies. For example, R. L. T. Smith offered testimony and evidence regarding his confrontation with Fred Beard and WLBT practices that stood in stark opposition to the narratives offered to the FCC on typed station letterhead. Other witnesses testified to program disruptions and alterations officially denied by broadcast managers. Then again, black Mississippians often provided narratives admittedly contingent on memory — frequently without written corroboration or documentation — while station accounts supported by logs, letters, and other documents denied their historical and political contingency and were largely of the staff's own creation.

And so the petitioners were not surprised to learn in May 1965 that the commission majority would fail to fully consider the stories and testimonies of their witnesses: such nonrecognition was the commonplace.

The station's moment of regulatory victory was short-lived. In 1966, the U.S. Court of Appeals for the District of Columbia rejected the commission's ruling regarding legal standing; granted a measure of legal recognition to the petitioners grounded in the discourses of consumerism; and agreed with the commission dissenters that there was enough evidence to merit an evidentiary hearing on relicensing (see chapter 2). The court explicitly reversed the FCC's licensing order and remanded the matter to the commission, while retaining jurisdiction to dispose of the case. Thus, by court order the FCC held formal hearings in Jackson, Mississippi, during May 1967, calling witnesses and reviewing new legal briefs as well as those materials submitted in earlier challenges.

The court charged the commission with investigation of fairness doctrine concerns, black access to station facilities, and address of whether or not the broadcaster had acted in good faith dealing with racial representation. Extensive documentation and testimony was submitted from both sides of the debate. On 27 June 1968 the commission majority announced that they had reconsidered all relevant evidence and then published their decision. Given the commission's history and handling of the case, few were surprised that the regulators decided to grant a full, three-year license renewal to the embattled station.

In a departure from their extraordinary claim of sensitivity to racial tensions that was stated in defense of the 1965 renewal, the 1968 decision justified relicensing due to an absence of significant "corroboration or substantiation" of petitioner allegations. In short, the FCC claimed that charges against the station had not been proven. Echoing the FCC hearing examiner's conclusions released in 1967, the commission majority summarized:

> Examiner Kyle determined that the allegations made by the interveners, which were of a sufficiently serious nature to merit an evidentiary hearing, were neither corroborated nor substantiated at the hearing. Rather the examiner concluded that the record demonstrated that WLBT had consistently afforded the right of expression over its facilities to persons of contrasting views to those expressed over the air . . . and that the record was devoid of any evidence that WLBT misrepresented either to

the viewing public or to the Commission, its programming policy with respect to racial issues or that it did not act in good faith in the presentation of programming on that issue. . . .

We are in agreement with the examiner's conclusion that the interveners failed to corroborate or substantiate virtually all of their allegations upon which the hearing was predicated.[52]

This argument stood in uneasy juxtaposition to the commission's 1965 decision. The earlier ruling had granted only a probationary short-term license, telling the station that the "asserting of ignorance . . . or of reliance on [misleading] labels is over," and demanding that it "immediately cease discriminatory programming patterns."[53] In 1968 the commission reexamined many of the same complaints that commissioners had defined as serious and troubling just three years prior, yet now dismissed them as lacking any evidentiary base. Angry dissenting commissioners Kenneth Cox and Nicholas Johnson attacked this contradiction: "The Commission's former show of concern for the public interest has been replaced by all-out indifference. In May 1965, the Commission found WLBT's performance sufficiently disturbing to warrant a special, short-term, probationary renewal. In June 1968, the Commission looks over the same record and declares it clean enough to justify a routine, rubberstamped, 3-year renewal."[54] Again, in regard to the FCC's decision, the station's petitioners were far from surprised. It had been evident to them early in the hearings that the commission was grudging in its grant of a hearing and that the appointed hearing examiner, Jay D. Kyle, brought into the hearing room considerable animus aimed at the station's challengers and their arguments.

During the two and a half weeks of testimony eleven witnesses appeared for the station challengers and twenty-four for the station. In the case of station witnesses, although attorneys had attempted to bring in African American witnesses supporting WLBT, only one black witness testified.[55] The eleven witnesses providing testimony for the interveners included the original petitioners — Reverend R. L. T. Smith, Dr. Aaron Henry, and UCC representative Everett Parker — as well as Tougaloo College president Dr. A. D. Beittel, civil rights worker Andrew Young, and three other local black residents. All of these witnesses faced rigorous cross-examination by both station counsel and attorneys from the FCC's broadcast bureau, which was made even more hostile through the rulings and comments of hearing examiner Kyle.

Before the hearings began Kyle made a series of key procedural rulings that put the interveners at a severe disadvantage and essentially ended any hope of a successful license challenge. Kyle ruled that "material regarding civil rights in Mississippi which did not relate" to either of two narrowly defined "fairness" issues — the airing of all sides of controversial issues or facilities access to all segments of the community — would not be accepted. Further, he ruled that any voluntary statements not made in direct response to questions of counsel would not be allowed.[56]

Perhaps most crucial of all, Kyle and the commission preempted damning testimony against the station through the establishment of an extraordinarily strict standard and burden of proof for the petitioners. Working with this standard, the hearing examiner and commission majority routinely refused to accept oral testimony as evidence, even in cases when such testimony was not challenged or contradicted by the station's representatives. The examiner repeatedly dismissed detailed testimony that in his estimation lacked a precise recall of times, dates, and other details, or further corroboration. Within this legal framework, much of the petitioner testimony describing discrimination and station complicity remained formally at the level of allegation and was viewed with suspicion, although emerging patterns and themes were clear.

Andrew Young, then the executive director of the Southern Christian Leadership Conference, was just one of several witnesses who received reprimands or criticisms from the FCC hearing examiner or commission attorneys for perceived vagueness or provision of materials deemed "unrelated to the issues" at hand. In comments to UCC attorney Earl Moore, and later Young, the presiding examiner voiced a familiar criticism of petitioner testimony: "And the witness also used the word 'guess' a minute ago and that is not good, Mr. Moore. Let's tie it down to the places and this station. All we are concerned with here is WLBT. That is all we are concerned with. I don't want any witness to deal with the realm of generalities, so tie it down as to what he had done and what he has not done and then he may be cross-examined and it may be rebutted. There are to be no voluntary statements of witnesses so you are limited to the questions of Mr. Moore and later Mr. Miller and Mr. Kehoe."[57]

Ruth Owens, director of public relations at Tougaloo College until 1965, was one petitioner who brought not only a detailed memory of station offenses, but precise written records regarding station incidents. She had found local programming so outrageous that she had privately decided to keep written notes, including precise times and dates, regarding some of the station's particularly offensive practices. As she testified, FCC attorneys attempted to discredit her accounts. Shortly before she was called to testify in the hearing room, at least one attorney approached her, and seeing the diary in her hands, charged "you just wrote those notes down here, didn't you?" Owens responded she had not, and that indeed the notes had been put on paper for some time. In her testimony she charged that the station had failed to carry public service announcements that she had personally issued for Tougaloo events, and then documented instances in which WLBT personnel had failed to use courtesy in addressing local African Americans.[58] In response the FCC attorney attempted to weaken Owens testimony by questioning why some instances she mentioned were documented — that is, described in detail on paper — and others were not.[59]

When a discrepancy arose regarding the use of the term "nigger" by Tom Q. Ellis on the *Comment* program, Kyle's ruling again epitomized the commission's treatment of intervener witnesses. Although WLBT news director Richard Sanders maintained he had never heard station employees use the term, three witnesses testified that both Ellis and announcer Alon Bee had used it. Kyle acknowledged that Bee's use of the term was unrefuted, then he invalidated the testimony as hearsay: "A glaring weakness of the interveners evidence here is that, as in many of their allegations, they did not pinpoint specific times when certain events supposedly occurred thereby unfairly depriving the applicant of an opportunity to properly rebut such allegations."[60]

R. L. T. Smith was in the midst of testimony when examiner Kyle made one of many rulings excluding the information provided by local citizens. Smith, who offered testimony characterized by the commission as vague and lacking detail, certainly carried enough detail into his description of the WLBT premises and the station's on-site supremacist Freedom Bookstore to raise the ire of Kyle. The examiner issued a warning to UCC attorney Moore that explicitly articulated his perspective as well as that of the commission majority: "Well, I want you to keep in mind, Mr. Moore, the issues, all parties will stay on the issues. I have no authority to broaden any issues or enlarge any issues. . . . I don't want a lot of ramification, Mr. Moore. I just want you to stick to the issues."[61]

Watching Jim Crow

It bears repeating that in calling the petitioners and critics of the station back to the issues Kyle was demanding that diverse practices and experiences of those practices be translated and condensed into very constricted, formally constituted considerations. By telling the petitioner's lead attorneys that he didn't "want a lot of ramification," Kyle cast an emphasis on what one analyst termed "an examination of particulars rather than an evaluation of the total effect of past programming."[62] Rather than examine larger patterns of practices, individual practices divorced from earlier contexts were to provide conclusive insight into institutional behavior.

This was analogous to a reliance on a few selected police department documents to assess long-standing department practices toward people of color. Various parts of the whole, stripped of their historical context and definitions, were examined through the technically adjusted microscope of administrative procedure. This disaggregative work translated that which was familiar and urgent to the petitioners into the unrecognizable and irrelevant. The relevant cohesions informing everyday experience were taken apart and their meaningfulness was reworked by a set of values and politics formally denied.

In the person of examiner Kyle the commission exercised one of the legal institution's most dramatic and important powers — namely, to renominate and rearticulate everyday concerns — thus forcing them into strangely deadening contexts removed from their original locale.[63] Throughout the hearings Kyle repeatedly defended his decisions and limiting judgments as mandated by court directive and the demands of administrative procedure. Such justifications provided a thin formal veil for the particular interests and politics of the agency. Long before the hearing examiner issued his official decision or the commission majority concurred, the petitioners acknowledged that the hearing and commission decisions process must simply be endured as prelude to yet another, 1969, federal court appeal.

DATA THAT MATTERS

Certainly as the FCC began investigations into the practices of WLBT in the sixties, local African Americans gave voice to specific, concrete, articulate knowledges regarding the station and its practices. However, these were knowledges devalued or disqualified within the processes of administrative law: memories of suspicious omissions or absences; memories that were never officially documented or transferred into the bureaucratic record, but rather communicated orally and circulated throughout local communities.

What the commission's handling of African American testimony in this case points to, among other things, are differences in ways of knowing as well as differences in the epistemological frames employed in evaluating disparate knowledges. Cultures frequently differ in their choice of "data that matters,"[64] and this fundamental tension was made manifest throughout the WLBT licensing fight. On the one hand there was the "permanence" and authority associated with written documentation, offered often by the station and its advocates, and on the other hand was the "transience" and lack of authority that officialdom associated with orality and intervener memory. This tension underlined the incongruity of localized communal credibility and generalized legal authority. For FCC examiners and attorneys what mattered most was not the credibility of a witness within her/his community or social space, but rather what seemed to many petitioners to be arbitrary and superfluous — a precise notation of times, dates, and durations corroborated by written documentation. In the practice of administrative law these "precise" knowledges were deemed the guarantors of truth and were categorized as substantial and authoritative in the final analyses.

These technologically based assessments negotiated existing tensions between orality and literacy. Privileging printed documents and their ostensible precision corresponded with the primacy of literacy within Western culture and law. In investigating this primacy in *Orality and Literacy*, Walter Ong discusses the historical shifts from orality to literacy, showing how orality values very different types of thinking than does literacy. Ong echoes philosopher Jacques Derrida's insistence that "writing is 'not a supplement to the spoken word' but a quite different performance."[65]

By focusing attention on predominately oral cultures, Ong argues that oral peoples most frequently view the categorical (rather than situational) thinking characteristic of contemporary legal reasoning as unimportant and trivializing. Empathetic and participatory, rather than objectively distanced, knowing and learning are held paramount.[66] Ong also observes that earlier cultures that knew the technology of writing did not assume that written records had more force than spoken words as evidence of a long-past state of affairs. Rather, they often assumed quite the opposite, especially in court and legal settings: "Witnesses were prima facie more credible than texts because they could be challenged and made to defend their statements, whereas texts could not."[67] He goes on to caution that "persons whose world view has been formed by high literacy need to remind themselves that in functionally oral cultures the past is not felt as an itemized terrain, peppered with verifiable and disputed 'facts' or bits of information. It is the domain of the ancestors, a resonant source for renewing awareness of present existence, which itself is not an itemized terrain either. Orality knows no lists or charts or figures."[68]

Most of the black witnesses submitting testimony or comments were not only literate but well educated, and were considered all the more threatening for embodying these qualities. But the cultures of most black Mississippians were also rich with connections to oral traditions, and it was the oral testimony offered by petitioners as key evidence that FCC examiners and station supporters assessed as lacking. Evident within this assessment was a racially marked politics of documentation, a supposedly neutral proceduralism promoting particular interests by putting the differences between orality and literacy into play.

For most of the petitioner witnesses the precise details, lists, charts, and figures so highly esteemed by commission attorneys and official legal culture were of less value than other more pragmatic, holistic knowledges. The memories held were common themes valued by the speakers and their community, not verbatim recall.[69] The oppression emanating from powerful dominant institutions encouraged a healthy skepticism regarding the truthfulness of "precise" official knowledges and warned against the recording of contrary and accusatory data. Oral practices meant that supremacist surveillance had no records for review and reprisal. Instead, within these traditions, knowledges that powerful institutions neglected or refused to formally recognize were hidden, cultivated, maintained, and circulated — knowledges that were officially effaced but remained stubbornly attached to specific contexts and experiences.

As the regulators went point by point through petitioner testimony and memory they refused to consider these contexts, but instead dissected and tore apart that which memories had brought together. Dissatisfied with the generalizing nature of historical memory, those working within the administrative process began to separate and recategorize these local knowledges, demanding higher levels of precision and exact agreement in historical description. The commission's hearing examiner repeatedly warned movement leaders such as R. L. T. Smith and Ed King that the administrative matters under consideration had nothing at all to do with civil rights and that any testimony explicitly linked to civil rights concerns would be disqualified.

This was the awkward technique of law through which the FCC attempted to renegotiate its relationship with wide-ranging civil rights and racial justice concerns. Of course, the matters under consideration had everything to do with civil rights, and the politics and race struggles of the moment were a prime concern of the commission. The agency had recognized as much. In its 1965 decision the FCC had explicitly justified the relicensing of both Jackson stations in civil rights terms, noting that its streamlined investigation was motivated primarily by the "urgency" of local race relations. Social discourses external to the legal structures of concern had been recognized, making a recuperation of institutional authority seem necessary three years later. While local race relations remained "urgent" in 1968, perhaps even more urgent than 1965, the commission majority now recognized the "supplementary" discourses of local race relations as profoundly threatening to its authority and legitimacy.

Of course, the agents of state law consistently attempt to efface the fundamentally social constitution of their actions. To appropriate Stanley Fish's more general remark regarding the law's operations, the commission is an example of a prominent legal institution that "wishes to have a formal existence." It does not want its policy or decision making declared subordinate to nonlegal structures of concern, or recognized as dependent on "supplementary" social discourses for definition and nomination. Such recognition, while always present on some level, must remain below a critical threshold before it profoundly threatens institutional authority and legitimacy. Thus the commission was forced to continually create and recreate itself out of the social materials and forces that it was also obliged to deny as fundamental to its usefulness and meaning.[70]

In this case, state agency decision making would be redefined, in the words of hearing examiner Kyle, as having "nothing to do with civil rights." Fearing the increasing mobilization, intervention, and power

Watching Jim Crow

of civil rights and minority activists, the agency worked to thwart these new citizen petitioners, all the while denying the commission's strategies of regulatory retrenchment.

DISAGGREGATING AND WRITING THE PAST

The commission's handling of the anti-licensing petitioners provides a vivid illustration of how liberal legal and regulatory institutions rely on proceduralism joined to scientific rationalism and other forms of "instrumental reasoning" in "merely another form of politics that postpone or obscure moral and political actions under the cloak of a supposedly universal neutrality."[71] As one theorist has put it: "Scientific rationalism, that way of knowing which imperializing power has developed so successfully, works through separation and categorization; indeed its motto, both politically and epistemologically, is 'divide and rule' . . . [because it] exerts its control over the world by dividing it into ever smaller categories, by drawing ever finer lines of distinction."[72] By separating everyday experiences and memories of civil rights struggle from the struggles surrounding the station, commission examiners invoked notions of objectivity, a "desirable" disinterest, and simultaneously attacked the countermemories so important to the complainants.

In the present and past this practice of "dividing" — what Supreme Court justice Thurgood Marshall termed "disaggregation" — has been employed in a variety of legal forums to take apart that which has been experienced whole and to isolate experiences from their meaning-giving contexts.[73] As critical legal theorists Kimberlé Crenshaw and Gary Peller have argued, disaggregation's primary move is to divorce the effects of racial power from their social context and from their historic meaning.[74] Such a decontextualization of social events from their space and time leaves only a "hollow, analytic norm of 'color-blind' — an image of racial power as embodied in abstract classifications by race that could run either way, against white as easily as against blacks."[75] These same decontextualized events, stripped from time and space, are effectively recontextualized and "transformed" as they are inserted into the epistemological systems of legitimated institutions such as law.[76]

The FCC's handling of African American concerns in this case, and the disaggregation employed by the commission, represented a symbolic and literal isolation of, and from, African American lives. Although the commission's logic and strategies demonstrated creative variations, the 1965 and 1968 decisions were consistent in their refusal to recognize the actual voices and lived experiences of black Mississippians. Presented with evidence that was achingly concrete — painful memories of exclusion and verbal assaults — the legal examiners drew "ever finer lines of distinction" between memories that would be considered "true" — that is, legally admissible — and those that would be, along with the televised images of African Americans, simply omitted.

The late Ralph Ellison was one among many African American voices who responded to such problems of white omission and nonrecognition with exceptional power. In his potent novel *Invisible Man* Ellison's black protagonist witnesses a cop kill his friend, and the author uses the character's voice to call attention to the historiographic problem that continues to echo both inside and outside of legal institutions: "All things, it is said, are duly recorded — all things of importance, that is. But not quite, for actually it is only the known, the seen, the heard and only those events that the recorder regards as important that are put down, those lies his keepers keep their power by. . . . Where were the historians today? And how would they put it down?"[77] As Ellison observes so powerfully, all historiography (and that certainly includes my project) is partial — it is abstracted and invested in the politics of the present. And, officially, the "lies [that] keepers keep their power by" are produced via powerful, legitimated technologies that construct and enable levels of recognition.

As the fate of Jackson television was contested in hearings, courtrooms, and less formal settings, three dominant tactics were deployed in response to petitioner testimony and demands — maneuvers that are often aligned with the defense of white privilege today: nonrecognition, formal recoding, and disaggreggation. Histories offered to the representatives of government and law enforcement were frequently ignored, or were recoded and/or stripped of social contexts. Official or legal recognition, then as now, was a technically complicated, multifaceted problem, engaging politics on multiple institutional levels. And interveners were forced to ask themselves, when formal recognition was finally won, how were their arguments and perspectives defined relative to their social and historical locations?

What some have termed "nonracist" or "inferential" racism denies

Watching Jim Crow

its power and presence via claims to nonracial processes and concerns. In this case, concrete, specific knowledges and memories were ignored, devalued, disqualified, and/or socially dislocated within the "non-racial" processes of administrative law. And because local voices of color have so often been subordinated to the formal requirements and language of dominant institutions, the problem of translating historically marginalized voices and concerns into the taxonomies and terms of industry, law, and state regulation remains an enduring concern.

CHAPTER 5

Blacking Out

REMEMBERING TV AND THE SIXTIES

A motivating problem within this study, at least during my first travels to the state, was what I perceived to be a lack of primary paper records providing insights regarding African American resistance to racist media practices during the sixties. I wondered, given the practices I describe in the past few chapters, why there was not more "documented" resistance to the consistent racism and unvarnished hate made manifest in sixties broadcasting? Where were the organizational notes and records of those that opposed and strategized against the broadcasting status quo?

Initially I thought such questions regarding African American and rights alliance resistance might be addressed via discovery of some hidden paper trail or some bit of undiscovered writing. I assumed that written records of efforts undertaken by local activist churches and civil rights organizations must exist. But I came to realize that given the climate of terrorism existing in the sixties, these organizations would have been extraordinarily courageous, if not foolhardy, to preserve documents detailing complaints, challenges, and strategic interventions leveled against very powerful institutions. In the moments of white terrorism and surveillance, the transience of oral communication was one of its tactical strengths. "Unofficial," unwritten oral communications, quickly distributed via social networks, meetings, and telephone, were at the center of civil rights interventions.

Thus I moved to oral history with an aim of more fully recognizing the particular voices and histories marginalized by Jim Crow by grounding them in larger social and historical contexts. I attempted to situate concerns regarding television, past and present, alongside other social concerns and conditions, placing the viewing, discussion, and analysis of television within a larger habitus.[1] Although a few white Mississippians are represented in this chapter, I was particularly interested in what black Mississippians engaged in sixties activism remembered regarding television, because the station battles centered on the televisual treatment of African Americans. I initially sought out those who had signed the locally circulated petitions during the early sixties calling for federal or FCC investigation of the Jackson stations. Inevitably this led me to others who were not necessarily signed petitioners but who graciously offered their stories to me. The majority of those interviewed were teachers, ministers, or acknowledged coordinators of local civil rights activism, although some outside both "the movement" and these vocations are represented. For various reasons, I had greater access to an educated and professional population.[2] In oral history interviews, I consistently asked participants to talk about "growing up" in Mississippi and about their memories regarding local television and the challenges to the station. I also solicited discussion of other media, mediated representations, and race relations.[3]

Frequently I heard stories that spoke of the essential actions of "domestics," teachers, and female professionals in the local civil rights fight. The scope and value of women's participation in the freedom struggle has often been neglected in the widely circulated histories concentrating on particular personalities such as Martin Luther King Jr. or Stokley Carmichael and the predominately male leadership of large civil rights organizations. But more recently civil rights historians have come to explicitly note that, in the words of John Dittmer, "wherever one looked in Mississippi in the 1960s, women were in the forefront of the movement." Particularly in the Mississippi delta, women "constituted a majority at the mass meetings, did voter registration work, [and] led marches to the courthouse."[4] As Mississippi SNCC worker Lawrence Guyot has put it, "it's no secret that young people and women led organizationally."[5]

Historiography based largely on oral sources, perhaps due to its relative independence from organizational archives celebrating male leaders, has been important in bringing women's voices to the fore by pointing to the crucial, yet less-publicized, role of women in organizing and advancing the black freedom fight. For example, the excellent oral history, *My Soul Is Rested*, provides a number of important narratives offered by women such as Fannie Lou Hamer, Ruby Hurley, and Mary Dora Jones.[6] In this chapter, excerpts from my conversations with Ineva May-Pittman, Mary Ann Henderson, Juanita Jefferson, Jeanne Middleton, and Barbara Barber provide additional insights regarding women's activism and memories of the sixties and television viewing at home in Jackson.

Almost all of the oral history excerpts used in this chapter and the next were recorded in conversations with longtime Jackson residents. Specifically, these chapters derive from approximately twenty extended interviews I recorded, primarily in the state of Mississippi, during the summers of 1992 and 1993. They raise important questions regarding contemporary problems, as do all good stories and histories, and no doubt point to many others that I do not discuss but that will be noted by differently situated readers. To the degree that the histories represented here depart from dominant narratives regarding racial and cultural "progress" or widely distributed accounts of a civil rights "past," they also represent "countermemories," those which rely on the local and personal rather than on an alliance with dominant or institutional knowledge. Although often marginalized in historiography, such memories are, as George Lipsitz clarifies, "not a rejection of history, but a reconstitution of it." And such "ways of remembering and forgetting" can be powerful tools in contemporary cultural contestation.[7]

DIALOGIC HISTORY

Memories rooted in oral history rather than written records acknowledge what writing effaces — their interconnection with time, as well as the dynamics and subjectivity of all memory. In contrast to the seeming stasis or immutability of something written, orality foregrounds memory as the only means of structuring and recalling the past.[8] In contrast to a literacy that values distanced analysis and knowledge abstracted from its immediate arena of social negotiation, predominately oral cultures most appreciate concepts used in situational, operational frames of reference that remain close to lived experience and familiar human interaction, consistently situating knowledge, in the words of Walter Ong, "within a context of [social] struggle."[9]

These epistemological tensions, long evident in law's prioritization

Watching Jim Crow

of literacy over orality, have increasing resonance in current historiographical debates. Those defending traditional historical research approaches often remain cautious or skeptical regarding oral histories, insisting that written sources provide the standards by which other memories should be evaluated. What is neglected, or left unproblematized in such arguments, is the historical and social construction of all texts, written and oral, and their necessary interaction with memory. Within cultures that prioritize literacy and written precision it is often forgotten that written observations, no matter how contemporaneous, also represent partial and selective memories — the traces and recuperations of things experienced and past, understood within the contexts of the present.

As historians working with oral history have observed, it is problematic to view research based on oral sources as supplemental to other types of historical documentation, or as offering a direct, relatively unmediated account of personal experience. Rather, the selective, synthetic, and generalizing nature of historical memory should be recognized.[10] As A. Portelli states plainly, "oral sources are not objective. This of course applies to every source, although the holiness of writing sometimes leads us to forget it."[11] Rather, oral sources are artificial, variable, and partial — artificial in the sense that they are generated in the present as the result of directed dialogue; variable in that no two interviews or dialogues are exactly the same; and partial in the sense that the total population will never be heard, but rather selected voices are analyzed.[12] These characteristics may be considered weaknesses only if an objective historiography is assumed. Within alternative theoretical frames offered by contemporary historians of culture, they are productive reminders of present-past relations, the dynamics of human memory, and the partiality of any historical knowledge. In recognizing the fragmentary nature of any historical project, scholars can look to oral sources with the aim of broadening participation in the processes of historical interpretation, thereby providing readers with alternative visions of the present and past.[13]

Oral history and its dependence on memory have an uneasy relationship with objectivist historical projects because conversations regarding memory force the speaker's subjectivity into history. Oral history is history spoken in the present, in dialogue, and within a relationship to another person. It undermines the position of the historian as an external and omniscient narrator — someone who would claim to stand apart from her or his sources, outside of any relationship, beyond observer, to object. Rather, oral histories are explicitly relational, and "the narrator is pulled inside the narration, and becomes part of it."[14] Accordingly, the dynamics of the interviewer-interviewee relationship must be reflected on and examined.

As I spoke with Mississippians about the sixties, television, and their lives, I found in myself an unsettling tendency to mirror the very practices I have criticized. Much like the administrative agencies discussed earlier, I found myself using interviews to seek additional historical documentation — to fill what I perceived to be historical gaps or faulty memories. As a scholar invested in writing I often felt the tension and frustration of working with oral histories that were aggregative and that resisted quick classification. Although I began with discrete, neatly defined questions and topics for discussion, the processes of human dialogue quickly blurred what I had abstractly categorized. And the histories I heard, given my relatively narrow research parameters, were, in a sense, excessive — always exceeding my own expectations and lines of inquiry, offering more information, insight, and reflective analysis than I could fairly represent. Out of many hours of rich conversation, only traces and excerpts of lively interaction are offered here. Language, with its representational limits, fails to capture much within a complex social interaction, and the emotional and nonverbal are certainly less lively, and often invisible in transcribed excerpts describing powerful social phenomena of the present/past.

Not unlike the FCC investigators and courts, I found myself attempting to break apart or disaggregate holistic historicized descriptions to address those questions and topics in which I was most interested and invested. The questions and structures of knowledge I offered others were sometimes met with puzzlement, and inevitably forced interpretive frames on experiences never contemplated by those interviewed.

Although I was hoping to focus on rich memories of local television, I instead found that our dialogues often concentrated on childhood memories, job experiences, or more commonly, sixties activism aimed at institutions other than TV. Because Jackson was the site of repeated civil rights clashes and direct-action campaigns, I heard vivid recollections of the nonviolent efforts directed toward local businesses, churches, public schools, and parks. The small-scale yet sustained struggles by blacks for improved education, public facilities access, and political power were frequently mentioned. I also heard stories regarding movement interventions and the supremacist violence that met such efforts: the arrival of the freedom riders in 1961 and 1962, the Tougaloo students' library sit-in, the Woolworth's lunch counter sit-in, and of course, the bold campaigning, sudden death, and funeral of Medgar Evers. All of these events were prominent, along with those less public, in memories offered of the early sixties. The struggle over local television was not forgotten but rather was a memory interwoven with all of the other markers of a much larger fight.

Because the challenge to broadcasting in Jackson was just one small part of a multifrontal attack on Jim Crow, in this chapter I extend discussion of the historical contexts in which television and popular culture became fronts for progressive challenge. The conversations that follow also locate the prioritizations of local activists and provide glimpses of how television was viewed in some Jackson households in the early years of local broadcast service.

DOING THE BEST WITH WHAT YOU'VE GOT

As I talked with local civil rights workers in Mississippi about the much-publicized efforts of northern students and racial justice organizations (such as the United Church of Christ) beginning in 1963 and 1964, I was met with reminders of larger and longer historical contexts. Expressions of gratitude for migrating northern activists were common, but also were consistently accompanied by emphases on the earlier black efforts that opened the way for mid-sixties campaigns.

I was frequently reminded that "the whites didn't make us aware we were unhappy." For example, George Owens, president of Tougaloo College during the mid-sixties, had the following response when I talked with him about the perception that civil rights gains occurred largely as a result of "outside activism":

Well, that's . . . the general notion around the country that a bunch of young white liberal kids up north decided one day that they would go down south and mobilize those blacks to get their rights and independence. And we hadn't felt any concern about it, until these young liberal white kids came down here — which is not true. Even some whites claim that Medgar Evers was not taking care of business until they came in and told him what to do, which is all a bunch of hogwash. The thing of it is, it's almost like kids of today's generation saying to me, even though I'm 73, "I wouldn't have taken that stuff from those white folks back there in 1930. I wouldn't have taken it." Well, like Thurgood Marshall says, "You do the best that you can with what you've got." And what we had, we used. We weren't satisfied. We were fighting everywhere every way we could and as effectively as we could.[15]

Other civil rights activists, such as Ruby Hurley, have echoed Owens's specific observation regarding dissatisfaction and rights struggles around Jackson more generally. As Hurley, an NAACP pioneer in Alabama, has put it, "I think young people need to know, and some older people need to know, that it didn't all begin in 1960."[16] When Everett Parker and the United Church of Christ initiated the formal FCC petition process against Jackson television in spring 1964, they entered an environment in which black Mississippians had previously voiced dissatisfaction with local broadcasting and print media. Medgar Evers and others had, to paraphrase Owens, "done their best with what they had," petitioning the FCC, leading voter registration drives, and campaigning for black dignity and recognition years earlier. Important activist groundwork had been done and foundations laid for eventual legal challenges. As was discussed earlier in this project, challengers to the broadcasting status quo did not wait for northern organization intervention, although they often sought out such alliances.

Aaron Shirley, a Jackson physician long concerned with public health issues, also spoke of pre-sixties efforts and awareness within black communities. As the cofounder of the Vicksburg, Mississippi, civil rights newspaper, the *Citizen Appeal*, Shirley offered particularly powerful stories regarding local black activism speaking to the need for alternative media sources and communication efforts by early movement participants:

There were complaints aimed at one of the other stations even before the United Church of Christ. I've actually forgotten what it was. In some of our opinions, WJTV was even worse than WLBT in its programming biases. So it didn't take the United Church of Christ to convince us that things weren't the way they should have been. It took resources to make things change. But like I said, we started the [civil rights] newspaper (the *Citizens Appeal*) way before that. That was a result of

Watching Jim Crow

my being displeased with the media and the way it was treating things. It's not as if Everett Parker made us aware that we were unhappy. [laughter] But that was a resource that came.[17]

The memories of Owens and Shirley both prioritize and make explicit the early efforts of black Mississippians who cultivated environments in which further activism and northern reform efforts could bear fruit. And both Owens and Shirley trace the motivation for these struggles to the deep dissatisfaction of African Americans suffering under Jim Crow segregation.

Speaking specifically about media practices, Shirley remembers the censorship of crucial materials and news stories addressing white-on-black violence as a primary concern motivating the publication of the *Citizens Appeal*. He recalls that such attacks were not covered or addressed by local high-circulation print or broadcast media. With others he remembers the local industry's disregard for black suffering and struggle. In the eyes of some Mississippi media professionals even white-on-black murder was unworthy of journalistic attention. Charles Cobb, a student volunteer and "outside agitator" who came to work in Mississippi in 1962, has recalled, "[The] winter of '63 the whole state was being swept by this wave of violence against blacks, and it was directly related to the voter registration effort. Southwest Mississippi to the Delta, churches were being bombed, economic reprisals were being effected, killings were happening. Most of those killings, we couldn't even get out the information about them. Because it was clear, unless you were somebody famous, no paper or TV station was very interested that a person like Lewis Allen was killed down in Amite that winter."[18]

Such memories of journalistic omission remain common, offered within the context of a more holistic assessment of media and their interaction with the freedom movement. Statements regarding the racism of WLBT and other television stations were frequently placed in a comparative dialogue addressing other media, as well as other movement concerns and strategies. Some remembered that the offenses of local television frequently paled in comparison to the threatening diatribes and supremacist cheerleading in Jackson's daily newspapers, the *Clarion-Ledger* and the *Daily News*. For example, a local minister remembers that while fear limited the activists' public outrage regarding most media treatments, all of the dominant local media were generally slanted toward segregation and television was only very slightly better than newspapers. Aaron Shirley also spoke about television's relative importance at the time:

> Shirley: At one point there was talk, and I don't know exactly . . . about the possibility of cancelling subscriptions to the *Clarion-Ledger*. That was, I recall, something that was discussed . . . the notion did come up about the possibility of folks cancelling their subscriptions. I don't think it ever got anyplace. To be frank, when I think back and think about prioritizing, that was one of the painful things, but there were so many other things that we considered more urgent. We knew that we could impact with a boycott over [at the] Emporium. The Emporium was a department store where we couldn't try on things. Couldn't try on a hat. So we knew if we boycotted the Emporium we could have a direct, instant, impact. Subscriptions to the paper, I don't know. I can't perceive it as having the same impact as putting up a picket line around a department store.
>
> Classen: Was it your impression that there were relatively few black households in the early sixties that had a television, or that subscribed to the local newspaper?
>
> Shirley: No. In the early sixties folks had televisions. I had rabbit ears [antenna], but televisions were an essential bit. As bad as newspapers were, [with] television at least you got the national perspective — you got information.
>
> Classen: So in some ways television offered a perspective that local newspapers wouldn't?
>
> Shirley: Yes. They had to carry the evening news. So many times we learned more about Mississippi watching NBC or ABC news than we did watching the local programs.[19]

Shirley's memories of network newscasts and the attention they received in the black community are very similar to other historical accounts of African Americans gathering around television sets to watch Martin Luther King Jr. or student activists on the national network news.[20] Generally speaking, while local television offered much that offended, its racist censorship was far from perfect. And local stations, often unwittingly, provided glimpses of black dignity and of the possibilities of "something larger" outside the segregated neighborhoods of Jackson.

In a city dominated by white supremacist journalism, it was network news, not local, to which African Americans paid close attention and that prompted anxiety for local white censors. Station manager Beard

Watching Jim Crow

of WLBT was frequently criticized not only by Jackson activists but also by his fellow Citizens' Council members for failure to remove programming deemed damaging to council interests. As the council was well aware, in the brief moments that black Mississippians viewed other African Americans engaged in a larger freedom fight, a knowledge and power dangerous to white supremacy was circulated. Control of television or broadcasting in efforts to reproduce particular sets of knowledges was always partial and imperfect. As semanticist S. I. Hayakawa observed in his essay "TV and the Negro Revolt," by 1963 it was already too late for segregationists to undo the influence of national television, for blacks had been able to use the same communication technology as whites and thereby gain knowledges previously segregated and employed to white advantage.[21] As "dangerous" knowledges gained circulation, social change was produced.

Stories and remembrances of African Americans gathered around an early sixties black-and-white TV are common in existing civil rights histories. For example, Harvard Sitkoff, in *The Struggle for Black Equality*, recounts the words of Cleveland Sellers, a student activist in North Carolina, who remembers "rushing to the student union to view the [network] news broadcasts . . . With the exception of the announcer's voice, the lounge would be so quiet you could hear a rat pissing on cotton. Hundreds of thoughts coursed through my head as I stood with my eyes transfixed on the television screen. My identification with the demonstrating students was so thorough that I would flinch every time one of the whites taunted them. On nights when I saw pictures of students being beaten and dragged through the streets by their hair, I would leave the lounge in a rage."[22] While no former students I interviewed offered such vivid accounts based on experiences in Jackson or at Tougaloo, it is clear that network newscasts dealing with white-on-black violence or civil rights struggle, when aired, received the same intense attention and sense of self-identification in the houses and dorms of black Mississippians — as did positive representations of black politicians, artists, scholars, and professionals.

A common memory in Jackson is one of families and friends gathering together around the television to catch that rare view of "Martin," Nat King Cole, or Sammy Davis Jr. People were routinely called out from other rooms and telephoned by friends and family when televised blacks appeared. One reason such moments remain memorable is because they were so extraordinary. And next to such exceptional moments, televisual "blackouts" of African American entertainers and civil rights reports are perhaps the most prominent collective memory of black Mississippians addressing segregationist TV. Positive black spokespersons, perspectives, and concerns were consistently (but not perfectly) omitted, interrupted, or blocked from view by the local stations. As I asked longtime residents of the predominantly black neighborhoods of west Jackson to talk about local television, it became clear that this practice, a central point of complaint in the 1960s FCC hearings, was, and is, most memorable. Aaron Shirley remarked: "[In the local television] programming, if there was going to be a network program that . . . they knew might have integrated characters — they would bump it. And sometimes they would shaft them during the broadcast. If they slipped through, sometimes the [program] would just switch off and they'd go on to something else. And, of course, the only black involved in local broadcasting — he had something that has to do with a Saturday program of blues. More like what you'd refer to now as an *Amos and Andy* type thing. . . . He would tell comical jokes and made a poor image for black kids. . . . There were two major stations, and that was the only black show, period."[23]

For Barbara Barber, a retired elementary school teacher, and her niece, Jeanne Middleton, a professor of education at Millsaps College in Jackson, there were similar recollections, but also memories of their old household, neighborhoods, and gatherings around the television set. Their remarks placed television viewing within a domestic setting — one of family and friends as well as fear and intimidation. As we discussed the short-lived *Nat King Cole Show*, I remarked that I would be surprised if such a show ever aired in the Jackson market:

> Barber: No, they wouldn't play anything like that show. And every time someone would come on, the TV would go off.
> Middleton: Oh, yes, that's so true. We always thought it, but I wondered . . .
> Barber: I wondered . . . it was strange . . .
> Classen: Tell me about that.
> Barber: Whenever a black person would come on in any kind of a positive role . . .
> Middleton: Anything about black people.
> Classen: Like in a network news program?
> Middleton: Yes, something would happen to the television.

Barber: Yes. Well, some kind of a special-type thing where maybe Roy Wilkins or somebody was speaking . . . Ralph Bunche or somebody . . . and then the TV would just go off.

Middleton: A lot of snow, interference.

Barber: Snow, interference, yes.

Middleton: And then that "Ready Kilowatt" [character] would come up, and put up a little sign: "It ain't you, it ain't me, it must be them."

Barber: Speaking of the network.

Middleton: Speaking of the network, who interrupted the broadcast. And it just used to happen, so it was like a little in-house joke: "Oh, it must have been something about black people, because they're messing up the TV." Now whether it was, maybe you could research it and see.

Barber: Yes . . . [longtime WLBT weathercaster] Woody Asaf would probably be the only one left who would know. We would get on the telephone and call each other. . . . Now that's strange, isn't it? That a black person would come on . . .

Middleton: That a black person would come on TV . . .

Barber: Whatever he was doing, no matter what — if he was acting a fool, as gramps would say — we would get on the phone and say, "turn on channel three."

Middleton: We'd call somebody. We'd yell and say, "Come watch TV."

Barber: "There's a black person on."

Middleton: And the whole house would stop . . .

Barber: To go watch TV.

Classen: So like when Ed Sullivan would have a black entertainer like Sammy Davis Jr. on.

Barber: Yes. Oh, especially Ed Sullivan. We never missed Ed Sullivan's show. Never.[24]

Of course, such bits of oral history speak not only about the nature of local television, but more generally of past and present social experiences, including those of family. Television viewing, sometimes conceptualized as a solitary activity involving passive individual viewers, was often remembered as a collective, explicitly social, activity. This was certainly the case in the late fifties and early sixties, when access to the technology was still somewhat limited and neighborly invitations to view television were frequently extended to those without sets. Residents of west Jackson remember viewing programs collectively, and that entertainment in black communities centered on the family and its spaces. Much of this was made necessary by the strict limitations and patterns of segregation. As Barber and Middleton remembered:

> Barber: And all through the years black children have been protected by their parents. These children were especially protected, because when they came home they partied in the backyard or all went to the movies. Rarely did anyone go anywhere alone.
>
> Middleton: It was a segregated society. We couldn't go to the city zoo, to the park, so your family would have the neighbor kids over and you would have a barbecue in your backyard, it was that kind of thing.[25]

It was within this paradoxically restricted yet liberating space of the black family and neighborhood that the exchange of countermemories and counterhistories could be nurtured. While white segregationist pressures were oppressive, they were also limited in their cultural policing capacities. What is remembered, by at least some longtime residents of Mississippi, is that black neighborhoods offered one of the few safe areas where counternarratives and pleasures specific to the black community could be enjoyed. Longtime Mississippians told me about terrible childhood memories of white abuse, usually at school or in public places, that were experienced alongside many happy moments of recreation produced with few material means within the safe backyards and residential spaces of the black neighborhood.

In terms of public spaces the Farish Street district in downtown Jackson, the primary area of black business and entertainment, was exceptional. Many remembered the Farish area as "lovely" and as a source of black pride. The retail outlets and professional offices were viewed with considerable nostalgia and fondness. Clothiers, physicians, dentists, lawyers, churches, news periodical services, a mortuary, and a black theater, the Alamo, were all located on or in close proximity to Farish Street. In its offering of news periodicals, both legal and underground, the district is also remembered as a vital information center. Here black Mississippians could talk, shop, worship, enjoy entertainment, and conduct business segregated from at least some forms of white oppression.

The information exchanged and distributed in this segregated district—for example, through a variety of national black press magazines and newspapers—cultivated the ironic situation in which a resourceful minority could often be better informed regarding national and global politics than were the wealthier, privileged whites managing state institutions and enforcing segregation. While the immediacy of information available was often problematic given segregationist control of broadcasting, several interviewees talked with me about the ways that they anticipated reading and discussing newspapers like the *Chicago Defender* and *Pittsburgh Courier*. Such publications offered very different perspectives on Mississippi and on worldwide black empowerment movements than did the provincial Hederman press.

Still, I was reminded not to romanticize such cultural spaces and practices. Interviewees discussed the pervasive sense of suspicion that existed around areas like Farish Street and that coexisted with everyday life. As most I talked with made abundantly clear, I had little appreciation for the atmosphere of fear that was cultivated by violent state-sanctioned racism. This heightened fear and risk hung over any appearance of black activism. The Sovereignty Commission worked constantly to infiltrate black neighborhoods, groups, meetings, churches, and social spaces using a variety of strategies, including the active recruitment and financing of black informers. Many within Jackson, both white and black, did not know whom they could fully trust. Several black Jacksonians told me personal stories of white terroristic responses to those within their family and circle of friends. Others talked of pervasive anxiety, partial information, and distrust. As Barber and Middleton put it while talking to me about meetings, mediated information, and fear:

> Barber: We had heard the freedom riders were coming, you really didn't know too much about it because you had no way of knowing, you see. You don't have those things on TV, what it's all about, the real side. You don't have that on radio. And if you were not attending meetings . . . the NAACP would have meetings at certain churches. That's the only place our meetings could be held — churches.
>
> Classen: Right.
>
> Barber: The Pearl Street church was the number-one church where all their meetings were held, and unless you could go there and be instructed on what was going to happen, we really didn't know. And of course as I've said before, a lot of us stayed away because of our jobs. So we would only learn about what someone else told us. As I said before, this person that I worked with, whose father was highly involved, would inform us, and she could only inform us so far

because somebody on the faculty was informing too. You know, we had a lot of informers, about what was going on and who said what. You call in the next day and "I heard you did so and so and so, or you did so and so and so." It was really hard to even know what was going on. I remember a friend who was called in and questioned because she parked her car near her home — which also happened to be close to a movement meeting place.

Classen: Did that build division within the black community? That you didn't know whether you could trust other people you were with?

Barber: I don't think there was as much division then as there is now, really. I don't think there was as much.

Classen: It seems more pronounced now?

Barber: I guess so. People are going so many different ways with their own programs now.

Classen: Right. . . . Do you remember [sixties network television documentaries] giving you any kind of encouragement?

Barber: When television came along and you saw all of these things in the outside world, and what was going on . . . a lot of people attribute it to what's happening now with the young men, killing and what not, you know when you see certain things and certain places — you don't have them, you're going to figure a way to get them. Some people figure that's the way to get what they want. But, yes, television was an eye opener for a lot of people, for all of us to see what was going on in the outside world, so to speak.

Classen: So you think that's an accurate assessment that many people in the state were complacent because they didn't know that their lives could be otherwise, until they had been able to see it?

Barber: I would think that's a good . . . I think so. Complacent may not be the word, it may be that you just don't know. And for lack of a better word, ignorance as to what was going on.

Middleton: Yes, I'm just realizing that fear . . .

Barber: Fear was the main thing.

Middleton: When all the power, everything is owned . . . if you're an independent shop owner, you've still got to get your electricity from the power company and those people.

Barber: Groceries.

Middleton: And you know, your groceries. You look back historically, that historical period, say from 1900 to 1945, that preceded the flowering of the movement — an extremely repressive time in history marked by lynchings and terrorism. I was a teenager at the time, but even as a child I had heard stories from my grandmother and my grandfather, so . . . we probably need to find another word, it's not complacent, but it's a sense of the reality of it, and we are not playing games here. Because you know of somebody who was lynched, or was maimed, or who did lose their job, you know, it's not fun and games — this is serious.

Barber: It's for real.

Middleton: It's for real. So you didn't enter into it lightly.[26]

Harassment, physical violence, and loss of employment were possible reprisals that local African Americans knew all too well. Black parents trying to feed and house a family, already suffering from the conditions of segregation, knew that job termination was quick and irreversible for those who made their protests too visible. Juanita Jefferson was employed as a domestic worker in sixties Mississippi and talked with me about the fears of unemployment and of the violence against black children:

Classen: Maybe you could help me with one of the problems that I have. . . . I've been a bit surprised as I've talked to black residents of Jackson that were involved in the Movement, that were very concerned about civil rights, that there wasn't more attention toward the media and toward changing the media. . . .

Jefferson: I don't know if I can help you, but I can try. I think that a lot of people just like me, did not have a set, and they didn't realize what the situation was, and they were afraid. Some were afraid to get involved. Because some of the people that could have been involved, you see, they were involved in working in . . . people's homes, or working for their friends, and they would lose their jobs. So that kept a lot of people back from doing a lot of things. . . . They needed their jobs and their little twelve dollars a week [salary], and that kept a lot of them back. And a lot of them were single parents, and they needed that little money for their support. . . . I was blessed when I first came to Jackson because my mother kept my son. And so it was just me, see, I didn't have to worry about somebody killing him or harming him while I was gone . . . and a lot of people were not that blessed.[27]

Sam Bailey, a longtime member of the Jackson branch of the NAACP, talked of the 1950s and the secret meetings of the organization. He also spoke about public reactions to Medgar Evers:

Bailey: One thing he would always say, my man Medgar Evers, "Are you a member of the NAACP, are you ready to vote?" . . . things he was going to ask whoever he met. And he had so many people who would keep away from the vote. They'd run if they saw him coming, and they would run across the street. People would say names at him. They felt for you, but they were scared of their jobs, and that made it very unpopular, you know, that your own people would run from you, and try to hide from you when they see you coming. Like a religious fanatic.

Classen: It must have been difficult.

Bailey: It was difficult.

Classen: To see people running away when you . . .

Bailey: Running. Then you start to call them Uncle Toms, because they were, you know, making a good living, and they would tell, and go down and talk about you, you know, anything that happened in your community. And then the police would get your [auto license] tag, if you went to a NAACP meeting they would get your tag number and turn it in. If you worked for the state or school system, you were fired. And you hadn't done nothing but attend a meeting. And all those things happened.[28]

These memories and others depict the public terrain of popular culture as extraordinarily dangerous. Simply talking about local television or newspaper accounts was an activity filled with risk. The most casual expression was anything but "free." Rather, it was watched, guarded, and contained, albeit imperfectly. Segregationists were always monitoring and attempting to infiltrate the activities of the Jackson movement and its sympathizers. Spies, both black and white, listened carefully for any departures from the official state segregationist line. As a retired black minister remarked regarding the spying and the use of African American informants: "Ain't no way in the world that the white man would come down in the black community and know how to find everything, unless somebody told him. And that's exactly where it was back in those days. Somebody would tell them."[29]

In this environment, black Mississippians knew they were surveilled as they shopped downtown, sat in the segregated section of the movie theater, gathered for church, or participated in any type of large group activities. More than that, they knew they were watched and heard within their own homes and neighborhoods. The extravagant efforts of white segregationists to infiltrate all aspects of black life spoke volumes regarding supremacist fears — fears of an emergent black power, integration, and a society without strong racial barriers. White surveillance and spy activities were explicitly concerned with gathering information. But they were even more concerned with the transmutation of their own integrationist anxieties into strategies and forms of fear that would terrorize, divide, and paralyze black activism.

Ineva May-Pittman was just one of the interviewees who spoke of this oppressive surveillance and its implications for her career. She recalled being summoned to the school superintendent's office after driving her mother to an NAACP meeting place in Jackson, the Masonic Temple. Although she stayed in the car and never entered the building, the mere proximity to black activism was enough to prompt swift interrogations by school officials. Such seemingly innocuous behaviors had significant repercussions.

Joining the present and past, May-Pittman explained to me that she never has been seriously considered for a school principal position because of her civil rights activities. "That was held against me by the power structure and I was told that, and another lady that was a teacher also was told that we would never be principals because of our activities."[30]

It is also clear from the recollections of professionals such as WLBT's Hewitt Griffin that within local media outlets supremacist surveillance was particularly pronounced. Jackson's *Clarion-Ledger* and *Daily News* regularly unleashed vitriol against all sorts of integration and racial activism. Still, they were also taken to task when their coverage or commentaries were viewed as "out of step" with the Citizens' Council agenda. As one University of Mississippi professor noted, by 1959 the council had "created a climate of fear that has strait-jacketed the white community in a thought control enforced by financial sanctions, and has undone most of the improvements in race relations made over the last thirty years."[31] Together, Jackson's radio, television, and dominant press institutions fought hand in hand with the white Citizens' Council against contrary voices while seeking to expose departures from the approved state line.[32] The segregationist charge to local journalists and media managers was contradictory and impossible to perfectly fulfill, as media institutions were encouraged to simultaneously silence and expose voices contrary to the racial status quo.

In this climate of fear and racial orthodoxy there was a practical impatience with integrationist efforts entailing extensive legal or bureaucratic obstacles. Instead, there was a keen focus on changing segregationist practices and institutions such as the retail Emporium, where, as Aaron Shirley put it, "direct, instant impacts" could be realized. Activists in Jackson were not alone. Elsewhere in the black freedom fight, students and other groups had grown weary of working through, or more often against, officialdom and lengthy legal procedures, and increasingly they opted for direct-action campaigns. The direct-action campaigns undertaken by the SNCC and other student groups pointed to impatience with legal and legislative strategies.[33] Describing the impact of Martin Luther King Jr. and Montgomery on black middle-class youth, Sitkoff writes:

> Disappointed with the NAACP's inability to provide immediate relief from the yoke of discrimination and oppression, they yearned to take to the streets. They bitterly decried the lack of racial progress in the late 1950s, yet optimistically believed that by using the strategy fashioned by Martin Luther King in Montgomery they could topple Jim Crow, quickly and throughout the South. King's prediction to the annual convention of the Fellowship of Reconciliation [FOR] in mid-1959 that the coming years would witness mounting black "direct action against injustice without waiting for other agencies to act" defined their propensity. His thundering peroration to the FOR — "We will not obey unjust laws or submit to unjust practices" — adumbrated their cause.[34]

From Jackson, in the light of the official rebukes that the FCC and Washington had already delivered to Medgar Evers in the 1950s, any changes in local television practices following the course of administrative law appeared extraordinarily expensive and elusive. Further, administrative law formally addressed a very limited terrain of struggle. The representation (or nonrepresentation) of African Americans on local television was horrible, but so were many other aspects of black life in an oppressive society.

In his memoir *Growing Up Black in Rural Mississippi*, Chalmers Archer Jr. remembers watching childhood motion pictures that offered disturbingly "happy stereotypes, Aunt Jemima and Rastus, Little Black Sambo and Mammy. . . . But there were more pressing concerns. Like the involuntary servitude all around us."[35] Other popular mediated offenses of the sixties are often remembered with a similar perspective. Some institutions of oppression, less ensconced in formal protections and requirements than the media industry, could be more directly attacked. For example, the Jackson Movement and the Tougaloo College students used boycotts and other disruptive strategies to attack retail trade and other important components of the existing power structure.

Of course, Tougaloo students were responsible for one of the direct-action campaigns engaging television that was commonly remembered by those I interviewed — namely, the disruption in 1963–1964 of segregated entertainment and of appearances by television, governmental, and musical celebrities. Most everyone I talked with smiled and fondly remembered the last-minute cancellations of the *Hootenany* and *Bonanza* stars, for example. The events are remembered as brief moments of positive integrationist empowerment. Still, strategically such activism was not directly aimed at station or network programming, or solely at local television, but rather played out on the more immediate and easily infiltrated terrain of live local performance.

Understandably, in comparison to the threats and problems facing African Americans in sixties Mississippi, offensive television fare is remembered as a relatively minor concern. Mary Ann Henderson, a longtime Mississippi resident and expert in audience research, along with her spouse, Gordon Henderson, a political scientist who taught at Jackson's Millsaps College, offered the following perspectives as local white supporters of the movement who volunteered to enter the local television fight:

> Classen: So you think there might also have been a type of fatalism on the part of the black community, in terms of getting . . . media issues resolved?
>
> M. A. Henderson: . . . Actually TV was a relatively minor thing. It was irritating, but it wasn't threatening survival. And there were other things that were threatening survival. . . . I'm sure they didn't realize how useful it would be if the station did have to shape up.
>
> G. Henderson: There was one more thing, too, and that is that I think you have to recognize the extreme measure of political powerlessness that characterized blacks in Mississippi at that time. I did not feel at all politically powerless. I felt very powerful. I knew I was one person — I was a member of a minority [movement]. But it was a very distinguished minority. I thought this thing [the license challenge of

WLBT] had a chance of being pulled off. Blacks, even when they were demonstrating at the time, needed strong leaders like [SNCC head] Bob Moses to reassure them every day that there was a remote chance that some of this was going to work; or some of the other people . . . there were many, many blacks who completely shied away because they saw no point to it. School integration started with how many kids, three, in 1964? It was a very small number. I'll bet you it wasn't more than five. But the first thing that happened was that, you see this black kid now going to this all-white school. "What's her name, and whose maid is her mother?" So they had reality facing them everyday. This was viewed as a threat to the power structure, which still at that point it was. It wasn't beginning to crumble in 1964. Maybe it was beginning to get a bit tattered. It took the Voting Rights Act of 1965 to make any fundamental difference, and that was the beginning of ultimate change. It did not come easily or quickly. But that was 1965, that was a whole year after.

Classen: Yes, I think that's worth my thinking about further. It's something that I think I've not appreciated enough up to this point — just the degree of powerlessness that the black community felt at this period of time. It's surprised me, as I've talked to people who remember this time. . . . I was surprised for example, there weren't local black church meetings that addressed these kinds of issues [of mediated racism] . . .

M. A. Henderson: It was just a relatively minor problem. They focused on the things that were important to them.

G. Henderson: Black churches were having meetings almost nightly to protest, for example, the closing down of the swimming pools. But that was something, again, that you do, and [that] could take a small hard-core band to do it, and have it organized by somebody like Bob Moses or some of the other black leaders, like Marian Wright [Edelman], or whomever. And that was possible. But this [station challenge] was just outside the realm. You had [federal district court] Judge Harold Cox calling them chimpanzees in the courtroom. They were used to being put down. I'm not exaggerating. He did that with the self-assurance that this was a perfectly acceptable thing to say. He had to be ordered by the Fifth Circuit Court of Appeals to cover up the slave auction mural behind his bench that he was so proud of.

M. A. Henderson: At that time, speaking of closing the swimming pools, they closed the swimming pools rather than integrate. In fact, the mayor even had the benches taken out of the park so that black people couldn't sit down next to white people.

Classen: Because parks had been integrated?

M. A. Henderson: Well — they were trying to get them integrated. This was before the Civil Rights Act. That wasn't until Lyndon Johnson signed it, in 1964. They were having park bench sit-ins, as well as dime store sit-ins, and church sit-ins, and library sit-ins. The public library was not open to blacks.

G. Henderson: That was a terrible scene.

Classen: The library? In terms of the police response to the demonstrators?

G. Henderson: Yes. And the library patrons and staff.

M. A. Henderson: So they were focused on things that would give a more immediate reward. Which was very sensible. You go after the FCC, you may not hear from them for five years. It's very expensive to do it.[36]

Others made this observation, too. Direct-action interventions cost little and eschewed dependence on expensive trained "experts." In contrast, going before the courts was a high-priced, risky excursion into foreign, often hostile, territory. George Owens underscored the expense of formal legal undertakings and the limited resources of the local nonviolent movement, as follows:

There were people doing challenging things. We had Dr. [Gilbert] Mason down the coast early on, [in the] NAACP, challenging the segregation of beaches down the coast. You had things going. But [Everett] Parker and those had the money and the resources and some know-how. So we used what we could where we found it. They didn't come wake up. It was a case of using what you had where you found it. What we had during that time, we had no black lawyers. We had three — but they were tied up in all this litigation, because the outside lawyers had to work through them. [Attorneys] Jess Brown, Jack Young, and Carsie Hall were all tied up. So that was one of the goals we set for ourselves when I became president [at Tougaloo College] in 1964. To try to put in place some indigenous skilled people, lawyers, doctors. . . . And we did.[37]

Some of the key resources and expertise Owens refers to came from skilled women working behind the scenes and the public leadership of men. Although the vast majority of Jackson's ministers, doctors, lawyers, and civic leaders were men, in the early sixties women were assuming important roles, including those of leadership, in the Mississippi civil rights fight. Many women not in leadership or the public eye formed the organizational backbone for activism and projects in Jackson, as well as elsewhere throughout the state. For example, Mary Ann Henderson was one of a number of particularly talented Mississippi women aiding integrationist efforts in Jackson. Henderson had survey and measurement expertise after working for the A. C. Neilsen company, and volunteered to work with the UCC television monitoring project. With her husband she trained other local women and men to do the precise task of charting and analyzing hundreds of hours of television programming.

Also in Jackson, Doris Allison served as a student leader for the North Jackson chapter of the NAACP and was vitally involved in effective direct-action campaigns aimed at changing the business community and retail store practices. In various conversations I listened to local residents remembering women students at Tougaloo, such as Dorie Ladner, Joyce Ladner, and Joan Trumpauer, who were key leaders in the Jackson Movement. And they remembered, as well, other women who either led or were key participants in church sit-ins and other direct action protests.

Many women also helped the movement in a more quiet fashion by providing food, clothing, housing, and transportation for freedom workers, and by organizing church meetings, working in voter registration, and providing alternative communication networks. As mentioned earlier in this project, Clarie Collins Harvey, a prominent businesswoman and owner of Collins Funeral Home on Farish Street, was the founder and leader of Jackson's Womanpower Unlimited, a network of women who offered critical support services and supplies to civil rights workers, beginning with the jailed freedom riders in 1961. Harvey, A. M. E. Logan, and Thelma Sanders have been locally recognized as the principal leaders of the group, although among the two to three hundred women affiliated with Womanpower many served on committees without holding office.[38] Women working as maids during the day quietly organized, administered, and served the cause of civil rights interventions after hours. As Harvey recalled in another oral history project:

We considered ourselves the major support group behind all of the five or more activist groups that were strategizing the Movement. We were the ministry to them for healing, for food, for money, for love, for whatever a caring community they needed. . . . We'd have them in churches in the neighborhoods where they were. The problem was that we had to do it all in the midst of earning our daily bread — you see we had to work early in the morning. First thing I'd do in the morning when I'd get up, I'd start talking to our women and who was going to do what, who was going to see about that during the day. Then I'd have to come to the office and work all day with families in making funeral arrangements and direct funeral services and all the rest of it. Then at night there were the mass meetings, the rallies, and then there was more planning . . . you know, eighteen, twenty hours a day, whatever.[39]

The active participants in Womanpower Unlimited are too numerous to list here, but included several of the women that I interviewed, such as A. M. E. Logan and Ineva May-Pittman. May-Pittman was also very active in the NAACP, and she traveled to Gulfport in 1962 or 1963 to attend the organization's state meeting — mindful that such an action could mean immediate termination of her job as a Jackson public school teacher. She told me about the dangers and tensions of traveling, with two other black women, to the Gulfport conference, attending the meeting, and "making statements" of black dignity:

So then we went on [the bus] and when we got down there they still had the separate waiting rooms but it was a choice situation. You could choose to go on the black side or you could choose to go on the white side — you know, the previously all white side. So, we chose to go on the white side to claim our luggage. There were blacks there, they were all on the other side, you understand. But we went to claim our luggage. Nobody bothered us or anything, but we were making a statement because that was giving those blacks courage to see that you could do it and they weren't going to bother you. Now sometimes they would bother you. But they didn't bother you nasty. . . .

At that time it took a lot of courage for us to go down there in a situation like that, because we could have easily stayed at home. But we wanted to go, and we went and we met these black lawyers down there. And they were surprised to see us because they knew if the powers to be up there knew we were down there teaching at some NAACP meeting, we were as good as fired. So they asked us if we were members of the NAACP, and at that time we had cards, and they said "I'll tell you what you do — you all burn those cards." They said, "because we have enough cases . . . rather than to have to come to you all and rescue you if they fire you. Burn you all's cards." . . .

But anyway, we didn't burn our cards. We figured that we were grown, and teaching that we had the right to make the decision that we wanted to make. And we made that decision, we were going to stand by it.[40]

Similarly, Juanita Jefferson, A. M. E. Logan, Aurelia Young, and others told me of transporting, housing, and assisting freedom workers, knowing that they were under the constant surveillance of the Citizens' Council or Sovereignty Commission spies. Cars distinguished by their white passengers in an otherwise black neighborhood would often remain parked outside their homes for long periods of time. More explicit threats were common.

Facing severe consequences and risks these women and many others quietly, and without much recognition, organized, motivated, and supported direct-action campaigns that too often were attributed to a few charismatic male leaders. Like some Tougaloo student groups, these small coalitions of women in and around Jackson represented direct action in its most efficient form. Independent from larger male-dominated organizations, they worked quickly and cooperatively, without territorial infighting, to see local interventions succeed.[41]

THE PRESENT PAST

Sitting in the Tougaloo College campus home of Henry Kirksey, I expected to hear some interesting stories regarding the *Mississippi Free Press* — the paper the former educator and state senator had briefly edited. I had sought him out, along with other experienced broadcasting and print professionals, to talk about the historical trajectory of various Jackson media. Excerpts from these conversations, focusing on media institutions, identities, practices, and trends, appear at the beginning of this final section of the chapter. Yet, while Mr. Kirksey obligingly answered such questions, the stories and perspectives I heard while talking with him and other black Mississippians, rather than simply "adding in" to my local television and press history, implicitly argued that my conversational aims were often too narrow, abstract, and mediacentric. In conversation, I consistently found that the media histories I thought I would write were impossible to extract from reflections on race, everyday life, and politics. The battles and changes targeting local television were described as "of a piece" with larger civil rights struggles — past and present. Accordingly, this chapter moves, along with the flow of conversations, into more holistic comparisons of past and present rooted not just in media practice and consumption but also in other aspects of everyday life.

Mr. Kirksey has been a highly visible activist for civil rights over the past thirty years, and in recent years he served as a legislator in the Mississippi State Senate. From 1964 to 1965 he was the editor of the *Free Press*, and I asked several questions specifically regarding the history of mainstream and alternative media in Jackson's past. However, beginning with comments regarding the racial surveillance manifest in Mississippi's former spy agency, the Sovereignty Commission, and African American complicity with the commission, Kirksey quickly connected concerns regarding black identity and complicity with white supremacist interests to the present. He reminded me that an enduring problem — the lack of African American control over, and ownership of, important media properties — was very much manifest in contemporary Jackson.

> Classen: I was wondering if you could talk a little bit about . . . the kind of environments that local blacks found themselves in [during] the early sixties, in terms of the way that the dominant press, the *Clarion-Ledger*, the television stations, and so forth, were framing issues and were talking about the local black community.
>
> Kirksey: . . . The Sovereignty Commission was the modus operandi in the State of Mississippi during that period of time when WLBT was being challenged and the other . . . ways and means for our communicating with blacks during that period of time were being sought. . . . But equally important, blacks, some blacks, were taking advantage of the fact that ways and means were being provided for blacks who were supportive of the Sovereignty Commission to get monies to do what they wanted. . . . What I guess I'm getting to is during that period of time it was exceedingly difficult, in terms of your question about how you're going to get this publication distributed, how you're going to get any information. It was difficult to get people to help in any way. As a matter of fact, more often than not when people see me coming, and especially when they see Medgar Evers coming this way, they went the other way. If they were in public employment. So, it was a difficult period of time for blacks in this state to even communicate with themselves.

Blacking Out

Classen: Certainly you must have been talking to people in the community during this time and I'm wondering how widespread do you think the dissatisfaction was in the black community about what they saw on television, and what they heard on radio?

Kirksey: Well, you know, I think it was generally widespread — but the fear among blacks in that period really meant that you would never get a real honest to God assessment of how blacks really felt because blacks were afraid to talk to one another. Even in the same household they were afraid to mention things that might be considered controversial. So it was a dangerous thing, and that's why Medgar Evers is so revered — [and why it] is that he did what he did in spite of the dangers of that period. It was just a dangerous thing in any organization, fraternities, sororities, and what have you, to speak about anything that was contrary to the way that whites wanted things to be run. And especially about the government. Just don't get yourself involved in anything that the whites were interested in. Talk black stuff.

Classen: So even though there was a lot of anger and frustration about what was going on, being printed in the *Clarion-Ledger*, being shown on television, things newscasters were saying on the local TV stations, . . . the majority of black citizens would just kind of keep that to themselves because it was dangerous to talk about your complaints.

Kirksey: Yes. So, it was only a few who were pushing and mainly they were able to push because they had these contacts with national organizations like the church [UCC]. And that basically would provide the means by which the suit was brought that changed things for WLBT, but, eventually — I might add this because I think that it's important — the change that came about at WLBT is not as fundamental as it would appear to have been or be. Blacks are supposed to be 51 percent owners, and that's a joke, because the blacks are not 51 percent owners. . . . Now what I am saying is that basically these people who got the [ownership] positions were really given a position to sort of go along with what the owners of that corporation wanted. WLBT is not, is not a black station by any stretch of the imagination. As a matter of fact, I rarely watch WLBT now because in my view . . . some of those other stations have better programming for blacks.

Classen: What other stations do you think do a better job?

Kirksey: Well, there is WJTV and WAPT. Both are in my mind doing a better job in many areas than WLBT.

Classen: Including covering black issues? They do a better job?

Kirksey: Yes, yes, as good a job at any rate. I guess the bigger difference is WLBT's resources are greater. I think it's a wealthier station and they get more people out and they, I think, are able to hire some reporters that are better trained, better qualified to do the job. But if you're really looking at what is being covered and then compare WLBT's coverage with some of the other stations, you'll find that WLBT is not a black perspective station.[42]

Interestingly, the former *Free Press* editor made these observations in 1993 while the station was still, by FCC and federal legal standards, "minority owned," and several years before the year 2000 sale of WLBT and its parent company, Civic Communications, to the Liberty Corporation of South Carolina—a company lacking the "minority" designation. Kirksey was, and remains, concerned about the ways in which black Mississippians did, and continue to, "sell out" to white interests. He is convinced that WLBT's African American owners represented white, rather than black, interests. Kirksey contends that white power has historically divided African Americans, prompting the betrayal of black interests—a point made dramatically evident as he wove together with his cautionary comments regarding problems in broadcasting the stories of black Sovereignty Commission spies working for segregation.

A bit later in our conversation Kirksey remarked that "not just then but even today, a part of my whole thing is about the role of blacks in the whole scheme of things and the thing that hurts most . . . is the role of blacks who are supportive of what the hell is going on."[43] His portrayal of black Mississippians, past and present, highlights profound political differences within this racial formation, and the problems surrounding and emanating from such deep divides. Kirksey's wariness regarding the power and presence of white supremacist–black complicities is historically well grounded. White supremacist power has long been manifest and reproduced in its use of "divide and rule" strategies.

Echoing Kirksey was the well-known civic voice of Charles Evers, one of Mississippi's first black disc jockeys and, later, general manager for Jackson's public radio facility, WMPR-FM. As Medgar's brother and a former city mayor and politician, Evers has long attracted public attention and controversy within the state. During the seventies, Evers, Aaron Henry, and other prominent Mississippians were part of various "minority-controlled" ownership groups vying for FCC grant of the WLBT license.

Evers met with me in the station offices of WMPR, and at one point, I asked him about the present status of WLBT:

Classen: Would you call it a black television station?

Evers: Ownership, or just operated? . . .

Classen: Operated, the way it operates.

Evers: No, I think it's just a television station operated according to the FCC guidelines and from what I can see it includes everybody, so it wouldn't be a black station. Ownership is good, but, I mean, as far as programming, I would like to see it come back to what it was when we were trying to get it [in the seventies].

Classen: The reason I ask that is because I've talked to a couple of people who say this is not a black television station at all, it doesn't serve black interests at all, and I was wondering if you had a reaction to that.

Evers: I agree partially. I don't get into the black community as much as I should. I admit that channel 12 is a little more involved and 16 is really good, but channel 3. . . . They've got a CEO down there who is black . . . and he has gotten rid of more blacks that we had down there. . . . Well we have less black people now than they did before he came on, and that's because of the way he thinks. . . . It may be still 51 percent [black owned], but it's still being controlled by whites, and I guess that's where they're going. I'd like to see it controlled by blacks and supported by whites, we need that.

Classen: Who do you think controls it in the white community?

Evers: The guy in Texas, the millionaire that's backing [WLBT manager] Frank Melton is in control, there's no question about that.[44]

Evers and Kirksey's concerns regarding African American control of majority-black-owned broadcast stations were spoken at a moment in which the proportion of such properties owned and controlled by historically disadvantaged groups was very low. Since the National Telecommunications and Information Administration began collecting data on "Black, Latino, Asian and Native American" ownership of commercial broadcast stations in 1990, it has found that "minority" broadcast ownership has remained consistently low, never exceeding 3.1 percent. And the percentages of "minority" ownership have dropped still further since the passage of the Telecommunications Act of 1996. Greater ownership concentrations within and across industry sectors have been the legacy of the 1996 act, and nonwhite owners have testified to its adverse effect on efforts to further diversify ownership and programming.

The comments of Kirksey and Evers further complicate these discouraging studies by pointing to "race" as a social construct that should be evaluated in the light of local performance. They implicitly challenge the contemporary practice of formalizing racial identities and constructing policy taxonomies with little sensitivity to evolving daily concerns and experiences confronting marginalized groups. The Jackson residents suggest that "black" broadcast stations by practical definition are those that routinely engage the "black community" in and around their city, expressing and addressing their particular, but disparate, concerns. Kirksey's and Evers's focus is on the performance or enactment of racial affiliation in contrast to the static definitions and identities offered by administrative law. In our discussions they portrayed the state's definitions and operationalization of race (pertaining to federal authorization/licensing) as deadening and unresponsive, implicitly proposing that broadcasting be evaluated and defined in the light of performance connected to community interests and problems. Along with others I interviewed, Kirksey and Evers reminded me that understandings of "blackness" are inevitably connected less to formal legal nominations than to daily practice.

Kirksey's and Evers's insights resonate with the work of critical theoreticians who have warned against essentializing racial identities or categories. Instead their exhortation is to recognize such identities as dynamic, power-infused constructs that interact with class, religion, gender, and other social differences realized in the everyday. They rearticulate the argument that whiteness and blackness are, according to John Fiske, "better defined by what they *do* than by what they *are*," even while it is still important to "recognize that whiteness uses skin color as an identity card by which to see where its interests may best be promoted and its rewards distributed."[45]

Progressive policy responses to these identity dynamics do not include the complete abolition of affirmative action or racially targeted incentive programs, as many conservatives increasingly insist. Rather, they include policies that explicitly connect licensee identity and broadcast license allocation to what stations *do* — that is, to local broadcast practices and their address of diverse social demands. What Henry Kirksey draws our attention to is the vital point that a black station is not one nominally "owned by blacks" but instead one that consistently interacts with, and engages, local black communities, however those communities define themselves and their varied concerns.

In December 2000 I returned to Jackson, and during that visit talked with Walter Saddler. Saddler was able to offer a rare perspective regarding local broadcasting expectations and practices because he was one of the first African American reporters to work full-time at Jackson station WJTV (channel 12) in 1972. He worked in Jackson broadcasting ever since that time, eventually becoming director of community services for channel 12. When asked about contemporary Jackson television, he stated, "I see some disturbing changes taking place. A lot more representation [of African Americans], not only in the news, is needed. If we're not careful, we'll find ourselves back in sixties-type problems." Saddler told me that local television had been healthier, in terms of ethnic diversity and opportunities, in the past, and that more recently a "steady erosion in African American employment," joined to wider attacks on affirmative action, had him very worried. He spoke of local stations offering "false impressions and optical illusions of black involvement and investment in the black community." In contrast to such practices, which he believes are growing and only fostered by distant, group ownership, he told me that "TV's role is to *bring out* the problem. Your role [as a broadcaster] is to work on it. People in television must have knowledge and *empathy*."[46] Saddler speaks of these characteristics and this approach to the black community as in decline.

Saddler is keenly aware of trends and professional norms within commercial journalism that limit African American vocational advancement. As a beneficiary of affirmative action and federal Equal Employment Opportunity (EEO) programs in the seventies, he remembers earlier decades with fewer black journalists but greater promise for significant industrial change.[47] The full impact of the 1999 elimination of the FCC's EEO guidelines, coupled with increasing industry conglomeration, is yet to be seen, but many fear that employment opportunities for those speaking to communities of color and their concerns will continue to decrease. And, as the veteran reporters I interviewed would be quick to note, those culturally impoverished by the lack of professional journalistic diversity are not only blacks but all races.

Saddler, Evers, and Kirksey observe that local broadcasting has changed in recent years, and from their perspective not for the better of journalism or of service to the local African American community.

Watching Jim Crow

Certainly some powerful components of this change include the global restructuring of broadcast/media ownership and the failure of large commercial media interests to hire and support journalists asking hard questions regarding racial justice. The days of local stations working with relative autonomy from other stations are now gone in this new era of converging electronic media and global journalism, and Jackson's television stations have become part of large, growing broadcast groups that wield power by negotiating and purchasing syndicated packages and other programming as a group rather than as individual players in the market.

In working with programming tailored less to individual regions and particular metropolitan markets than to abstracted demographic targets, local station programming is less distinct, idiosyncratic, and unpredictable, and less likely to be significantly "out of line" in the ways that WLBT was during the fifties and sixties. Contemporary station group programming certainly can be, and sometimes is, racist in power and effect — but not often racist in the crude fashion of a Fred Beard editorial. As Hewitt Griffin, former WLBT programming director told me, "it couldn't happen now, I don't think." When I asked him why WLBT was targeted during the sixties instead of WJTV he said: "The bottom line was that of all the billions of words and everything else, Fred Beard took a television station and made it his own personal propaganda machine. . . . It was a sign of the times; it was a hallmark of the times. It couldn't happen now, I don't think. . . . I think that television has come to a point in its early adolescence, well, in its early adulthood now . . . where it's turned its destiny over to just a lot of people, the bean counters — the Lawrence Tisches and the Cap Cities, and the GE folks, you know. Man, it's just making money. And, of course, the audience is so fragmented nowadays, I can take my clicker and I can go wherever I want."[48]

Griffin's comments suggested an interesting mix of personal relief and loss. Lost are the times when stations had distinct, identifiable, personalities and programming choices, and purposes beyond "just making money." Thinking back to his tenure as a white employee of Lamar Broadcasting during the mid-sixties while WLBT was under federal pressure to reform its ways, Griffin remembered the constant stress of that moment and was relieved to be past that contestation. But he also mourned the transfer of local broadcast stations to "just a lot of people," "bean counters" without any particular broadcast experience or commitments to particular communities. As local stations become extensions of, and outlets for, huge media and journalistic organizations, it is not surprising that the Jackson *Eyewitness News* nightly production looks much like "eyewitness news" elsewhere. As one Jackson friend sighed and remarked in a recent phone call, "our news now looks pretty much like everyone else."

While the comments I've highlighted reveal ambivalence regarding local broadcaster performance or dissatisfaction and calls for change, it should be noted that some I talked with pointed to WLBT with a sense of accomplishment—for its present practices as well as its historical legacy. For example, Aaron Henry, who was one of the minority owners mentioned, characterized the contemporary station as a point of pride, perhaps flawed in its efforts yet impressive and positive in many regards. Some told me that the present station offered an impressive number of news anchors and announcers of color, as well as features targeted at Jackson's black communities. Still, those who assessed the station in these more positive terms often grounded their evaluation in the stark contrast of the present and the station controlled by the Citizens' Council in the sixties.

Most commonly what I heard was an assessment of local broadcasting that spoke of improvement but not sufficient change. Woven throughout the interviews there was the theme of promises and potentials unrealized. The dream of the local media activists in the sixties, that of progressive broadcast stations that consistently engage and invest in local minority communities, has remained largely a dream, or where it has been realized has been disrupted by economic and industrial reconfigurations. The economic and structural changes in broadcasting engage many social dynamics other than race and ethnicity and certainly are not reducible to these concerns. Still, such changes may be racist in effect, if as feared they erect even more daunting barriers to ownership and control by particular historically disadvantaged groups.

In this environment of structural and covert discrimination, I found people like Charles Evers who said that they will fight for control of local broadcast interests. Shortly after I interviewed Evers in his radio station offices, he went on air with his regular call-in show, *Just Talk*. One of the two discussion items on his program agenda was the way in which another prominent black Jacksonian, WLBT manager Frank Melton, was using his televised editorials to "ride blacks." Evers pointedly asked, "Why are only blacks showcased in television news crime coverage?" Later, after briefly recounting the way local blacks successfully fought for and won the WLBT license, he pledged, "We're not going to allow you [Melton] to take WLBT and bash on people you don't like." For more than an hour callers responded to Evers, the majority of whom affirmed his criticism of a television manager who seemed too willing to focus only on the worst events and elements in Jackson's black neighborhoods.

Certainly there is much to criticize when one views the terrible poverty and crime afflicting predominately black neighborhoods in and around Jackson. But, of course, the important questions are who and what is criticized and how those criticisms are made. Evers and others in Jackson's black communities are understandably concerned about the representations of blackness and crime that frequent local broadcasts and editorials. At times, the broadcast content seems not at all removed from the 1960s, when "black" equalled "crime" and social unrest. More than one black resident I talked with asked rhetorically where the media coverage of white involvement in drug trade and violent crime was to be found.

This is a vexing representational problem not confined to Jackson, to Mississippi, or to the South. The enduring problem of racializing crime and politics in both network and local news production has been widely observed. One of the most recent major surveys of black images on U.S. television has concluded that in network news productions addressing politics blacks are depicted "as sources of disruption, as victims, or as complaining supplicants. . . . One gets the impression from the overall pattern in these reports, in other words, that . . . in what really counts, blacks are takers and burdens on society."[49] And in studying local TV news, this research team also noted a practice eerily consonant with racist practices of the past — the failure to name and personalize African American subjects in news stories. Just such professional choices, as described earlier in this project, motivated the legal challenges and black community calls for integrity and respect aimed at WJTV and WLBT. But Robert Entmann and Andrew Rojecki, writing almost forty years later, summarize that "white victimizers appear as personalized, named individuals while black victimizers are more often depersonalized, nameless threats depicted in mug shots cut from a generic stripe of common criminal."[50] To the degree that such practices are still evident in Jackson telecasts they evoke memories that seem far past, but are not past at all.

CHAPTER 6

Not Forgetting

"We can't let people forget, else we go back." As we ended a phone conversation Aaron Shirley reiterated this point. In particular, he told me it was important that people remember what was accomplished in Jackson television during the 1970s, in the wake of the sixties' challenges. Beginning in the early seventies, central Mississippians experienced a very different type of local television, literally seeing the fruit of more than a decade of resistance to segregationist programming. In 1971, when the FCC placed WLBT under the control of an interim nonprofit management group, Communications Improvement Incorporated, the organization moved quickly to hire William H. Dilday Jr. to lead the station. In doing so, it became the first U.S. commercial television station to employ an African American general manager. Black employment at the station increased by more than 20 percent during the decade and included the placement of several people of color in managerial roles.[1]

Local programming, news, and public affairs productions were revamped. Under new management the station worked to expand the range and scope of serious public debate. It produced programming openly discussing the chronic problems confronting city and state. A morning talk show, *Coffee with Judy*, increasingly took on community problems such as mental health care and literacy, as did local news.[2] Local public affairs programs such as *Probe* and *Inquiry* invited controversial guests for interviews and made efforts to find representatives across the political spectrum from ultraconservative to liberal.[3] An interracial children's show, *Our Playmates*, was locally produced, and to this day it is remembered fondly by many in Jackson's black community as a positive step forward.

Given the degree of change this program revamping reflected and encouraged, it is not surprising that the "new" channel 3 met a rough reception. Some local advertisers boycotted the station, and longtime station employees bristled (or sometimes left) when faced with the prospect of working with many new, less-experienced employees of a different race. Hewitt Griffin, program director at the station through the late sixties to early seventies management transition, described these station changes as "traumatic," and states that he initially "hated" Dilday before a later rapprochement and friendship developed. He remarked, in retrospect, "as is often the case, it was the fire that forged this station to become what it turned out to be, which has been one of the best television stations in the South."[4]

Many local viewers regularly and loudly complained that a very good station had been replaced with an incompetent and politicized one. Briefly, WLBT's ratings slipped. Some used the slur "nigger news" in reference to channel 3 journalism, and the complaint that "niggers" or "negroes" had taken over control of a previously high-quality station endured in numerous letters written to the FCC through the early 1980s.[5] Still, after a rocky start, the station's ratings returned to the market's top, and channel 3's disciplined efforts to include conservative as well as more liberal perspectives garnered respect and (sometimes begrudging) praise alongside increasing audience numbers.[6]

Thus, a station singled out by activists and the federal government for its stark use of exclusionary and insular programming transformed into one marked by racial inclusion, wider public access, and invitations to debate enduring social problems. As historian Kirsten Fermaglich has observed, the change in station management was a key component in the changing of Jackson's public sphere from the sixties to the late seventies. Due in part to local broadcasting's changes, she writes, many (but certainly not all) white Jacksonians understood "the public sphere" very differently by 1979 than they had a decade earlier. They had moved from an understanding of a sphere "dominated and regulated by the elite whites of the community to one that included blacks and hailed open investigation."[7]

To the degree that this shift in understanding the public sphere and local broadcasting occurred, it was prompted by no single factor or personality and no single organized campaign, but rather by a multifrontal attack on local segregation and institutions of white supremacy, including local television. These powerful institutions were confronted by a variety of interventions, resistances, and petitions, involving the strategic employment of alternative, often low-tech, media, direct action, and formalized legal challenges. All of these interdependent discourses converged at a moment in time to prompt change. In particular, the stations were confronted by the intersecting activities of three groups — local activists, reform groups, and federal jurists. All three of these groups were necessary for reform, even though the motivating visions and agendas for the activists, reformers, and jurists were in frequent disagreement. For example, Medgar and Charles Evers, as well as R. L. T. Smith, focused their activism on access to broadcast outlets, motivated by a desire to more frequently and publicly connect black voices to ongoing debates and social crises concerning voting, educational opportunity, and public employment. The United Church of Christ's interventions, according to their key advocate, Everett C. Parker, were primarily motivated not only by goals of racial justice but by the prospect of constructing new legal precedents that would reform national broadcast policy, thereby increasing citizen standing to address federal administrative agency actions. And the federal court, as discussed earlier, acted as a mediator primarily interested in stabilizing and calming racial tensions and local conflicts via the exnomination of race and racialized conflicts in and around Jackson. In the place of "race and rights" tensions, the court embraced and rearticulated a politically popular "consumerism" in its decisions.

As Jackson's problems were repositioned and redefined within the realm of administrative law, specific concerns and problems would further be abstracted, losing the specificities of particular differences within a certain time and place.[8] Thus, all television viewers in central Mississippi, regardless of race, politics, or social power, were primarily nominated as "consumers." In the case of the Mississippi station challenges, the alignment of consumerism with local civil rights and communication access interests was sufficient to prompt some measure of reform and change. However, this alliance lacked the vision and collective strength necessary to force radical changes in the social formations undergirding local racist broadcasting or the structure of domestic commercial television.

The activisms of the moment were certainly essential in bringing about local broadcasting reform and change, but at times they were far removed from the problems or policies most directly connected to television. In Jackson, the alternative *Mississippi Free Press* published a few movement letters and editorials addressing local broadcasting

Watching Jim Crow

practices, and petitions regarding the licensing and practices of WLBT and WJTV were circulated and signed at NAACP and Jackson Movement meetings, but these petitions were few among many appeals. I was surprised to find so few archived documents speaking to the problem of broadcast or media representations, much less any campaign plans or organization for local media reform.[9] Black Mississippians and civil rights activists were vitally concerned with popular media productions and representations, but also felt that it was unsafe, impractical, and/or unproductive to directly attack the most powerful and wealthy institutions for segregationist representation. And other movement problems and concerns had more immediate claim on their time and energies. Instead, as discussed earlier, some movement participants took their direct-action interventions to concert venues and specific locations of public performance.

I was reminded of broadcasting's "secondary status" within Mississippi's movement activism when I talked with Aaron Henry in his Clarksdale drugstore. As often as I tried to bring him back to the topic of media advocacy and change during the sixties, he would remind me that he, and the Mississippi movement, were primarily about voting, employment, poverty, and education. As he told the story, the dramatic challenges and changes within Jackson television were but a sidebar to the main narratives regarding fights for other civil rights. Changes in local television practices were not foremost in the minds of Jackson's movement leaders, nor were they foremost in the mind of Henry. Rather, the press of Henry and many others toward civil rights, and more specifically, changes in everyday practices and policies governing voting, economics, and education, created an environment in which limited media activism, the interventions of the UCC, and the federal courts would together produce changes at the state's most powerful television outlets.

Thus, if this particular bit of history offers a historical model for broadcasting change or reform, it is a holistic model in which popular media practices are not the initial point for activism. Rather, they are intertwined with concerns of greater social salience such as poverty, hunger, crime, education, and health care. In the multifaceted address of such social problems, local media practices also become targeted and legitimate civil rights issues only as they are integrated within larger issues and contexts. The study of the Jackson station histories, as well as other histories of media change and reform in the sixties and seventies, points historians to the conclusion that if such change is divorced from connections to larger social movements and concerns, very significant alterations in national and local broadcast policies and practices are unlikely.

Put differently, significant changes in broadcasting policies never stand alone. Rather, they are imbricated within larger social concerns, visions, and movements. While hardly new, this point is often lost on those of us who too often confuse a mediacentric approach for a more sophisticated holistic study of television, and it is even more often neglected by contemporary media policymakers who place faith in studies and policies that isolate media use and industry practices from their larger contexts of meaning.

Media scholar Chon Noriega implicitly warns against such media-centrism and makes similar observations regarding the relationship of media reform and social activism in his study of television, the state, and the rise of Chicano cinema during the sixties and seventies. Noriega observes that the histories of the past four decades tell us that significant broadcast reform is less connected to direct government intervention than to public protest and direct-action campaigns.[10] He writes that during the sixties and seventies, "the social pressures that changed communication policy in the first place [were] . . . the rise of civil disobedience and outright violence acted out in public space and refracted through the mass media, which prompted courts to intervene and redefine the 'public interest' in order to selectively incorporate and diffuse social movements."[11] Of course, the catalysts for the direct-action campaigns as well as the rhetorical and strategic violence employed were seldom conditions in broadcasting or particular media sectors. However, social activists inevitably engaged contemporary media practices and practitioners, and sometimes did so using a "discourse of violence [that] worked because it walked hand in hand with an immediate, palpable, and visible social crisis."[12]

In Jackson, the changes that came to local television during the late sixties and early seventies can be fairly described as reformist — an incorporation of activists, movements, and discourses deemed threatening to the state and other powerful interests in a moment of crisis. Certainly, as others have described in some detail, the employment, programming, and public affairs changes evident in Jackson and elsewhere in the heyday of early seventies broadcast reform were heartening for many yet fundamentally flawed and too short-lived.[13] While

　　　　　　　　　　　　　　　　　　　　Watching Jim Crow

within the national scope of the reform movement some broadcast stations were forced to change their programming and employment ways, the structure, primary institutions, and economic bases of U.S. broadcasting were not changed or even seriously challenged. Rather, individual stations, including several southern broadcasters considered particularly egregious in their practices, were separately targeted for reform. Successful regulatory corrections to such "bad members" of the broadcasting industry thus encouraged understandings of the "punished" broadcaster as truly exceptional, and of the broadcasting system as one that works to correct its problems. Broadcast changes were thus to be atomized rather than systematic.

These criticisms of reformism in general, and more specifically the flaws within seventies broadcast reform, are important and convincingly made. But they discount more vexing questions regarding the relative importance of local difference and change within the national and global milieus, as well as inevitable historiographical negotiations between macro and micro analyses.[14] Structural and political economic criticisms become more complicated and problematic when placed in conversation with the experiences of the everyday in a particular time and place. Such conversations yield better understandings of how individuals negotiate industrial, institutional, legal, and economic structures, how they are transformed in and through these everyday negotiations, and how they influence the processes by which media structures and institutions evolve.[15] As Marc Raboy and his coauthors have written, "While political economy's attention to the unequal distribution of power across social and economic structures is crucial . . . this same stance has closed off a more subtle view of the local interactions that take place on the contradictory terrain of culture, where the effects of structures are translated into lived experience."[16]

Certainly, sitting in a Jackson living room in the early 1970s and viewing WLBT's William Dilday forcefully editorialize for more resources in Jackson's poor black neighborhoods, when a short while earlier a predecessor worked to block all positive African American appearances on air, was *felt* as radical — profoundly and fundamentally different for viewer citizens in ways that are simply lost in macroeconomic and structural analyses. Less than a decade before Dilday took his post the Jackson stations were so entrenched in segregationist interests that most Mississippians believed that changes at the stations, on even a lesser scale, would be simply impossible; indeed, the state's

WLBT sales manager Jack Goebel (left) and general manager
William H. Dilday.

most powerful media outlets were widely deemed unassailable. For the
practices of the Jackson stations to change as they did involved a
dramatic transformation of local policy and politics, interacting with
other movements in the social world. A radical change was accomplished in a particular sphere, time, and place, even though consequent
changes in federal law and policy moderated and shifted the focus of
the Jackson activism.

The significance of these changes are not lost nor have they faded
with time among the activists I met. Instead they say that a chief civil
rights concern is that of holding onto and advancing the cultural gains
that began to flower in the seventies. Black Mississippians I talked with
who were employed at WLBT and WJTV still remember the seventies as
dramatically and wonderfully different from the broadcast environment just a few years prior. For them and for others the changes in
Jackson television felt radical, even if historically contingent and too
short-lived. Walter Saddler, one of the earliest African American employees of the Jackson stations, is among those who remember the
seventies as filled with a sense of black empowerment and excitement,

Watching Jim Crow

with professional and productive discussions of race and racism and the promise of further progressive change.

Sadly, he now refers to the seventies as a moment very different, and more promising, than the present. Even though majority-black corporations were awarded the license of WLBT subsequent to a 1979 FCC decision, the seventies are still remembered as a decade that was exceptional for the station's service to diverse Jackson communities. Three decades later, Saddler joins Shirley in voicing concerns that television broadcasting in Jackson might be "going back" — in part because of increasing corporate consolidation, production centralization, and other dynamics connected to national and global media ownership and control.

REREGULATING JACKSON'S "MARKETPLACE"

In 1996, while I listened to citizens express concerns that Jackson television might be in danger of "going back," President Bill Clinton was signing a massive new bill promising to move national broadcasting and telecommunications forward. The Telecommunications Act of 1996 would, the chief executive opined, "strengthen our economy, our society, our families, and our democracy." Further, the legislation would "provide consumers greater choices and better quality in their telephone, cable, and information services . . . [which] puts us squarely on the road to a brighter, more productive future."[17]

By reinvoking the rhetoric of consumer choice and benefit used so effectively by John F. Kennedy, President Clinton both called on and reiterated discourses of consumerism in a legitimization of a sweeping neoliberal reregulation of American telecommunications and broadcasting. This act has had, and will continue to have, significant consequences for all U.S. broadcasting interests and "marketplaces," certainly including those in Mississippi. The bill is, in essence, a massive overhaul of the long foundational 1934 Communications Act regulating domestic telecommunications. Constituted with an unquestioning embrace of long-assumed commercial commitments, the 1996 act formalized the corporate liberal vision of a "deregulated" marketplace that, if left unfettered by the state and significant social obligations, would somehow magically and meaningfully serve those who engaged it not only as consumers but as citizens with diverse social interests and demands. Clinton gave voice to the vision of giving more power to this "freer marketplace," which in turn would not only aid consumers looking for better and less-expensive products but also "strengthen our society . . . and our democracy."[18]

One irony connected to these remarks and their underlying perspective is that the 1996 act, like much important telecommunications legislation and "deregulation," was negotiated and written — ostensibly to "strengthen democracy" — outside the purview and notice of the great majority of Americans. Certainly the federal government and its representatives claim that its hearings and debates regarding the act were open and on public record. But on a practical level, those outside the conventional policymaking communities found, and for a variety of reasons continue to find, full information and access to key policymaking information and agents to be a very difficult undertaking.[19]

For information and insight regarding such sweeping legislative change, most citizens understandably rely on commercial journalism. But, not surprisingly, the 1996 act and its key assumptions and components received very little commercial journalistic coverage prior to its codification. The industries pressing Congress for deregulatory changes and further economic advantage were less than keen on the idea of reporting regarding their own lobbying campaign and the potential pitfalls of a complicated reregulatory scheme. When the massive piece of proposed legislation was discussed in the press, it was tellingly defined as a business or technological, rather than public policy, issue.[20] Thus, at the time of its formation most citizens simply did not know that Congress was writing law that would have profound implications not only for how and at what costs people receive information but also for cultural production and relations.

As civil rights advocate Mark Lloyd has put it, regarding the wider issue of national communication policy debates, the debates in this democratic nation to which citizens are too infrequently invited are ones regarding "who gets to speak, at what price, and to whom."[21] Instead, very typically, within a sphere of select technical, political, and legal "experts" rather than broader public discussion, the 1996 act's regulatory template was formed and certified as necessary for a time filled with changing technologies and increasing global competition.[22]

Ostensibly created in response to scientific and technological complaints regarding the antiquated 1934 Communications Act, the 1996 act is just one of many state actions that regulators or legislators

Watching Jim Crow

have taken in recent years to "deregulate — or, put differently, to "re-regulate" — broadcasting.[23] Certainly it should not be singled out as the sole expression or reproduction of corporate liberalism in recent years. However, it is an exemplar of the state's inconsistent exercise of power in the constitution of broadcast licenses and the spectrum as private rather than public resources, enabling extraordinarily large and wealthy businesses to gain ever more resources and capital. The act reproduced powerful discourses allowing large media corporations greater power and opportunities to further concentrate property ownership, greater security in the holding of their licenses, and more broadcast spectrum.[24] Subsequent to the legislation's passage, a large quantity of broadcast spectrum — parts of the electromagnetic "airwaves" formally declared to be publicly owned — were, and continue to be, auctioned off or leased away to commercial conglomerates. In radio, all national ownership caps were removed, encouraging in recent years the phenomenon that is Clear Channel Incorporated, a single corporate entity with ownership of approximately twelve hundred local radio stations. In television, ownership groups substantially increased their broadcast holdings and continue to lobby Congress and initiate lawsuits against the government for removal of even very modest existing ownership limits.[25]

As telecommunications policy analyst Patricia Aufderheide has summarized, despite the promises of the president and Congress, in the midst of all this corporate consolidation residential customers have not been well served. She notes that these media users have not been seeing more choice in cable and local telephone service, while at the same time "very large firms have become much larger, without either offering new commercial services or expanding their social obligations."[26] The FCC, an agency that was largely supportive of the 1996 act, in its 1998 biennial report addressed changes in local broadcast radio by saying that "it appears that while there may have been a number of salutary effects flowing from the consolidation that has taken place since 1996, largely in financial strength and enhanced efficiencies, it cannot be said that consolidation has enhanced competition or diversity, and indeed, may be having the opposite effect."[27]

These pitfalls of "deregulation" have, again, been almost completely predictable and predictably downplayed in mainstream commercial media journalism. Such failures to meet the promises of more open and vigorous competition could be foreseen in part because the new and invigorating "competition" promised is a curious phenomenon — one that is strange to classic capitalist theory. Within the model of competition formed by the 1996 act a handful of enormous, vertically integrated media conglomerates such as News Corporation, Time Warner, and Disney, all owners and part owners of multiple communications-related companies, are freed to have their broadcasting companies further "compete" with their own companies in film, cable, telephone, computer publishing, internet service, and consumer electronics. And, to the degree that News Corporation, Time Warner, or Disney companies actually contest across conglomerate lines, it is very likely, due to the multiplication of joint ventures and cross ownerships of properties and products across those same lines, that the "competition" engaged is far from what is envisioned when people think of classic entrepreneurial capitalism. In fact, it is difficult to conceive of how any small entrepreneurial broadcasting or cable group would be comparatively advantaged by the 1996 act or through it enabled vigorously to "compete" directly today against the likes of a News Corporation.

In this environment minority broadcasters have consistently made the point that media consolidation has decreased broadcast competition and diversity. A minority broadcast ownership study undertaken by the National Telecommunication and Information Administration (NTIA), published in 2001, reports that:

> NTIA has consistently heard from minority owners about consolidation's detrimental impact on their ability to compete effectively against better financed non-minority station owners. . . . Relaxation of the ownership rules and consolidation have contributed to higher station prices. The skyrocketing prices, in some instances up to 20 times or more the amount of the station's actual cash flow, have exacerbated minority broadcasters' historic difficulty accessing sufficient capital for entry or expansion. . . . Panelists echoed concerns about the loss of diverse sources of information relevant to minority communities and the lack of outlets for local issues. Some feared without media ownership, minorities are virtually powerless to present positive images of their communities.[28]

The concerns alluded to here are familiar ones. They speak to the same fear I heard implicitly expressed as I talked with those concerned about racial justice. Having experienced a broadcast industry and environ-

Watching Jim Crow

ment led by elite white interests, there are many in Jackson and its surrounding areas who are deeply troubled by the prospect of a "return to the past" in the ownership or management of Jackson's television and radio industries.

These concerns are strong in part because they pertain to property and the ways in which white privilege has been historically reproduced. This privilege, manifest in historical patterns of broadcast property ownership and management, undergirds present concerns regarding the relationship of racial difference and inequality to property and class. Given the state's legal constitution of broadcasting, the radio and television licenses necessary for operation in Jackson and elsewhere are increasingly treated as private property, and because this is the case property claims are constantly at stake — at the same time official government studies conclude that "minority" ownership of commercial television stations in the United States is less than 2 percent, the lowest level measured in the last decade.[29]

When the U.S. commerce secretary Norman Mineta releases such statistics while speaking of our nation's "long standing commitment to minority ownership in the broadcast industry,"[30] one is prompted to wonder where and how such a commitment lies. The history of the present tells us that the regulators and legislators of the state, working within the guiding lights of corporate liberalism, enthusiastically construct legal regulatory plans that routinely work against such diversity "commitments," although most often without any explicit mention of race, ethnicity, or diversity. "Deregulatory" schemes, for example, have most often acted as formalized technologies for the perpetuation of an exnominated racial-ethnic privilege that has marked U.S. broadcast law and regulation since its inception. The consequences of such (de)regulatory actions are evident in cities across the country, and certainly can be seen in Jackson where small ownership groups and standalone operations have, in recent years, been increasingly targeted for takeover by larger conglomerates and station groups.

LEAVING JACKSON

On 20 June 2000 the Jackson *Clarion-Ledger* announced that WLBT-TV was again changing owners. The announcement confirmed the station's merger in a $204 million cash transaction, with Cosmos Broadcasting, a subsidiary of Liberty Corporation, owner of a fifteen-station television group.[31] Frank Melton, the principal owner and president of Jackson-based Civic Communications Incorporated, announced that he felt "very, very good about the sale," adding that he had been searching for a corporate partner for two years, in order to address "growing industry consolidation."[32]

This action came as no surprise in light of the industrial-regulatory environment just described. Jackson's other commercial television stations had in recent years become affiliated with large media conglomerates. WJTV aligned with another large regional corporation, Media General, and WAPT-TV joined the ranks of Hearst-Argyle stations. Further, these three longtime network affiliates were joined in by WB and UPN network affiliates, WDBD-TV and WXMS-TV. Pegasus Communications Corporation, the distributor of DIRECTTV digital satellite services, purchased WDBD and WXMS as part of its investment in "emerging networks." In this "marketplace" WLBT's Melton felt the press to "consolidate." As the contemporary commercial television market in Jackson exemplifies, in today's broadcasting environment to operate as a stand-alone station, or even a small station group, is truly the exception to the rule of commercial profit and "competition." Local television stations apart from large and increasingly consolidated national and international media conglomerates seem to be a dying breed.

The demise of locally owned and operated broadcast properties is not simply an economic phenomenon, but also one related to industrial organization and culture. The corporate form of organization, increasingly defined as "inevitable" due to its increased "efficiencies," tends toward, in the words of Thomas Streeter, "vertical integration, bureaucratic rigidity and hierarchical organization, oligopolistic market behavior, large size, and in general, replacement of open, entrepreneurial competition with what historian Alfred Chandler calls the 'visible hand of management.' "[33] As stations lose independence and their entrepreneurial organization, they take on more standardized corporate identities, programs, and formulas.

This is not to say that WLBT or other Jackson stations were not marked by such managerial cultures prior to the most recent corporate consolidations. However, the quality and degree of centralized managerial controls are clearly changing. The Jackson stations now answer primarily to distant corporate offices that oversee a dozen or dozens of

Watching Jim Crow

local stations and use some version, for example, of the "eyewitness news" formula in local news telecasts. Certainly this is not, in every case, an entirely negative practice. For example, in the case of race and its broadcast representations, flamboyant and overt demonstrations of racism, such as those performed by Fred Beard, are less likely to be explicitly linked to station management and local production. Corporate managers, following established commercial formulas and consultancy plans, work to eliminate any high-risk connection of such extremism or radical discourse to local outlets. Thus, the sympathetic airing of an openly racist rant from the sixties is unlikely, but so is "radical" programming that would sympathetically side with say, leftist Chicanos or African Americans, and so are productions that would take up the troubling questions of enduring structural racism in Mississippi and elsewhere. Journalistic formulas with a nonconfrontational commercial appeal are the rule for corporate profit.

What I heard during this project was that even prior to the recent management changes, station declarations that WLBT was "black owned and controlled" left many in Jackson's progressive and African American communities increasingly dissatisfied. As I discuss in the previous chapter (and which is also discussed at some length in the NTIA document), simplistic definitions of "black" and "minority" ownership or control are increasingly problematized. These definitions especially are challenged in cases where citizens and careful observers suspect that the use of token or figurehead minorities in management conceals a power structure that is less concerned with investment in communities of color than with quick profit. During my interviews in Jackson, the CEO and general manager of WLBT, Frank Melton, was often identified as the center of public controversies involving the station. Although Melton has many enthusiastic supporters in both black and white communities, critics point to his provocative editorials and attacks aimed at black neighborhoods, black crime, and the malfeasance of black officials as an appeasement of powerful white interests — both historical and financial. They make the point that this issue is especially clear when such attacks are contrasted with the lack of such condemnations aimed at powerful white institutions. Some I talked with went so far as to explicitly say that Melton was not really in control but rather simply a black ventriloquist for distant white power brokers. But whether or not one accepts these personal criticisms, the more important observation is that many in west Jackson and elsewhere simply believe that in the wake of the sixties station-licensing fights and the promise of progressive programming manifest in the seventies, WLBT as a voice for the historically underrepresented has been a disappointment. In their view, the station has failed to adequately address enduring local problems that have hit communities of color particularly hard, such as poverty, public health neglect, defacto segregation, and decaying city infrastructure.

Thus it is understandable that the change of ownership, the moving from a small, locally based corporation in charge to a large regional ownership group headquartered in South Carolina, has again raised serious questions regarding this long-contested station's relationship to its local minority communities. Some individuals long affiliated with WLBT or its licensing battles reacted to news of the Liberty merger with sadness and anger. In the *Clarion-Ledger* Charles Evers stated: "I am appalled. There were many hours of sweat and protest to get the station minority owned, and now someone is coming in and taking it away. I guess Aaron Henry and Medgar are rolling over in their graves. It's a slap in the face to minorities. It's not great out there now, but it's better than it was. There are only a few blacks in management at the station, and now its only going to get worse." William Dilday, who was replaced at the end of the seventies and the interim licensing period by Melton, also stated in the *Clarion-Ledger* that he was "surprised" and "sad" to hear news of the merger.[34]

What one sees in the Jackson television market is viewed by many as a movement in a backward direction that effectively erodes the gains and claims established in earlier times. Several viewers and journalists talked with me about the local stations' lack of public affairs programming addressing minority concerns and crises. To cite one example, Walter Saddler, a widely respected veteran reporter and former news anchor at WJTV, has seen his public affairs programs, which frequently address controversial issues of importance to the black community, effectively sequestered away in an early-morning programming slot on Saturdays. This is not to say that WJTV management is comparatively insensitive to or uncaring regarding communities of color; rather, it is to point to some of the consequences of the standardization of local station programming following corporate models for profit maximization. So, for example, when Saddler produced a provocative program on the coercive displacement of poor black farmers from their long-held lands to make way for a giant new Nissan car plant not far from

Jackson, the program was aired only once — at six o'clock on a Saturday morning. While the station gave the story the conventional "balanced" coverage on its evening newscasts, more investigative, substantive treatments of the issue would likely have seemed out of place with the station's other news "product" given the move of local newscasts increasingly toward standardized formulas, shared video feeds, and seemingly interchangeable news readers with only a fleeting connection to their local communities.

Such trends prompt Saddler to mourn the "rootlessness" of contemporary local television journalism and the ways in which such practices discourage personal and corporate investment in Jackson's poorest communities. Another African American journalist, when asked how the corporate takeovers of the local stations influenced station editorial control, remarked that "corporate fingerprints" were now "all over the stories" produced and that, particularly in the case of investigative news series, nothing was produced until the corporate center gave the project a green light. Taken together, the environment described makes it easy to understand how the takeover of local "black owned and controlled" stations by very large, distant, historically white-managed corporations seems to many like a step back in time. As William Dilday poignantly summarized his response to the WLBT sale, "I'm never happy to see minorities lose control of any company, but I guess they did it for the money."[35]

"PRODUCERS" AND "CONSUMERS" REVISITED

Dilday's lament regarding loss of control speaks to his implicit recognition of a formative dichotomy that pervasively informs understandings of popular culture — what Streeter has discussed as "the production/consumption divide" foundational to U.S. commercial broadcasting. This bifurcation is commonplace but is neither "natural" nor an inevitable outcome of history. Rather, it is a dominant social discourse, shaped by capitalist pressures dating back to the Industrial Revolution and the creation of privatized domestic space: "In theory this social innovation separated the public world of work, markets, and politics from the world of the nuclear family. Concretely, it enabled new arrangements of space, time, gender, and labor, with complex manifestations. Both the practice of funding broadcasting by 'selling audiences to advertisers' and the radical separation of transmission and reception that constitutes broadcasting itself are premised on the production/consumption divide."[36]

As Streeter's words explain, the reiteration and reproduction of divides between transmission and reception or production and consumption also help to underwrite broad acquiescence to the idea that the public's principal role in regard to broadcasting is not production or even productive but rather is passive and primarily a matter of listening and viewing. Certainly the cultural work of the reader/viewer is important and productive, but those that economically profit from this "work" routinely fail to recognize it as such, and have unequal power to influence broadcast content. Indeed, the citizen-consumer is often rhetorically wooed and flattered by advertisers and industry, but is not imagined as one that should, or will, have decision-making power beyond a very limited sphere of activity.[37] As Streeter argues: "Addressing people as consumers is not the same as addressing them as say, citizens or souls. The variability of the meaning of 'consumer' takes place within certain boundaries and is shaped by certain pressures. . . . Generally, though, the key defining characteristic of 'consumers' is that they are not invited directly into decision-making processes concerning production."[38] Nor do dominant "consumer" discourses, with their focus on the activities of consumption, often encourage scrutiny of the larger social institutional structures in which we all live.[39]

For these and other reasons, the production/consumption bifurcation has long been a problem for media activism, influencing how such activism is conceptualized as well as its actual practices and goals. This dominant logic has encouraged activists, government, and others to define those advocating media change as residing on one side or the other of the production/consumption binary — often positioning nonindustry voices within historically limiting consumer definitions. In this way, advocacy and activism are routinely circumscribed.

The state's relationship with broadcast "consumers" has been historically complex and problematic. As I have demonstrated, it is a relationship in which state agencies and agents have historically employed "consumer" definitions and "consumerist" discourses in the management of racialized threat. Certainly, problematic and reductionist discourses of consumerism and "the consumer" are not simply confined to, or even primary to, agents and agencies of the state. As Foucault reminds us, such regulatory discourses circulate in multiple

Watching Jim Crow

and capillary ways, always connected to social power.[40] Nonetheless, the history examined proffers a prime example of the ways that state regulators have routinely dismissed the abilities, insights, or initiatives of citizen activists, particularly those lacking experience or expertise in particular types of policy/legal language, as they mobilize around the strategic tropes of consumer rights or consumerism. At the same time, state employment of consumerist discourses has opened strategic, vital spaces for social change.

Certainly in the WLBT case this was repeatedly evident, but it was shown most dramatically in the varied activities of the FCC and court of appeals. The FCC announced early in the license challenge process that local citizens, "consumers," had no legal right or "standing" to challenge, or even formally participate, in local licensing decision making. Such decisions were to be made exclusively via a dialogue of administrative agency experts and those in the producerly realm. And when the commission announced this decision to deny citizen access to such decision making it was not performing in a particularly peevish way or taking a bold new stance, but rather simply reproducing the legal means and logic by which producers and consumers had been routinely divided off from one another and consumers defined out of particular activities.

Even when the subsequent 1966 federal court decision (see chapter 2) on station licensing granted legal standing to citizens, it took pains to entirely limit their definition and activities within "consumerism." Social differences, tensions, and issues of justice fueling citizen cries for change were homogenized and elided in the articulation of distinctly "consumerist" concerns such as a fair return on their economic investment in television hardware.

Actions by the FCC in this case also illustrate how the state has often reproduced and strategically deployed discourses defining consumers as relatively unqualified, uninterested, or naive in their address of industry choices. The commission, ostensibly designed to govern and regulate communications on behalf of "the people" rather than industry alone, has long evidenced a distrust or indifference toward those who offer substantive criticism (beyond that of excessive advertising, sex, or violence) of the industries' offerings and programming plans. In this case (see chapter 4) the commission revealed a particularly hostile attitude and rhetoric aimed at citizens speaking to long-existing patterns, not just isolated instances, of local broadcast injustice and racism. By employing a rationale of technical and legal requirements, the commission worked to dismiss serious observations, evidence, and arguments provided by citizens asking for substantive programming and operational changes.[41]

In having done so, the commission provides us with an example of its often-explicit commercial commitments and also demonstrates how the public policy process itself functions as a technology for, in the words of Roopali Mukherjee, "the production and legitimation of particular [racialized] knowledges," and for the formation, mobilization, and discipline of racial subjects.[42] Mukherjee provides in her work on California in 2000 examples of how federal and state policy processes operate precisely in this way. She implicitly encourages readers to follow and further scrutinize the historical trajectories of such policy technologies that are all the more efficient for their implicit and explicit claims of political abstinence.

Still, in a particular place and time, the Jackson activists embodied not only a savvy and strategic use of "consumerist discourses" but also a creative resistance to the binaristic logic of the historical consumer/producer divide. By clearly focusing on the material and social constraints on consumption, their productive activities put the lie to the dominant myth of the homogenized, universal consumer. In working with alternative media and creating spaces for spontaneous cultural performances at Tougaloo and elsewhere, the Jackson students and station challengers were both "consumers" and "counterproducers." In their production and reproduction of popular culture they effectively called into question the dominant production practices and policies as they connected to consumption and undergirded segregation.

The stories of this study not only highlight such strategic gains but also animate the serious risks and consequences for contemporary identity politics within the play of dominant consumerist discourses. Even when consumer movements have enjoyed success — and they did in the late sixties and seventies — it has often come at the price of displacing more pressing social concerns. Those advocating substantive changes often must strategically both employ and reject that which makes them a "consumer," by recognizing the historical limitations and dynamism of "consumerist" advocacies.

Today, in the climate of increasing deregulation and global corporate conglomeration, the "consumerism" that served in past decades to bring partial and contingent progress to African American citizens

Watching Jim Crow

seems even more problematic in its reiterations — lacking, among other things, the support once offered inconsistently by vital federal institutions such as the appellate courts. However, the histories offered in this volume and elsewhere will hopefully spark alternative views of the present, in which, for example, "citizenship" and "consumer" are less juridical or formal state pronounced positions than they are nominations employed strategically within local, translocal, or regional campaigns for alternative cultural resources and venues.[43]

Critical policy debates that engage "citizens" and "consumers" with little or no formal policy expertise must, as I suggested earlier, reexamine their frequent mediacentrism and their peculiar taxonomies and terms, and strive to engage people within their larger sphere of social concerns. In the study of these concerns, the employment of anthropological and enthographic audience research methods has been a particularly welcome contribution to critical media research. But, at least in U.S. academies, it has too seldom been connected to policy studies.

Work in the past few years has, however, effectively advocated for the productivity of such a scholarly synthesis by arguing that critical attempts to study social demands might productively reorient the policy research domain dominated by industry interests and market demand concerns. As one study put it: "Intervention in policymaking should be connected with the ways in which citizens continue to live out the structures of government. . . . Researchers must recognize that it is not fruitful to study either policy or media use without taking both into account."[44] The cultural studies emphasis on audience and reception studies could, and should, be joined to an investigation of the policy environments in which not only is media content negotiated but also citizen definitions of the public and private, as well as their identities, needs, and aspirations.

REMEMBERING TODAY

During the years addressed in this volume, consumerism was a converging set of discourses enjoying a time of cultural power and notice that made it an attractive political force. But even during the sixties, consumerist campaigns were recognized as essentially reformist, and prominent African American leaders consistently reminded journalists and young followers that those engaged in the freedom fight were engaged in a battle for more than being able to sit at a lunch counter or enter an entertainment venue. Austin Moore and the few Tougaloo College students and staff members who joined him in "the cultural and artistic agitation" campaign recognized the importance of cultural and entertainment venues in the struggle against white segregationism but also argued that their activism was about much more than standardized consumer rights, access to better commercial goods, and admittance to musical concerts: it was about fundamental connections between popular culture and human dignity. Ella Baker, a leader of the SCLC and early direct-action campaigns, famously wrote that the activism of young people was "concerned with something bigger than a hamburger. . . . The Negro and white students, north and south, are seeking to rid America of the scourge of racial segregation and discrimination."[45] And in 1961, Malcolm X remarked that hundreds of years of racism and labor exploitation were "worth more than a cup of coffee at a white cafe. We are here to collect back wages."[46]

Now, as then, property and visions of property are inextricably tied to notions of justice and dignity. According to Streeter, "property is not just a technicality of the law . . . [it] remains an ideological linchpin of contemporary social relations. Consciously or not, property touches on central questions of justice and social vision."[47] Knowing this less through abstract argument than through the experiences of everyday life, those concerned with racial justice in Jackson continue to publicly connect their concerns with property and social justice to local cultural institutions such as WLBT. They also call on people to remember: to remember how race and racial concerns have historically been addressed in the regulation of popular television; and to recall the ways in which race has inevitably been a part of the social and political constitution of popular television in particular times and places.

Aaron Shirley's specific admonition is that we remember the gains of the past to enable and empower our visions in the present. In the case of WLBT-TV, unofficial direct action activities and formal legal activism complemented one another as part of a multifrontal, sustained campaign. While these intersecting campaigns did not bring an immediate halt to segregationist practices or racist policies in the state, they prompted change and were a vital part of the larger ongoing struggle against white supremacy and its institutions.[48]

The victories won and the changes made in Jackson television came at a considerable cost and only after very long and complicated fights, but they offer those fighting for progressive change both hope and a historically informed view of the challenges and dangers to be faced. They remind us of the historical stakes, including "property" and "human dignity," in play.

Because television remains a vital social institution that reproduces particular understandings of race, racial power, and identity, the struggles over local television continue, as do hegemonic negotiations of historical white privilege. What is at least tacitly acknowledged in these engagements is that while television is commonly regarded as a corporate technology and an increasingly conglomerated business, it is far more: it is something that people do. Fundamentally, it is a practice of our social imaginations that is inextricably bound up with particular, disparate identities, values, memories, and understandings. And as the Jackson activists still remind us, television is a social activity that can, and should, explore new and different ways of understanding ourselves and others.

Chronology

The fifties and sixties civil rights movement, while national in impact, was hardly a singular intervention. Nor, in the words of Melissa Fay Greene, was it a series of neatly "distinct and strategic skirmishes" that achieved "well-anticipated goals."[1] Rather, the movement was a synergistic conjuncture of myriad, often disparate, local struggles.[2]

In this project I focus on local civil rights struggles in and around Jackson, Mississippi, during the fifties and sixties, but I do so while recognizing that these conflicts were only part of a complicated social aggregate. Because the integrationist campaigns to change Jackson television and popular entertainment occurred within a complex period of social change, and because these efforts offer a plenitude of events and activities for ongoing study, I offer the following, admittedly partial, chronology.[3]

1953

JANUARY Mississippi's first television station, WJTV, goes on air in the state capital of Jackson, initially operating on UHF channel 25. The station is owned by the Hederman family, which also owns and operates two Jackson daily newspapers, the *Daily News* and the *Clarion-Ledger*. Station WJTV is affiliated with the CBS television network.

DECEMBER Station WLBT-TV goes on air in Jackson, operating on VHF channel 3. Lamar Life Broadcasting Company, a subsidiary of Lamar Life Insurance Company, which also operates radio stations WJDX and WJDX-FM, owns the station. All three stations are located in a new "little Radio City" complex adjacent to Jackson's downtown district. Station WLBT-TV has a primary affiliation with the NBC television network, and Fred Beard is its general manager.

JANUARY   Medgar Evers, with assistance from the NAACP, attempts unsuccessfully to enroll at the University of Mississippi law school. He later accepts an invitation to become the NAACP field secretary for Mississippi.

MAY   The U.S. Supreme Court votes unanimously to declare separate educational facilities inherently unequal, and declares that racial segregation "is a denial of equal protection of the laws" in *Brown v. Board of Education*. Many white Mississippians, fearing the consequences of racial integration, begin to refer to May 17, the day of the Court's public decision, as "Black Monday."

JULY   Robert "Tut" Patterson calls together a small group of men in Indianola, Mississippi, to mobilize legal, nonviolent white resistance to school desegregation. Approximately seventy-five Indianola whites join Patterson and his group later in the month to form the first Citizens' Council. Among the council's early public supporters are the Hederman family, owners of WJTV, and Fred Beard, general manager of WLBT. Months later Beard wins election to the board of the Jackson Citizens' Council.

1955

OCTOBER   The Washington bureau of the NAACP, alerted by its office in Jackson, begins correspondence with the Federal Communications Commission requesting an immediate investigation of Fred Beard and WLBT's programming practices. The bureau also requests action looking toward revocation of the licenses of stations WLBT and WJDX. Using supporting materials from a Jackson daily newspaper, the NAACP argues that Beard has cut off network programming addressing the racial integration controversy, including an ABC *Home* interview with NAACP general counsel Thurgood Marshall. The group further contends that the station has generally failed its fairness doctrine obligation to cover controversial issues of public importance and to allow reasonable opportunities for all sides to be heard.

1956

FEBRUARY   Station WLBT formally replies to the 1955 NAACP complaint. Later, the FCC defers any decision making, stating that the complaint would be considered when the station next filed an application for licensing.

OCTOBER Medgar Evers, Mississippi field secretary for the NAACP, informs the FCC that a program titled "The Little Rock Crisis," which aired on WLBT, presents a strongly segregationist perspective, to the exclusion of "the views of Negroes on this very vital issue." The NAACP and Evers ask for redress of this omission, specifically asking for time on behalf of "a group of Mississippi Negroes for the presentation of the Negro position."[4] This request is refused by WLBT.

MAY The FCC defers the license renewals of WLBT and WJDX, and requests that the stations respond to earlier NAACP complaints.

JULY The FCC, while admitting that WLBT's past programming content was "not entirely clear" to the commission, renews the station's license, arguing that "isolated" and "honest" mistakes by a station should not be a basis for license revocation. The administrative agency sends a letter to the NAACP concluding that, in regard to their earlier complaints, "the Commission is of the view that no further action is warranted on its part with respect to these matters."

MARCH Nine students from the predominantly black Tougaloo College, located just outside of Jackson, hold a sit-in at the city's whites-only public library and are arrested. The next day students from Jackson State University march toward the jail in protest and are stopped by police.

JUNE Freedom riders traveling on interstate buses enter Jackson to challenge local segregationist laws and are promptly jailed.

DECEMBER Medgar Evers and John and Eldri Salter lead a short-lived boycott of Jackson's Capitol Street, the white downtown shopping district that also benefits from black consumers. The merchants refuse to negotiate, and the effort receives virtually no attention from Jackson's radio or television stations, or its large-circulation newspapers.

The Reverend R. L. T. Smith, the first black Mississippian to run for a congressional seat in the twentieth century, appears on WJTV-TV for a thirty-minute political spot.

JUNE   Reverend Smith appears on WLBT for a second thirty-minute political spot, after a campaign of more than five months to pressure the station into this action. Smith is allowed to purchase the TV airtime the day before the election. Incumbent congressman and archsegregationist John Bell Williams defeats Smith in the election.

OCTOBER   James Meredith becomes the first African American to attend classes at the University of Mississippi, after a weekend of violent clashes between angry whites and federal forces. Mississippi radio and television stations offer extensive, often incendiary, coverage of the campus battle.

NOVEMBER   The FCC investigates eight Mississippi radio and television stations: WLBT, WJTV, WJDX-AM and FM, WRBC, and WSLI in Jackson, and WCBI-AM and FM in Columbus, concerning their role in instigating violence and broadcasting inflammatory editorials during the enrollment of James Meredith at the University of Mississippi. The commission requests further comments and explanations from the stations regarding their coverage.

The official bulletin of the North Jackson Youth Council, the *North Jackson Action*, declares an official start to the Jackson Nonviolent Movement's boycott campaign. This sustained campaign continues into spring 1963.

MAY   Jackson mayor Allen Thompson goes on local television to directly confront the Jackson Movement's boycott effort and its demands. Speaking of races living "side by side in peace and harmony," Thompson reiterates his refusal to consider the movement's agenda. Medgar Evers appeals to the FCC and local stations for equal time to reply. In his televised reply Evers appeals for an end to racial segregation and for increased black employment. The movement's direct-action efforts intensify, including sit-ins and marches.

JUNE   Medgar Evers is assassinated in the driveway to his home. Approximately five thousand black mourners join the funeral cortege and march from Jackson's Masonic Temple to the funeral home, fighting back when Jackson police attempt to disperse the crowd. A full-scale uprising is narrowly avoided.

JULY The FCC issues a public notice clarifying the need for balanced coverage of race-related issues under the existing fairness doctrine.

1964

JANUARY A small group of Tougaloo College students and staff begin a campaign of "cultural agitation," which effectively disrupts scheduled appearances of prominent artists, national leaders, and media personalities before segregated audiences.

MARCH Volunteers conduct a secretive monitoring study of local Jackson television stations WLBT and WJTV to be used later in the "petition to deny licensing" process. The station's challengers also begin to collect the statements and complaints of local African Americans regarding local television for submission to the FCC.

APRIL Local citizens, joined by the Office of Communication for the United Church of Christ, file official petitions with the FCC to deny the relicensing of WLBT and WJTV.

JUNE Hundreds of young women and men begin to arrive in Mississippi to work with local citizens during the "freedom summer" project.

JULY Congress passes, and President Lyndon Johnson signs, the Civil Rights Act. Soon after, the Mississippi NAACP issues a report stating that "Negroes are still in slavery in the state."

1965

FEBRUARY The staff of the Federal Communications Commission issues its internal report on WLBT. It recommends that the station's licensing be at least temporarily denied and hearings be held.

MAY The commission publishes its 1965 decision on WLBT — a one-year, probationary renewal with no hearings to be held. The station's challengers appeal the decision.

AUGUST President Johnson signs the Voting Rights Act into law.

1966

MARCH The U.S. Court of Appeals for the District of Columbia reverses the FCC's 1965 ruling regarding WLBT and remands the case for full hearings.

JUNE   James Meredith starts out on a one-man "March against Fear" but is wounded by a gunshot shortly after he crosses the Mississippi state line. Civil rights leaders, including Martin Luther King Jr. and Stokely Carmichael, continue the march.

1967

MAY   In Jackson, Mississippi, the FCC conducts formal hearings regarding the relicensing of WLBT.

NOVEMBER   The U.S. Commission on Civil Rights reports that by fall 1967 over half of the eligible black electorate had registered to vote. The Mississippi state legislature immediately enacts a series of laws aimed at diluting the black vote. John Bell Williams wins the state's governor race.

1968

APRIL   Martin Luther King Jr. is assassinated in Memphis, Tennessee. Massive uprisings take place across the nation.

JUNE   The FCC again decides to renew the license of WLBT, and again, the petitioners appeal.

1969

JUNE   The U.S. Court of Appeals for the District of Columbia again reverses the FCC by denying the relicensing of WLBT. The court then orders new comparative hearings to be held to determine who should receive the channel license.

1971

JUNE   Communications Improvement Incorporated, a nonprofit organization, is granted the license as an interim operator of WLBT.

1979

DECEMBER   After years of comparative hearings, the FCC decides to award licensing of WLBT to TV3, a largely local Jackson group that is 51 percent black and headed by Aaron Henry.

1984

APRIL   A Texas investment firm and a few Mississippi businessmen, including Aaron Henry, buy the WLBT station (and license) for an undisclosed price. The new owner, Civic Communications Corporation, claims 52 percent black ownership. Some black Mississippians, organized under the title of Coalition for Better Broadcasting, argue that these black ownership claims serve as cover for what is essentially a white-controlled corporation.

1986

SEPTEMBER   Civic Communications Corporation is bought out by Aaron Henry, station manager Frank Melton, and businessmen Charles Young and Owen Cooper. Melton announces that the station is 95 percent black owned.

2000

JUNE   Civic Communications Corporation merges with Cosmos Broadcasting in a $204 million cash transaction. Cosmos is owned and operated by the Liberty Corporation, based in Greenville, South Carolina.

NOTES

1 Historians have long recognized that the periodization of any study is the author's problematic, value-laden attempt at fixing time, and that is certainly true in this case. Most studies of the licensing challenges aimed at WLBT-TV have focused primarily on the 1960s and the activities of the courts and FCC. Some extend their examination through 1978, when the FCC assigned WLBT a new permanent license. I have chosen to concentrate on the fifties and sixties, from 1955 during the years of the first citizen challenges against Jackson television to 1969 when a federal court first vacated the station's license. I made this choice so as to focus on the integration of civil rights activism with legal and nonlegal interventions impacting local television.

2 Beard quoted in Charles E. Clift III, "The WLBT-TV Case, 1964–1969: An Historical Analysis" (Ph.D. diss., Indiana University, 1976), University Microfilms, no. 72–04612, 380.

3 Eudora Welty, *The Collected Stories of Eudora Welty* (New York: Harcourt Brace Jovanovich, 1980), 606.

4 Ibid., xi. In the preface to her collection of short stories, Welty explains that "Where Is the Voice Coming From?" "pushed its way up through a long novel I was in the middle of writing, and was finished on the same night the shooting took place. . . . The fiction's outward details had to be changed where by chance they had resembled too closely those of actuality, for the story must not be found prejudicial to the case of a person who might be on trial for his life" (xi).

5 Michel de Certeau, *The Practice of Everyday Life*, trans. S. Rendall (Berkeley: University of California Press, 1984), xi–xii.

6 Representation has been recognized as a central concept in cultural studies. For an introductory discussion of this concept, see Stuart Hall's anthology *Representation: Cultural Representations and Signifying Practices* (London: Sage, 1997). The mentioned issues of rep-

resentation are also briefly put forward by Ziauddin Sardar and Borin Van Loon in *Introducing Cultural Studies* (New York: Totem Books, 1997).

7 Thomas Streeter, *Selling the Air: A Critique of the Policy of Commercial Broadcasting in the United States* (Chicago: University of Chicago Press, 1996). In this paragraph I am using Alan Hunt's conceptualization of law as one constitutive mode of social regulation among many, as described in his *Explorations in Law and Society: Toward a Constitutive Theory of Law* (New York: Routledge, 1993). By drawing from and reinflecting readings of Foucault, Hunt argues that legal forms of regulation compete, conflict, and interact with other regulatory forms (315–20).

8 George Lipsitz writes that in the contemporary United States "white supremacy is usually less a matter of direct, referential, and snarling contempt, than a system for protecting the privileges of whites by denying communities of color opportunities for asset accumulation and upward mobility" (*The Possessive Investment in Whiteness: How White People Profit from Identity Politics* [Philadelphia: Temple University Press, 1998], viii).

9 John Durham Peters, *Speaking into the Air: A History of the Idea of Communication* (Chicago: University of Chicago Press, 1999), 3.

10 Michael Fletcher, "Kerner Prophecy on Race Relations Came True; Report Says Despite Progress, Foundation Finds 'Separate and Unequal' Societies More Deeply Rooted," *Washington Post* (1 March 1998): A6.

11 Aaron Shirley, interview by author, Jackson, Miss., 1 August 1992, 139–42. Page numbers following interview citations reflect the pagination of my transcriptions.

12 Willie Lewis, interview by author, Jackson, Miss., 13 August 1993, 20.

13 Stuart Hall, "The Whites of Their Eyes: Racist Ideologies and the Media," in *The Media Reader*, ed. M. Alvarado and J. Thompson (London: British Film Institute, 1990), 8–23.

14 D. Sears, "Symbolic Racism," in *Eliminating Racism*, ed. P. A. Katz and D. A. Taylor (New York: Plenum, 1988), 53–84. Powerful studies of racial inequalities in the United States have been published in recent years. For example, sociological and economic research has pointed to the economic and segregationist variables accompanying modern racism. Sociologists provide evidence of a growing black middle class but simultaneously point to increasing levels of black

poverty in urban centers such as Los Angeles (see Roger Waldinger and Mehdi Bozorgmehr, eds., *Ethnic Los Angeles* [New York: Russell Sage Foundation, 1996], 379–411, 451–55). Nationwide, levels of residential segregation in metropolitan areas have changed little in decades (see Douglas Massey and Nancy Denton, *American Apartheid* [Cambridge: Harvard University Press, 1993], 222). The overall division between rich and poor, both within and across racial lines, has widened, and a greater percentage of the population lives in poverty now than in 1968. The populations living in poverty are disproportionately people of color. In the Los Angeles metropolitan area where I live and work, for example, Mexican American earnings relative to that of European Americans are lower than they were two decades ago. There is little debate that the urban poor have become entrenched in inner cities marked by high unemployment and insufficient educational opportunity (see Alissa Rubin, "Racial Divide Widens, Study Says," *Los Angeles Times* [1 March 1998]: A20).

Over the past twenty years, "progress" in traditional "minority" communities can be seen, for example, in the enlarged and wealthier black middle class. Certainly there are some statistical and demographic indications of gains for some African Americans in the spheres of health care and economics. But it does not take much reflection to realize that, as *Newsweek* magazine put it, such announcements of progress are based on a "statistical profile of black Americans that, were it of whites, would be a source of horror and consternation" (Ellis Cose, "The Good News about Black America," *Newsweek* [7 June 1999]: 40).

15　David Kairys, ed., *With Liberty and Justice for Some: A Critique of the Conservative Supreme Court* (New York: New Press, 1993).

16　Roopali Mukherjee, "Regulating Race in the California Civil Rights Initiative: Enemies, Allies, and Alibis," *Journal of Communication* 50, no. 2 (2000): 42. The phrases "rugged individualism" and "nostalgic meritocracy" in the previous sentence also come from this analysis by Mukherjee of California Proposition 209, the so-called California Civil Rights Initiative (42–43).

17　See U.S. Department of Commerce, *Changes, Challenges, and Charting New Courses: Minority Commercial Broadcast Ownership in the United States* (Washington, D.C.: GPO, 2001).

18　Kobena Mercer, "1968: Periodizing Postmodern Politics and Identity," in *Cultural Studies*, ed. Lawrence Grossberg, Cary Nelson, and Paula Treichler (New York: Routledge, 1992), 431.

19   Willard D. Rowland Jr., "The Illusion of Fulfillment: The Broadcast Reform Movement," *Journalism Monographs* 79 (1982): 102–3.

20   For example, see Fred W. Friendly, *The Good Guys, the Bad Guys, and the First Amendment* (New York: Random House, 1976); Sydney Head and Christopher Sterling, *Broadcasting in America: A Survey of Television, Radio, and New Technologies*, 4th ed. (Boston: Houghton Mifflin, 1982); Barry Cole and Mal Oettinger, *The Reluctant Regulators: The FCC and the Broadcast Audience* (Reading, Mass.: Addison-Wesley, 1978); and Erwin Krasnow, Lawrence Longley, and Herbert Terry, *The Politics of Broadcast Regulation*, 3rd ed. (New York: St. Martin's Press, 1982).

21   Kathryn C. Montgomery, *Target: Prime Time; Advocacy Groups and the Struggle over Entertainment Television* (New York: Oxford University Press, 1989), 25.

22   Ibid.

23   Leonard Zeidenberg, "Struggle over Broadcast Access II," *Broadcasting* (27 September 1971): 24.

24   Krasnow, Longley, and Terry, *The Politics of Broadcast Regulation*, 56.

25   A number of works describe the seventies broadcast reform movement in some detail, including Montgomery's *Target: Prime Time* and Krasnow, Longley, and Terry's *The Politics of Broadcast Regulation*. Exceptional among these works is Rowland's *The Illusion of Fulfillment*, which offers not only an excellent description of these efforts, but an equally fine analysis.

26   Willard D. Rowland Jr., "U.S. Broadcasting and the Public Interest in the Multichannel Era: The Policy Heritage and Its Implications," *Studies in Broadcasting* 33 (1997): 106–7.

27   Horwitz, *The Irony of Regulatory Reform: The Deregulation of American Telecommunications* (New York: Oxford University Press); see also Horwitz, "Broadcast Reform Revisited: Reverend Everett C. Parker and the 'Standing' Case (*Office of Communication of the United Church of Christ v. Federal Communications Commission*)," *Communication Review* 2, no. 3 (1997): 344.

28   Rowland, "The Illusion of Fulfillment," 13.

29   John Fiske, *Power Plays, Power Works* (London: Verso, 1993), 252.

30   Nancy Partner, "Making Up Lost Time: Writing on the Writing of History," *Speculum* 61, no. 1 (1986): 110.

31   Hayden White, *Tropics of Discourse: Essays in Cultural Criticism* (Baltimore: Johns Hopkins University Press, 1978).

32   Michel de Certeau, "History and Science Fiction," in *Heterologies,*

trans. B. Massumi (Minneapolis: University of Minnesota Press, 1986), 202–3; Michel Foucault, *Discipline and Punish: The Birth of the Prison* (New York: Vintage, 1979), 30–31.

33 Craig Calhoun, Edward LiPuma, and Moishe Postone, eds., *Bourdieu: Critical Perspectives* (Chicago: University of Chicago Press, 1993), 4.

34 John Fiske, "The Culture of Everyday Life," in *Cultural Studies*, ed. Lawrence Grossberg, Cary Nelson, and Paula Treichler (New York: Routledge, 1992).

35 The following scholarly treatments of the WLBT-TV case during the 1960s offer the most detail and insight, and are among studies I refer to in various parts of this volume: Clift, "The WLBT-TV Case, 1964– 1969"; Cole and Oettinger, *The Reluctant Regulators*; Friendly, *The Good Guys, the Bad Guys, and the First Amendment*; Timothy R. Haight and Laurie R. Weinstein, "Changing Ideology on Television by Changing Telecommunications Policy: Notes on a Contradictory Situation," in *Communication and Social Structure: Critical Studies in Mass Media Research*, ed. E. G. McAnany, J. Schnitman, and N. Janus (New York: Praeger, 1981); Horwitz, *The Irony of Regulatory Reform*; E. Jones, "WLBT-TV, 1964–1979: A Case History of Progress" (master's thesis, Iowa State University, 1984); Krasnow, Longley, and Terry, *The Politics of Broadcast Regulation*; Ernest E. Phelps, "The Office of Communication: The Participant Advocate — Its Function as a Broadcast Citizen Group, March 1964–1971" (Ph.D. diss., Ohio State University, 1971), University Microfilms no. 72–4612; Rowland, "The Illusion of Fulfillment"; and J. Williams, "Improper Conduct: WLBT Programming and Operations, 1955–65" (master's thesis, University of Florida, 1987). Many other textbooks, histories, and broadcasting surveys only briefly mention or describe, usually in chapters dealing with television regulation, the station's struggles during the sixties.

36 Ian F. Haney López, *White by Law: The Legal Construction of Race* (New York: New York University Press, 1996), 114–15. This is not to say that "law" might not have foundations outside of present social discourses and contexts, but it is to recognize that those foundations are inevitably taken up and understood in present social practices and settings marked by human difference.

37 Hunt, *Explorations in Law and Society*, 304–5.

38 Streeter, *Selling the Air*, 86–69.

39 The intervention begun in the late 1970s known as Critical Legal

Studies (CLS) has made such observations in its analyses of contemporary legal liberalism. A common emphasis in this diverse intellectual work is the refusal to view state law, regulation, or policy as ahistorical or adequately self-descriptive. Scholarship in CLS rejects the view that law and policy, and their formalistic processes, are essentially neutral, value-free, and independent of underlying social relations and political forces (see David Kairys, ed. *The Politics of Law: A Progressive Critique* [New York: Pantheon, 1982], 930). Instead, law is defined as political in the broadest sense — embodying disparate, often contradictory, social visions. By abandoning the explanations of seamless formalism that suggest that law coherently follows its own internal logic and rules, CLS scholarship has offered a more fruitful tack, counseling readers "not to assume the coherence and consistency of legal discourse but to search out the resonances of the social, economic, and political struggles that reside behind the smooth surface of legal reasoning and judicial utterance" (Alan Hunt, "The Ideology of the Law: Advances and Problems in Recent Applications of the Concept of Ideology to the Analysis of Law," *Law and Society Review* 19, no. 1 [1985]: 16).

To appropriate critical assumptions regarding the social construction of formal legal texts such as FCC and court records is not to adopt the view that such legal texts (or professional or popular texts for that matter) simply reflect the social milieu. But it is to assume that the symbolic texts or productions of the 1960s were uneasy cultural sites just as problematic on many levels as the physical struggle of African Americans. The primary legal documents selected for analysis are not approached as self-evident in meaning or as reflections of true social conditions but instead as part of a discourse that itself participates in constituting social reality.

40 Mari J. Matsuda, "Public Response to Racist Speech: Considering the Victim's Story," *Michigan Law Review* 87 (1989): 2324.

41 Kimberlé Crenshaw and Gary Peller, "Reel Time/Real Justice," in *Reading Rodney King/Reading Urban Uprising*, ed. Robert Gooding-Williams (New York: Routledge, 1993), 64.

42 Fiske, *Media Matters: Everyday Culture and Political Change* (Minneapolis: University of Minnesota Press, 1994), 38–39.

43 Ibid., 162.

44 Chon A. Noriega, *Shot in America: Television, the State, and the Rise of Chicano Cinema* (Minneapolis: University of Minnesota Press, 2000), 181.

45 Although this project is shaped and informed by the perspectives and theoretical assumptions outlined above, empirical bases do matter, and a variety of archival, popular, legal, and oral history materials serve as primary resources for this project. These materials have been collected over the past ten years and are the fruit of my extended fieldtrips to Washington, D.C., and to Mississippi, as well as my studies at the University of Wisconsin — Madison.

My first step in this research, after reading the existing accounts of WLBT's history, was to thoroughly examine published federal court and Federal Communications Commission statements addressing the case. This was followed by extensive archival research and fieldwork. As mentioned previously, this project highlights the perspectives and voices of African Americans addressing the past and present. During two summers in and around Jackson, Mississippi, I was able to interview twenty-seven black Mississippians who offered memories of life, segregation, and television in the sixties. Twenty-four of these twenty-seven individuals offered extended interviews, some over two hours in length, that often resembled oral histories — tracing their lives in Mississippi from childhood to the present. Eight longtime white residents of the state, or civil rights activists who worked there, also graciously volunteered to be interviewed for this project. In almost all cases, the extended interviews were recorded and transcribed. Together, these individuals offered a wealth of oral histories, providing very different memories and perspectives regarding a particular case and moment in time.

In Washington, D.C., I addressed the WLBT case in interviews with Henry Geller, chief counsel for the FCC at the time; E. William Henry, chair of the commission during the crucial years from 1963 to 1966; and Lee Loevinger and Kenneth Cox, two other former commissioners. These interviews were complemented with additional archival work in the papers of E. William Henry, Lee Loevinger, Kenneth Cox, and Newton Minow at the State Historical Society of Wisconsin. In the area of official memos, hearing records, testimony, and papers addressing the station and the sixties licensing challenge, I reviewed all relevant FCC docket materials housed at the National Archives. While in the Washington area I also studied the papers of the national NAACP, housed at the Library of Congress, particularly those pertaining to Mississippi and field secretary Medgar Evers.

In the Jackson, Mississippi, area, two institutions offered a wealth of printed or written materials: the Zenobia Coleman Library at

Tougaloo College, in Tougaloo, Mississippi, and the state's Department of History and Archives, housed in downtown Jackson. The former offered extraordinary insight in its archives about the local Jackson movement, and the latter provided an extensive collection of alternative and mainstream Mississippi newspapers. Elsewhere in the state, I also found relevant materials in archival collections at Mississippi State University and Southern Mississippi State University. The latter institution has particularly rich archival offerings for those investigating Citizens' Council histories.

All of these materials, oral and written, offered indirect traces of the past, the clues used to construct larger interpretations and write larger histories. The method employed here is multiperspectival, ranging from local oral histories to the official statements of federal institutions.

46 Henry Kirksey, interview by author, Tougaloo, Miss., 18 August 1993, 24–26.

47 Juanita Jefferson, interview by author, Jackson, Miss., 5 August 1993, p. 24.

48 I have tried to address these ethical concerns, at least those regarding historiography, by circulating transcripts of the oral histories, as well as drafts of book chapters, to those who contributed to this project in Mississippi, along with a request for any corrections, additions, or feedback. Almost without exception I found the feedback to be supportive and positive, and I have tried to incorporate into this work all requested changes and corrections.

49 In recent years progressive advocates have enjoyed some gains arguing for further investment in Jackson's public schools. Jackson's Farish Street, a historical district of black culture and commerce, has also in recent years enjoyed more civic investment and public funding following decades of neglect. Perhaps, in fits and starts, there are reasons for optimism, but the decades of neglect and racial privilege cannot be remedied and tidied up easily. I continue to remember the remarks of southern writer John Shelton Reed, who visited Jackson during the same years I visited and lived there, that Jackson was a place of jarring contrasts, and that it was "the first place outside the Third World . . . where I've seen cigarettes routinely sold one at a time" ("Letter from the Lower Right: The Mississippi Hippies and Other Denizens of the Deep (South)," *Chronicles* [July 1993]: 47–48).

50 Jefferson, interview, 8.

51 Peters, *Speaking into the Air*, 269.

52 The ideas in this paragraph owe much to the concluding arguments in Ellen Seiter's ethnographic project, *Television and New Media Audiences* (New York: Oxford University Press, 1999).

53 Ien Ang, "Wanted: Audiences. On the Politics of Empirical Audience Studies," in *Media Studies: A Reader*, 2nd ed., ed. Paul Marris and Sue Thornham (New York: New York University Press, 2000), 482–91.

54 Seiter, *Television and New Media Audiences*, 139.

55 Ibid., 140.

56 Tougaloo College is a small liberal-arts institution located just outside the city limits of Jackson, Mississippi. It was founded in 1869 by the American Missionary Association "to respond to the needs of emancipated blacks immediately following the end of the civil war," and in the twentieth century has operated as an integrated, majority black institution. Clarice T. Campbell and Oscar A. Rogers, *Mississippi: The View from Tougaloo* (Jackson: University Press of Mississippi, 1979), xi.

57 In "Regulating Race in the California Civil Rights Initiative," Roopali Mukherjee first offered this insight in connection to policy making in her analysis of state referenda — namely California's Propositions 187 and 209.

58 William Faulkner, *Requiem for a Nun* (New York: Random House, 1950), 92.

1 : BROADCAST FOUNDATIONS

1 The activist referred to here is Myrlie Evers, now Myrlie Evers-Williams, past president of the NAACP and widow of slain civil rights leader Medgar Evers. Myrlie Evers, with William Peters, provides this account of fifties Mississippi along with a description of her late husband's efforts in *For Us, the Living* (Garden City, N.Y.: Doubleday, 1967).

2 John Dittmer, *Local People: The Struggle for Civil Rights in Mississippi* (Urbana: University of Illinois Press, 1994), 34.

3 Charles Marsh, "Jesus in Mississippi: The Civil Rights Movement as Theological Drama," *Books and Culture* (March-April 1998): 16–19.

4 MDAH, "Citizens' Council" subject file.

5 Ibid.

6 Taylor Branch, *Pillar of Fire: America in the King Years, 1963–65* (New York: Simon and Schuster, 1998), 182.

7   Evers, *For Us, the Living*, 175.

8   Ibid., 164.

9   James Silver, *Mississippi: The Closed Society* (New York: Harcourt, Brace and World, 1963), 4–10; Dittmer, *Local People*, 64–66.

10 Sam Bailey, interview by author, 3 August 1993, 6.

11 Charles M. Payne, *I've Got the Light of Freedom: The Organizing Tradition and the Mississippi Freedom Struggle* (Berkeley: University of California Press, 1995), 35–40.

12 Anne Moody, *Coming of Age in Mississippi* (New York: Dell), 123–26.

13 Payne, *I've Got the Light of Freedom*, 40.

14 Ibid., 54, 413ff.

15 Dittmer, *Local People*, 58.

16 David Halberstam, *The Fifties* (New York: Villard Books, 1993), 437.

17 "Till Case TV Play Causes Big Uproar," *Pittsburgh Courier* (12 May 1956), n.p.

18 *American Masters Presents: Rod Serling: Submitted for Your Consideration*, CBS Video, 1998.

19 MDAH, "Citizens' Council" subject file.

20 Silver, *Mississippi*, 30.

21 J. Fred MacDonald, *Blacks and White TV: Afro-Americans in Television since 1948* (Chicago: Nelson-Hall, 1983), 66.

22 The 4 January 1954, edition of the *Jackson Daily News* describes the new WLBT facility as "one of the finest television-radio installations in the South." As broadcast historian J. Fred MacDonald has detailed, "there were only thirteen southern market areas with TV by December 1949. While that represented 22.4 percent of all cities having television, only 4.5 percent of TV sets were in the South. . . . And given the freeze on licensing new stations by the Federal Communications Commission, not until 1953 was the South able to address this imbalance" (*Blacks and White TV*, 66).

23 WLBT station files. A third station, WAPT-TV, came on air in 1970 as Jackson's primary ABC affiliate.

24 Dittmer, *Local People*, 65. David Davies, ed., *The Press and Race: Mississippi Journalists Confront the Movement* (Jackson: University Press of Mississippi, 2001), 86–87.

25 *Jackson Daily News* (5 January 1954), n.p.

26 *Jackson Daily News* (12 January 1954), n.p.

27 Kirsten Fermaglich, "Never: WLBT-TV and the Changing Public

Sphere of Jackson, Mississippi, 1962–1978," paper presented at the Telling about the South conference, Charlottesville, Virginia, 1995.

28 Evers, *For Us, the Living*.

29 MDAH, "Citizens' Council, 1954–55" subject file; Neil R. McMillen, *The Citizens' Council: Organized Resistance to the Second Reconstruction, 1954–64* (Urbana: University of Illinois Press, 1971), 7.

30 MDAH, *Citizens' Council Forum*, films.

31 Marsh, "Jesus in Mississippi," 19.

32 Ibid.; Erle Johnston, *Mississippi's Defiant Years, 1953–1973: An Interpretive Documentary with Personal Experiences* (Forest, Miss.: Lake Harbor, 1990), 48–49.

33 Allison Graham, *Framing the South: Hollywood, Television and Race during the Civil Rights Struggle* (Baltimore: Johns Hopkins University Press, 2001), 41.

34 SCF, document no. 10-1-0-1-1-1-1.

35 Graham, *Framing the South*, 159.

36 Dittmer, *Local People*, 60, 65.

37 Davies, *The Press and Race*, 88–89. SCF, document no. 99-8-0-281-1-1-1.

38 Dittmer, *Local People*, 64.

39 As Dittmer notes (*Local People*, 30–31), before the sixties civil rights leadership was largely the province of male ministers, federal employees, and professionals. During the sixties more women emerged in leadership roles, and have been recognized, although not sufficiently, for having organized civil rights interventions. See also Vicki Crawford, Jacqueline Rouse, and Barbara Woods, eds., *Women in the Civil Rights Movement: Trailblazers and Torchbearers, 1941–1965* (Bloomington: Indiana University Press, 1990).

40 Charles Evers, *Evers* (New York: World, 1971), 99–101; Maryanne Vollers, *Ghosts of Mississippi: The Murder of Medgar Evers, the Trials of Byron De La Beckwith, and the Haunting of the New South* (Boston: Little, Brown, 1995), 69–70.

41 Evers, *For Us, the Living*, 211.

42 Vollers, *Ghosts of Mississippi*, 72, 86.

43 Dittmer, *Local People*, 50–78.

44 Ibid.

45 FCC, Memorandum of Broadcast Bureau, 1959, accession no. 173-82-20, box 7.

46 Ibid., 4.

47 The term "curious neutrality" is a variation on J. Fred MacDonald's description of southern television journalism of the time as exercising "studied neutrality" (*Blacks and White TV*, 70).

48 Johnston, *Mississippi's Defiant Years*, 71.

49 FCC, Memorandum of the Broadcast Bureau, 1959, accession no. 173–82–20, box 7.

50 Ibid.

51 NAACP, Evers correspondence, group III A-114.

52 Evers, *For Us, the Living*, 211.

53 FCC, accession number 173–76–12, docket 16663, box 58, vol. 10, exhibit 33.

54 TC, papers of R. L. T. Smith, box 1, folder 8. As broadcast historian Mary Ann Watson has written in "Eleanor Intervenes: A Phone Call from the First Lady Jolts the FCC to Action" (*Television Quarterly* [2001]: retrieved 15 July 2002 from http://www.emmyonline.org/tvq/articles/32-23-8.asp.), former FCC chair Newton Minow recalls firing off a terse telegram to WLBT regarding Smith's requested airtime, in response to a personal phone call from Eleanor Roosevelt.

55 Evers, *For Us, the Living*, 266–69.

56 Ibid., 268.

57 U.S. Commission on Civil Rights, *Window Dressing on the Set: Women and Minorities in Television* (Washington, D.C.: GPO, 1977), 2.

58 Ibid., 1.

59 Aaron Shirley, interview by author, Jackson, Miss., 1 August 1992, 126–28.

60 Paul L. Fisher and Ralph L. Lowenstein, *Race and the News Media* (New York: Praeger, 1967), 85.

61 Gordon Henderson and John Q. Adams, transcripts of oral history collection, Millsaps College, Jackson, Miss.

62 Everett C. Parker of the United Church of Christ remembers a meeting with NAB president Collins in which Parker made the suggestion that the broadcasting group send a letter to its member stations asking each station to pledge itself to diverse programming and further black access to local airtime. Parker recalls Collins as embracing this idea but that the initiative was stopped by the NAB board of directors (Horwitz, "Broadcast Reform Revisited," 315).

63 MacDonald, *Blacks and White TV*, 73.

64 Ibid.

65 Ibid., 70–71.

66 Martin Luther King Jr., as early as the years of the Montgomery

bus boycott (1956–1957), complained to church representatives and leaders that black representatives and issues were receiving terrible treatment on southern radio and television stations (Horwitz, "Broadcast Reform Revisited," 314).

67   Mary Ann Watson, "Eleanor Intervenes."

68   The commission's memo articulating federal fairness expectations, titled "Controversial Issue Programming — Fairness Doctrine," is found in *Pike and Fischer's Radio Regulations*, 25 RR 1899–1900 (1963).

69   Walter and Victor Reuther, with Joseph Rauh Jr., submitted a lengthy memo to Attorney General Robert Kennedy in December 1961 arguing for administrative actions to stop the "ever larger and growing . . . radical right." One argument that the Reuthers made, responding to extremist "anti-Communist" groups such as the Birch Society, the Schwarz Anti-Communist Crusade, and others, was that the FCC might reexamine its practice of allowing stations to give free time to the radical right without "comparable expression of the opposing point of view" (Victor G. Reuther, *The Brothers Reuther and the Story of the UAW* [Boston: Houghton Mifflin, 1976], 440). Such documented recommendations of the strategic use of "fairness doctrine" policy understandably bolstered claims that the rules were designed to target certain types of programming, and underline that policy is inevitably political.

70   SHSW, papers of E. William Henry, box 44, folder "Jackson, Mississippi."

2 : CONSUMING CIVIL RIGHTS

1   Also known as the 1963 March on Washington for Freedom and Jobs, this event is described by civil rights historian Taylor Branch as "the first — and essentially the last — mass meeting ever to reach the national airwaves" (*Parting the Waters: America in the King Years, 1954–63* [New York: Simon and Schuster, 1988], 876).

2   This description was included in a letter from NBC executive vice president William McAndrew to Tougaloo College President A. D. Beittel. The program was extraordinary but, perhaps, as Mary Ann Watson notes, not entirely altruistic, as NBC's heavyweight documentary was also a shrewd counterprogramming maneuver timed to air as CBS was launching its expanded evening newscasts (Watson, *The Ex-*

panding Vista: American Television in the Kennedy Years [New York: Oxford University Press, 1990]).

3   Harvard Sitkoff, *The Struggle for Black Equality, 1954–1992* (New York: Hill and Wang, 1993), 86.

4   FCC, accession number 173–76–12, docket 16663, box 58, vol. 10.

5   John R. Salter Jr., *Jackson, Mississippi: An American Chronicle of Struggle and Schism* (Malabar, Fla.: Krieger Publishing, 1987), 29–36.

6   Ibid., 36, 56.

7   John Salter recalls that a great majority of recruits to the Jackson movement were high school students, and that they had "reached the point where they perceived the injustices very clearly, and they also saw the vision very clearly. They just didn't feel inhibited . . . they were the backbone of the mass marches" (MDAH, Oral History of John R. Salter Jr., 29–30). In 1963, after his appointment as chaplain at Tougaloo, Reverend Edwin King also played a key leadership role in movement activities.

8   Salter, *Jackson, Mississippi*, 39, 51–52.

9   North Jackson Youth Council, papers of John R. Salter Jr., SHSW, box 1, folder 15.

10   Salter, *Jackson, Mississippi*, 101.

11   Ibid., 71.

12   Davies, *The Press and Race*, 44.

13   "Selma Stops Negro Fuss," *Jackson Clarion-Ledger* (22 December 1963): 14.

14   See the June/July 1963 editions of the *Jackson Clarion-Ledger* and *Jackson Daily News*. See also TC, papers of R. Edwin King Jr., box 8, folder 391.

15   Leaflet contents quoted as reprinted in *Mississippi Free Press* (21 March 1964), 1.

16   McMillen, *The Citizen's Council*.

17   SHSW, papers of John R. Salter Jr., box 1, folder 14.

18   Dittmer, *Local People*, 159.

19   TC, papers of R. L. T. Smith, box 6, folder 117.

20   Lizabeth Cohen, "Consumption and Civil Rights," paper presented at the annual meeting of the American Studies Association, Costa Mesa, California, 1992, 9.

21   Ibid., 8.

22   TC, papers of Reverend R. L. T. Smith, box 3, folder 28.

23 Juanita Jefferson, interview by author, Jackson, Miss., 5 August 1993, 6–7.

24 Robert Lampman, "JFK's Four Consumer Rights: A Retrospective View," in *The Frontier of Research in the Consumer Interest*, ed. E. S. Maynes (Columbia, Mo.: American Council on Consumer Interests, 1988), 19–33.

25 Ibid., 31.

26 Ibid., 29.

27 Michael Pertschuk, *Revolt against Regulation: The Rise and Pause of the Consumer Movement* (Berkeley, Calif.: University of California Press, 1982), 19.

28 David Vogel, *Fluctuating Fortunes: The Political Power of Business in America* (New York: Basic Books, 1989); David A. Aaker and George S. Day, eds., *Consumerism: Search for the Consumer Interest* (New York: Free Press, 1971), 49.

29 Cohen, "Consumption and Civil Rights."

30 Sitkoff, *The Struggle for Black Equality*, 86.

31 Silver, *Mississippi: The Closed Society*, 382.

32 Horwitz, "Broadcast Reform Revisited," 314.

33 FCC, testimony of E. Parker, docket 16663, box 56, vol. 4.

34 Clift, "The WLBT-TV Case," 16. Parker was especially interested in launching a license challenge in which his office could attempt to change the precedents defining legal standing for citizens. Parker's legal aim was to establish that the public should be formally recognized as a "party of interest" in all broadcast license challenges, and be granted the right to directly intervene in administrative agency (FCC) proceedings — a right long granted industrial representatives (Everett Parker, interview by author, New York, N.Y., 21 October 1993), 1, 14.

35 Parker asked not to know the names of the monitors employed, out of (the later justified) fear that he might be asked to testify against them or reveal their identities during hearings. Even today, although several of the monitors have discussed their own participation, the coordinators of the monitoring project, the Hendersons, continue to honor the volunteers' early request that their names not be released.

Dr. Gordon Henderson was a professor of political science at Millsaps College. Mary Ann Henderson brought valuable experience to the monitoring effort as a statistical analyst and former employee of the A. C. Nielsen Company.

36 Henderson and Adams, oral history collection; Horwitz, "Broadcast Reform Revisited."

37 Horwitz, "Broadcast Reform Revisited," 329, 341.

38 Ibid., 320.

39 To the chagrin of segregationist leaders, the 1964 petition made national press headlines and editorials within weeks of its filing. No doubt in part because of the UCC's connection to other branches of the mainline Protestant church, religious periodicals such as the *Christian Century* quickly sided with the petitioners in asking for comprehensive FCC hearings addressing station practices. The *Saturday Review* carefully followed and discussed the station challenges. And a variety of newspapers, large and small, offered editorial support for the petitioners' action. Church leaders made sure that these articles of support were forwarded to the FCC chair, E. William Henry (SHSW, Henry papers, miscellaneous correspondence, June–September 1964, box 48).

40 Horwitz, "Broadcast Reform Revisited," 320; Clift, "The WLBT-TV Case," 28.

41 FCC, Petition to Intervene and Deny, docket 16663, box 55, vol. 1.

42 Clift, "The WLBT-TV Case," 35, 54–55.

43 *Office of Communication of the United Church of Christ v. FCC,* 359 F2d 994 (2d Cir. 1966).

44 "Recent Developments — Administrative Law — Community Representatives Have Standing to Challenge FCC License Renewal," *Michigan Law Review* 65, no. 3 (1967): 518–31.

45 *Office of Communication of the United Church of Christ v. FCC,* 359 F2d 1002.

46 Ibid., 1000.

47 Ibid., 1000–1.

48 Ibid., 1000.

49 Ibid., 1003–4.

50 Elaborating on this rationale, K. R. Keller wrote that the court recognized that those previously narrow constructions of standing "had not achieved the desired result," ostensibly of serving the "public interest," and therefore was advocating a new standing construction (Keller, "The Law of Administrative Standing and the Public Right of Intervention," *Federal Communications Bar Journal* 21, no. 3 [1967]: 135). Even traditional legal analysts noted the court's lack of formal justifications in this shift, stating in one instance that the decision underscored the "burdensome and artificial construction of standing

requirements" ("Notes — Responsible Representatives of the Listening Public Have Standing as 'Persons Aggrieved,' " *Wayne Law Review* 13, no. 2 [1967]:), 384.

51 Thomas Streeter, "Beyond Freedom of Speech and the Public Interest: The Relevance of Critical Legal Studies to Communications Policy," *Journal of Communication* 20, no. 2 (1990): 44–45.

52 Kairys, *The Politics of Law*, 14.

53 Ibid.

54 Ibid., 17.

55 Further, the court's statements to the FCC regarding the strengths of the minority complaint provide evidence that the judges pondered the merits of the legal challenge when formal guidelines dictated that standing was to be determined a priori (*Office of Communication of the United Church of Christ v. FCC*, 359 F2d 1006–9). The court's concluding remarks underscored its concern as it surveyed the station's history and stated that "a pious hope on the Commission's part for better things from WLBT is not a substitute for evidence and findings" (1008). Critics noticed this formal transgression, questioning the appropriateness of court remarks suggesting how the FCC should have ruled in its initial statement regarding the WLBT license renewal. The *Michigan Law Review*, for example, remarked that the propriety of the court's approach was questionable "since policy determinations are clearly within the exclusive scope of the Commission's expertise" ("Recent Developments," 524). The WLBT case does not stand alone in regard to this type of formal transgression. In analyses of constitutional standing, for example, critics such as Mark V. Tushnet have argued that standing has become "a surrogate for decisions on merits" and that the law of standing "is little more than a set of disjointed rules dealing with a common subject" (Tushnet, "The New Law of Standing: A Plea for Abandonment," *Cornell Law Review* 62, no. 4 [1977]: 663). In this "surrogacy," standing law denies its social construction and social specificity, cloaking itself in an a priori rationale claiming a clean separation from consideration of contemporary social conditions.

56 Tushnet, "The New Law of Standing," 663.

57 William Boddy, *Fifties Television: The Industry and Its Critics* (Champaign: University of Illinois Press, 1990).

58 "Where, Might We Ask, Is the FCC?" *Consumer Reports* (January 1960): 9.

59 Ibid., 9, 11.

60 Pertschuk, *Revolt against Regulation*, 17–19.

61 Mark V. Nadel, *The Politics of Consumer Protection* (Indianapolis: Bobbs-Merrill, 1971), 42–43.

62 Aaker and Day, *Consumerism*, 10ff.; Ralph Gaedeke and Warren Etcheson, eds., *Consumerism: Viewpoints from Business, Government, and the Public Interest* (San Francisco: Canfield, 1972), 98; Vogel, *Fluctuating Fortunes*, 29.

63 SHSW, papers of E. William Henry, "Assistant for Consumer Affairs" and "White House Correspondence," box 76. Kennedy mentioned the All Channel Receiver Bill, then pending adoption by Congress, in his 1962 "Consumer Interest" address. In that speech the president also touched on other consumer concerns then being addressed by the administration, including television programming. In part, Kennedy stated, "the Federal Communications Commission is actively reviewing the television network program selection process and encouraging the expanded development of educational television stations" (Kennedy, *Public Papers of the Presidents of the United States: John F. Kennedy, January 1 to December 31, 1962* [Washington, D.C.: GPO], 237).

64 James L. Baughman, *Television's Guardians: The FCC and the Politics of Programming, 1958–1967* (Knoxville: University of Tennessee Press, 1985), 117–52.

65 Ibid., 123.

66 Ibid., 134.

67 Ibid., 135.

68 *Office of Communication of the United Church of Christ v. FCC*, 5 FCC 2d 37.

69 Everett C. Parker, "The Mississippi Television Station Cases," unpublished manuscript, 1972.

70 *Office of Communication of the United Church of Christ v. FCC*, 359 F2d 1005.

71 Julius E. Thompson, *The Black Press in Mississippi, 1865–1985* (Gainesville: University Press of Florida, 1993), 59.

72 U.S. Department of Commerce, *1960 Census of Housing*, vol. 1, part 5 (Washington, D.C.: GPO, 1963), tables 26–10, 26–15.

73 Streeter, "Beyond Freedom of Speech and the Public Interest," 60; Mark Kelman, *A Guide to Critical Legal Studies* (Cambridge: Harvard University Press, 1987).

74 Vincent Mosco, "Toward a Theory of State and Telecommunications Policy," *Journal of Communication* 38, no. 1 (1989): 118–19.

75 Branch, *Parting the Waters.*

76 David M. Chalmers, *And the Crooked Place Made Straight: The Struggle for Social Change in the 1960s* (Baltimore: Johns Hopkins University Press, 1991), 23, 40.

77 *Office of Communication of the United Church of Christ v. FCC,* 38 FCC 1153.

78 Thanks to an anonymous reviewer for suggesting I consider this parallel.

79 From their earliest years these broadcast mediums have been regulated as "interstate commerce" (Article 1, Section 8 of the U.S. Constitution). Thus, congressional and FCC oversight of radio and television has long been justified by broadcasting's commercial "nature."

80 Rowland argues along these lines in regard to the broadcast reform efforts of the sixties and seventies, highlighting "the symbolic dimension of the process, the significance of broadcast reform as part of an overall political legitimization — of ratification of prior structural arrangements and power allocations" ("Illusion of Fulfillment," 3). Examples of bureaucratic retrenchment in regard to citizen standing are perhaps most obvious in the FCC's erection of a procedural labyrinth for citizen petitioners, beginning in 1972 (e.g., see "The Public and Broadcasting — A Procedure Manual," *Office of Communication of the United Church of Christ v. FCC,* 37 FCC 2d 286, [26 September 1972]). In its complex "Procedure Manual" for citizens' groups, the commission made it clear that broadcaster performance inquiries were to be initiated by private citizens, not the commission, and that the burden of proof rested on the shoulders of challenging parties (Rowland, "The Illusion of Fulfillment," 17).

3 : TROUBLE AROUND THE PONDEROSA

1 FCC, accession number 173–81–67, docket 18845, box 23, vol. 18, folder 38, 4396ff.

2 Willie Lewis, interview by author, Jackson, Miss., 13 August 1993, 7.

3 Sam Bailey, interview by author, Jackson, Miss., 4 August 1993, 9.

4 George Owens, interview by author, Jackson, Miss., 5 August 1992, 59.

5 The "war of manoeuvre" and the "war of position" are metaphors used by Gramsci both descriptively and prescriptively in his discussions of social struggle and the state. The theorist argued that the "war

of position" was the more successful of the two in the context of modern capitalist societies. For a discussion of these concepts, see Joseph V. Femia, *Gramsci's Political Thought: Hegemony, Consciousness, and the Revolutionary Process* (Oxford: Clarendon, 1987).

6 Kimberlé Crenshaw, "Race, Reform, and Retrenchment: Transformation and Legitimation in Antidiscrimination Law," *Harvard Law Review* 101, no. 7 (1988): 1371. This essay was the reading that first prompted me to think of the relations of coercion, consent, and hegemony more carefully. In this volume hegemony is conceptualized, in the words of John Fiske, as the "process whereby the subordinate are led to consent to the system that subordinates them. This is achieved when they 'consent' to view the social system and its everyday embodiments as 'common sense' [or as] self-evidently natural" (*Television Culture* [London: Methuen, 1987], 40).

7 Grace E. Hale, *Making Whiteness: The Culture of Segregation in the South, 1890–1940* (New York: Pantheon, 1998), 125.

8 Robert Hooker, "Race and the Mississippi Press," *New South* (winter 1971): 56.

9 Dittmer, *Local People*, 75.

10 Quoted in ibid., 75.

11 SCF, document no. 1–83–0–2–1–1–1 (30 August 1964).

12 Ibid.

13 Ineva May-Pittman, interview by author, Jackson, Miss., 25 August 1993, 20.

14 SCF, document no. 1–14–0–1–1–1–1.

15 Hooker, "Race and the Mississippi Press," 56. Hooker estimated the 1964 *Advocate* circulation to be approximately four thousand, although it is doubtful that the paper had that many black readers. *The Advocate* was full of ads for white businesses and often filled pages with notices of black achievement and society events rather than coverage of controversy and social crisis.

Although Greene's paper received considerable support from white businesses and advertisers, the publisher also found other means of income. Alongside his newspaper duties, Greene accepted the role of Sovereignty Commission informant. On the commission payroll, he attended civil rights meetings and discussed various press coverage strategies with commission leaders. In explicitly aligning himself with an agenda of gradualism and a "friendly, respectful" attitude toward segregationist leaders, Greene would regularly rebut black activism and give further voice to "cooperative" segregation.

See Caryl A. Cooper, "Percy Greene and the *Jackson Advocate*," in *The Press and Race: Mississippi Journalists Confront the Movement*, ed. David Davies (Jackson: University Press of Mississippi, 2001), 55–84.

16 *Mississippi Free Press* (16 December 1961): 2.

17 John Salter, "Thoughts on the Mississippi Free Press," *Mississippi Free Press* (5 May 1963): 2.

18 "What's Not Said," *Mississippi Free Press* (26 October 1963): 2. Certainly the Jackson dailies were not the only large-circulation state newspapers marked by patterns of racist omission. In other Mississippi towns, civil rights periodicals such as the *Vicksburg Citizens' Appeal* enjoyed brief publishing runs — again, sparked into existence by deep dissatisfactions with the patterned neglect of stories speaking to white-on-black intimidation, violence, and oppression, as well as those pointing to black accomplishment.

19 Thompson, *The Black Press in Mississippi*, 74.

20 NAACP, papers of Medgar Evers, group III A-114.

21 Importantly, the *Free Press* was also the only Jackson newspaper to observe that efforts to revoke the broadcast licenses of WLBT and other Jackson stations were historically grounded in local black activism dating back to the fifties. The newspaper noted in its 13 June 1964 edition that such challenges had "been underway for some time" *before* 1964, and that these interventions were "initiated by pro-Civil Rights forces in the state."

Discussions of the United Church of Christ and its role in the WLBT-WJTV challenges are a key variable in Jackson press coverage. In the *Free Press*, the church is explicitly absent, never specifically mentioned but implicitly part of a national effort subordinated and subsequent to the license challenge brought by local labor and "Negro" organizations. Conversely, the *Jackson Daily News* coverage established the religious organization as solely responsible for the 1964 license challenges.

However, this seemingly contradictory treatment does reveal a consistency. By omission or commission the United Church of Christ is established as nonlocal — an "outsider." As the *Daily News* reminds us, more-specific labels for such organizations included "liberal do-gooders" or "outside agitators." Certainly, for aggressive white segregationists concerned about "state's rights" the symbolic and physical attacks against such "agitators" were aligned with the protection of the mythical southern "way of life."

Many black Mississipians, far less convinced that the southern "way of life" needed to be preserved, were also doubtful or critical of nonindigenous involvement in local concerns. For example, a review of oral histories and black autobiographies indicates that African American communities were deeply divided over the question of whether or not to solicit "outside help" during what became the Mississippi "freedom summer" of 1964.

It was during these months of contention and debate over "outside," particularly "northern," involvement that the United Church of Christ and its copetitioners submitted their initial challenge to Jackson's broadcasters. Just a few months after the petition was submitted, students from northern colleges and universities began to canvass Mississippi, establishing "freedom schools," community centers, and a variety of other services. As civil rights historians Henry Hampton and Steve Fayer note, "the press in Mississippi called the influx of northern students an 'invasion' " (Hampton and Fayer, with Sarah Flynn, *Voices of Freedom: An Oral History of the Civil Rights Movement from the 1950s through the 1960s* [New York: Bantam, 1990], 187).

Popular caricatures of the civil rights movement might lead us to believe that these "invasions" were feared by southern whites and applauded by blacks, but it is clear that many black Mississippians also perceived the activities of northern groups as threatening. White "freedom summer" workers met this perception in 1964. In one oral history collection, a summer project participant remarks that "the first problem was that we were white northerners there on a mission, so to speak — all of those things were fraught with danger for the people that we were talking to. . . . This was their lives, their land, their family, and they were going to be here when we were gone" (Hampton and Fayer, *Voices of Freedom*, 192). Hollis Watkins, a native Mississippian and black student activist, had similar concerns. Expressing his strong reservations about outsider involvement, he remarked, "Ultimately, when the people from the North would go back, people from Mississippi would have to start all over again, and go through that same rebuilding process. . . . We wanted to keep what we had in motion rather than stand the risk of destroying it and have to rebuild" (183). Within the Mississippi that these voices describe, the United Church of Christ advocates and legal representatives could certainly be perceived as northern reformers coming to the South with claims of good intentions yet involved only in short-term projects posing long-term risks and later leaving local blacks alone to suffer the consequences.

This description evokes the myth of the carpetbagger, a historical narrative that continued to have strong resonance for many in the South during the 1960s. In numerous Mississippi newspaper columns and broadcast editorials the term "carpetbaggers" or "carpetbagging" was made explicit and the mythology recalled. For white segregationists the "carpetbaggers" posed a threat to the southern "way of life." For many African Americans the mythology engaged fears of racist reprisal following northern reform. In particular, the segregationist-funded *Jackson Advocate*, in editorials aimed at black Mississippians, forcefully warned of the risks accompanying "carpetbagger" support.

22 NAACP, "Mississippi Pressures," group III A-232.

23 TC, papers of R. L. T. Smith, box 6, folder 117.

24 Evers, *For Us, the Living*, 267–68; Vollers, *Ghosts of Mississippi*, 107–8.

25 Vollers, *Ghosts of Mississippi*, 108.

26 Ibid.

27 Owens, interview, 66.

28 The Tougaloo "cultural agitators" and their supporters chanted this slogan after their successful interventions in local entertainment.

29 For more on the history and activism of Tougaloo College, see: Clarice T. Campbell and Oscar A. Rogers, *Mississippi: The View from Tougaloo* (Jackson: University Press of Mississippi, 1979).

30 Austin C. Moore III, interview by author, Jackson, Miss., 21 July 1993, n.p.

31 Reverend R. Edwin King Jr. grew up in Vicksburg, Mississippi, and, after leaving the state for theological training, returned to assume the post of the Tougaloo College chaplain in 1963. He was widely regarded as one of the state's most visible and committed activists for racial integration — one who "paid a heavy price for honoring his convictions" (Dittmer, *Local People*, 202). For an excellent discussion of King's activities and their grounding in Christian faith, see Charles Marsh, *God's Long Summer: Stories of Faith and Civil Rights* (Princeton: Princeton University Press, 1997), 116–51.

32 TC, papers of R. Edwin King Jr., box 2, folder 69.

33 Dittmer, *Local People*, 226.

34 Paramount, Desilu, MGM, Buena Vista, and Twentieth Century-Fox were among the major motion picture producers contacted by Moore in November 1963. In his letter to the studios he stated: "We are

asking all the major film producers to withhold their films from segregated theaters in the Jackson area. This would be what is needed to enlarge the audiences of our theaters to include Negroes. Please help us. We cannot risk arrest again — or possible violence. We can't do it alone. The key is yours" (TC, papers of R. Edwin King Jr., box 2, folder 68). Moore does not remember receiving any response from any of the motion picture producers, and there are no documents in the Tougaloo College archives that suggest otherwise.

The description of the interventions offered here, including the *Hootenanny* cancellation, as well as the situations surrounding the cast of *Bonanza* and the Al Hirt show, come from a combination of primary sources. Jackson's daily newspapers, the *Daily News* and *Clarion-Ledger*, as well as the local civil rights publication the *Mississippi Free Press*, were relied on heavily. In addition, materials from the papers of R. Edwin King Jr. at Tougaloo College provided key insights regarding Tougaloo activism.

35 Tim Brooks and Earle Marsh, *The Complete Directory to Prime Time Network TV Shows, 1946 to Present*, 5th ed. (New York: Ballatine, 1992), 409–10.

36 "Hootenany Called Off in Jackson," *Jackson Clarion-Ledger* (16 November 1963): 2.

37 TC, papers of R. Edwin King Jr., box 9, folder 450.

38 TC, papers of R. Edwin King Jr., box 9, folder 450; box 2, folder 68.

39 "Bonanza Family Won't Come Here," *Jackson Daily News* (23 January 1964): 6.

40 Irv Kupcinet, "Kup's Column," *Chicago Sun-Times* (22 January 1964): 44.

41 TC, papers of R. Edwin King Jr., box 9, folder 450.

42 "Furor Grows Hotter over Hirt's Pullout," *Jackson Clarion-Ledger* (27 January 1964): 8.

43 "Another Performer Cancels Show Here," *Jackson Daily News* (26 January 1964): 1.

44 *Mississippi Free Press* (1 February 1964): 2.

45 *Voice of the Movement*, newsletter of the Nonviolent Agitation Association of College Pupils (27 March 1964): 5–6.

46 MacDonald, *Blacks and White TV*, 81–82.

47 I borrow the terms and concepts in this paragraph from *The Practice of Everyday Life*, in which Michel de Certeau offers analysis of the ways in which "the weak" use that which is imposed on them. In elaborating on his differentiation of the subordinated's "tactics" from

the dominant's "strategies," the theorist writes that "the space of the tactic is the space of the other. Thus it must play on and with a terrain imposed on it and organized by the law of a foreign power. . . . It must vigilantly make use of the cracks that particular conjunctions open in the surveillance of the proprietary powers. It poaches in them. It creates surprises in them" (37).

48 TC, papers of R. L. T. Smith, box 6, folder 117.

49 Ibid.

50 Tom Ethridge, "Mississippi Notebook," *Jackson Clarion-Ledger* (6 February 1964): 8.

51 TC, papers of R. L. T. Smith, box 6, folder 117.

52 "Ask Bonanza Blackout," *Jackson Daily News* (31 January 1964): 1.

53 Ibid.

54 "Jackson Citizens' Council," *Aspect* (1 February 1964): 1.

55 "Hollywood Stars Not Needed Here," *Jackson Daily News* (13 February 1964): 6. As Ed King has noted in his unpublished account of this time, "for about ten years some white Mississippians had refused to watch the Ed Sullivan show because Negro entertainers appeared frequently (and were frequently blocked out by the local station claiming cable trouble)." King also recalls that some whites called the show the "N. L. Sullivan" show — the N.L. meaning "nigger lover" (TC, papers of R. Edwin King Jr., box 2, folder 69).

56 "Dislikes Sullivan and the Cartwrights," *Jackson Daily News* (28 January 1964): 6.

57 "No More Bonanzas on Sunday Nights," *Jackson Daily News* (28 January 1964): 6.

58 "Hirt Hurts Sick Children by Runout," *Jackson Daily News* (28 January 1964): 6. Although the reader nominates the NAACP as the activist force behind the recent cancellations, the NAACP had little to do with these interventions, at least in their initial stages. This attack on the organization was typical because civil rights organizations or efforts were frequently conflated by ardent segregationists, and attributions were made to the NAACP.

59 Tom Ethridge, "Mississippi Notebook," *Jackson Clarion-Ledger* (24 January 1964): 8.

60 "Voice of the People," *Jackson Clarion-Ledger* (28 January 1964): 6.

61 "Voice of the People," *Jackson Clarion-Ledger* (20 January 1964): 10.

62 "Voice of the People," *Jackson Clarion-Ledger* (24 February 1964): 13.

63 FCC, Testimony of Robert McRaney, docket 18845, box 24, vol. 22.

64 "Bonanza Family Will Appear Here," *Jackson Clarion-Ledger* (9 January 1964): 2.

65 Brooks and Marsh, *The Complete Directory to Prime Time Network TV Shows,* 1098.

66 Ralph Brauer with Donna Brauer, *The Horse, the Gun and the Piece of Property: Changing Images of the TV Western* (Bowling Green: Bowling Green University Popular Press, 1975), 130–35.

67 Ibid.

68 Ibid., 133.

69 SCR, document no. 99–36–0–66–1–1–1.

70 SCR, document no. 99–36–0–65–1–1–1.

71 MacDonald, *Blacks and White TV*, 78.

72 SCR, document no. 2–55–11–1–1–1.

73 "Mississippi Notebook," *Jackson Clarion-Ledger* (29 January 1964): 6.

74 Ethridge, "Mississippi Notebook" (24 January).

75 Charles Sallis and John Q. Adams, "Desegregation in Jackson, Mississippi," in *Southern Businessmen and Desegregation*, ed. Elizabeth Jacoway and David Colburn (Baton Rouge: Louisiana State University Press, 1982), 243.

76 Elizabeth Jacoway, "An Introduction: Civil Rights and the Changing South," in *Southern Businessmen and Desegregation*, ed. Elizabeth Jacoway and David Colburn (Baton Rouge: Louisiana State University Press, 1982), 8–9.

77 Ibid., 6.

78 Hale, *Making Whiteness*, 147.

79 Ibid., 133ff.

80 Jacoway, "An Introduction," 6.

81 Salter, *Jackson, Mississippi*, xxiv.

4 : PROGRAMMING/REGULATING WHITENESS

1 This quotation comes from a personal interview in 1993 with Barbara Barber and Dr. Jeanne Middleton at Jackson's Millsaps College. In the next chapter this memory is discussed and placed within the larger context of Mississippi in the sixties and the black freedom fight.

2 Hewitt Griffin, interview by author, Jackson, Miss., 17 August 1992, 31.

3 FCC, "Proposed Findings and Conclusions of UCC," docket 16663, box 58, vol. 10.

4 Ibid.

5 *Jackson Daily News* (25 March 1964), F6.

6 For further discussion of television and racial representation in the fifties and sixties, see MacDonald, *Blacks and White TV;* Fisher and Lowenstein, *Race and the News Media*; and Jannette Dates and William Barlow, eds., *Split Image: African Americans in the Mass Media* (Washington, D.C.: Howard University, 1990). The 1977 report of the U.S. Commission on Civil Rights, *Window Dressing on the Set,* also offers some discussion of this topic.

7 SHSW, letter to Sylvester Weaver, NBC papers, box 156, folder 56.

8 Boddy, *Fifties Television.*

9 Quoted in ibid., 198.

10 Michael Curtin, *Redeeming the Wasteland: Television Documentary and Cold War Politics* (New Brunswick, N.J.: Rutgers University Press, 1995), 41.

11 FCC, Intervener Exhibit no. 49, docket 16663, box 57, folder 12.

12 Ibid.

13 Stephen Whitfield, *The Culture of the Cold War* (Baltimore: Johns Hopkins University Press, 1991), 21.

14 FCC, Intervener Exhibit no. 46, docket 16663, box 57, folder 12.

15 Fisher and Lowenstein, *Race and the News Media*, 94.

16 Ibid., 84–85.

17 "Negras" was a common southern slurring of the word "negroes," considered by some, particularly older white southerners, to be relatively innocuous. But labeling, of course, is always an exercise in social power, and the rejection of the label "negroes," preferred by most black Mississippians, was never accidental.

18 Ruth Owens, telephone interview by author, Jackson, Miss., 30 August 1992.

19 FCC, "Proposed Findings, Civic Communications," docket 18845, box 25, vol. 25.

20 FCC, testimony of William Hodding Carter III, docket 18845, box 23, vol. 18.

21 Some may simply attribute actions described in this chapter to a racist institution, bureaucracy, or individual — a bigoted FCC, court, or judge, and deem that no further analysis is necessary. But, to repeat an important point, such individualized nominations, however accurate,

are inadequate for historical explanation, as they too comfortably elide the vexing complexity and scope of racial politics, difference, and racism. They fail to consider race as a multifaceted, socially contingent set of practices that touch and constitute all citizens in some way. It may be more comfortable to be sure that racist power is always neatly assigned, but the nomination of "racist" individualizes that which is fundamentally social.

22 FCC, memorandum (1959), WLBT license file, accession no. 173–82–20, box 7.

23 Ibid.

24 Clift, "The WLBT-TV Case," 17.

25 FCC, "Reply to Opposition," attachment F, docket 16663, box 55, vol. 3. Almost all official statements, testimony, and findings submitted to the FCC in the WLBT case are contained in FCC dockets 16663 and 18845, and are available through the U.S. National Archives in Washington, D.C. In this chapter, all testimony cited as "Reply to Opposition," may be found in the FCC papers titled "Reply to Opposition to Petition to Intervene and to Deny Application for Renewal," received 13 July 1964, docket 16663, box 55, vols. 2 and 3.

26 FCC, petitioner brief, docket 16663, box 54, vol. 5.

27 Clift, "The WLBT-TV Case," 43.

28 "Reply to Opposition," attachment G.

29 Ibid.

30 Noriega, *Shot in America*, 181.

31 Ibid., 64. Noriega's work offers an examination of this "insider/outsider" binary, drawing attention to its mutual, relationally dependent definitions and the imbrication of state discourses in the recirculation of such identities and understandings of identity politics.

32 "Reply to Opposition," attachment G.

33 Ibid.

34 "Reply to Opposition," attachment D.

35 "Reply to Opposition," attachment G.

36 Ibid.

37 FCC, letters to the Commission, docket 16663, box 55, vol. 3.

38 Ibid.

39 "Reply to Opposition," attachment E.

40 Ibid.

41 FCC papers, docket 16663, box 55, vol. 3.

42 Ibid.

43 Ibid.

44 Parker, "The Mississippi Television Station Cases."

45 *Lamar Life Broadcasting Co. et al.*, Memorandum Opinion and Order (adopted 19 May 1965), 38 FCC 1153.

46 Ibid., 38 FCC 1154.

47 Henry Geller, interview by author, Washington, D.C., 17 June 1993.

48 *Lamar Life Broadcasting Co.*, 38 FCC 1149, sup. 11.

49 Ibid., 38 FCC 1154.

50 *Lamar Life Broadcasting Co.*, 38 FCC 1154.

51 Clift, "The WLBT-TV Case," 55.

52 *Lamar Life Broadcasting Co.*, 14 FCC 2d 433.

53 *Lamar Life Broadcasting Co.*, 38 FCC 1154.

54 *Lamar Life Broadcasting Co.*, 14 FCC 2d 443.

55 Clift, "The WLBT-TV Case," 116, 129.

56 Ibid., 116.

57 Ibid., 121.

58 Owens interview.

59 Clift, "The WLBT-TV Case," 121.

60 Ibid., 166.

61 Ibid., 117.

62 Ibid.

63 Fiske, *Power Plays, Power Works*, 148.

64 Ibid.

65 Walter J. Ong, *Orality and Literacy: The Technologizing of the Word* (London: Routledge, 1982), 166.

66 Ibid., 45–52.

67 Ibid., 96.

68 Ibid., 98.

69 In his memoir, *Growing Up Black in Rural Mississippi*, Chalmers Archer Jr. has provided examples of this orality and the "patterns of truth" arrived at through spoken conversation. In introducing his work, he writes: "Because this is a family history, most of it is oral history, a compilation of many conversations and shared memories. And like many conversations, it may be rambling and repetitious at times. However, as in all good family talks, you detect patterns of truth and stir up shared family memories of your own" (*Growing Up Black in Rural Mississippi: Memories of a Family, Heritage of a Place* [New York: Walker and Company, 1992], ix, xii).

70 Throughout this paragraph I have paraphrased and applied the discus-

sion of Stanley Fish in "The Law Wishes to Have a Formal Existence," in *There's No Such Thing as Free Speech . . . and It's a Good Thing, Too* (New York: Oxford University Press, 1994).

71 Streeter, "Beyond Freedom of Speech and the Public Interest," 205.

72 Fiske, *Power Plays, Power Works*, 290.

73 As Crenshaw and Peller in "Reel Time/Real Justice" note, Thurgood Marshall used the term "disaggregation" in a dissent to the Supreme Court's 1989 decision in *Richmond v. Crison*, 488 U.S. 469.

74 Crenshaw and Peller, "Reel Time/Real Justice," 63.

75 Ibid.

76 For further elaboration on this "transformation," see not only Ong's work but also Michel de Certeau's discussion of "scriptural economies" in modern Western culture in *The Practice of Everyday Life*, 134–35.

77 Ralph Ellison, *Invisible Man* (New York: Vintage, 1990), 439.

5 : BLACKING OUT : REMEMBERING TV AND THE SIXTIES

1 As conceptualized by Pierre Bourdieu and other cultural studies scholars, the reference here to "habitus" refers to both social structures and actions — "the conditions in which one lives and the ways in which one lives in those conditions" (Fiske, "The Culture of Everyday Life," 163).

2 Altogether I conducted approximately thirty-five interviews, ranging from ten minutes to more than two hours in length, during summer 1992 and 1993 while living in Jackson. Most of the interviews represented in this project were one to two hours in length. In the process of editing, I found twenty conversations most useful and interesting.

All persons quoted in this and other chapters had opportunities to read the transcriptions of our conversation, and they were asked to suggest additions, corrections, or other changes — or to request nothing be used. Most also had an opportunity to review and comment on draft manuscripts of this and other chapters as the project evolved.

3 As much as possible I have chosen not to rework into general paraphrase and description my actual questions and interactive comments but instead include them as they occurred in conversation. Even though this may be less than flattering at times for the conversationalists, in making this choice I wish again to foreground the thoroughly dialogic nature of such projects and the ways in which both parties inevitably

lead, cajole, and prompt those with them in conversation. Certainly some of my questions are leading and perhaps patronizing. And, as we all know, at least in our more honest moments, the immediacy and dynamics of friendly conversation often produce interactions that are less than eloquent and fully sensitive to others.

4 Dittmer, *Local People*, 127. See also the collection of essays in Crawford, Rouse, and Woods, eds., *Women in the Civil Rights Movement*.

5 Quoted in Dittmer, *Local People*, 241.

6 Howell Raines, *My Soul Is Rested: The Story of the Civil Rights Movement in the Deep South* (New York: Penguin, 1983).

7 George Lipsitz, *Time Passages: Collective Memory and American Popular Culture* (Minneapolis: University of Minnesota Press, 1990), 213, 227.

8 Ong, *Orality and Literacy*, 42–49.

9 Ibid., 44.

10 Michael H. Frisch, *A Shared Authority: Essays on the Craft and Meaning of Oral and Public History* (Albany: State University of New York Press, 1990), 9–13.

11 A. Portelli, "The Peculiarities of Oral History," *History Workshop* 12 (autumn 1981): 103.

12 Ibid.

13 Frisch, *A Shared Authority*. A broader participation in the process of historical interpretation has been an aim in this project. Although I initially taped the interviews reproduced in this chapter several years ago, I have been able to stay in contact with some of the interviewees and have shared written transcripts of our taped conversations and/or parts of the manuscript of this book with most of those interviewed. Unfortunately, I have been unable to reestablish contact with a few people I interviewed, and some have died. As I have worked editing and rereading interview transcriptions, the generosity of content and perspectives offered have prompted a consistent awareness that my claims regarding others' perspectives recommend modesty because my interpretations, even given generous feedback, miss intended meanings and important perspectives.

14 Portelli, "The Peculiarities of Oral History," 105.

15 George Owens, interview by author, Jackson, Miss., 5 August 1992, 59.

16 Quoted in Raines, *My Soul Is Rested*, 137.

17 Aaron Shirley, interview by author, Jackson, Miss., 1 August 1992, 121.

18 Quoted in Raines, *My Soul Is Rested*, 247.

19 Shirley, interview, 126–27.

20 For example, see Sitkoff, *The Struggle for Black Equality*, 77–78.

21 S. I. Hayakawa, "TV and the Negro Revolt," *Television Quarterly* 3, no. 3 (1964): 23–25.

22 Quoted in Sitkoff, *The Struggle for Black Equality*, 78.

23 Shirley, interview, 119.

24 Jeanne Middleton and Barbara Barber, interview by author, Jackson, Miss., 19 August 1993, 14–15.

25 Ibid., 4.

26 Ibid., 2–4.

27 Juanita Jefferson, interview by author, Jackson, Miss., 5 August 1993, 17.

28 Sam Bailey, interview, by author, Jackson, Miss., 4 August 1993, 4.

29 Willie Lewis, interview, by author, Jackson, Miss., 13 August 1993, 11.

30 Ineva May-Pittman, interview by author, Jackson, Miss., 25 August 1993, 3.

31 Silver, *Mississippi*, 41–42.

32 Occasionally one of Jackson's two large-circulation newspapers would print a contrary opinion, often from a white "liberal" rather than a local African American, in the editorial pages of their publications. However, such writings were confined within the journalistically defined province of editorializing and opinion.

33 Sitkoff, *The Struggle for Black Equality*.

34 Ibid., 59–60.

35 Archer, *Growing Up Black in Rural Mississippi*, 63.

36 May Ann Henderson and Gordon Henderson, interview by author, Richmond, Ind., 18 April 1993, 177–79.

37 Owens, interview, 62.

38 Deborah L. Denard, "Womanpower Unlimited: A Case Study" (master's thesis, Jackson State University, 1976), 24–25.

39 Clarie Collins Harvey, oral history interview by John Dittmer and John Jones, Mississippi Department of Archives and History, Jackson, Miss., 1981, 32.

40 May-Pittman, interview, 9–10.

41 Dittmer, *Local People*, 98–99.

42 Henry Kirksey, interview by author, Tougaloo, Miss., 18 August 1993, 12–13, 16–18.

43 Ibid., 21.

44 Charles Evers, interview by author, Jackson, Miss., 25 August 1993, 12–13.

45 Fiske, *Media Matters*, 49–50.

46 Walter Saddler, interview by author, Jackson, Miss., 12 December 2000, n.p.

47 According to a summary of the year 2003 Radio and Television News Directors Association/Ball State University survey (conducted in the fourth quarter of 2002), U.S. broadcast stations were employing "the largest percentage of women news directors ever, but almost all the numbers for minorities — in both radio and TV — are down. . . . There was no good news for minorities in either radio or television. In television, the minority workforce dropped from 20.6 percent to 18.1 percent" (African Americans were 8.4 percent of the total, down from 10.1 percent in 1994). In radio, "the minority workforce continued its near-relentless slide, which started with the elimination of the EEO rules." The survey is available at: www.rtnda.org/research/research.shtml.

48 Hewitt Griffin, interview by author, Jackson, Miss., 17 August 1992, 49.

49 Robert Entmann and Andrew Rojecki, *The Black Image in the White Mind: Media and Race in America* (Chicago: University of Chicago Press, 2000), 8.

50 Ibid. This is not necessarily to generalize these findings to other specific local news productions. As Entmann and Rojecki write: "Whether local news [in Chicago] resembles that in other cities is open to question, of course, but research elsewhere has found similar racial contrasts" (79).

6 : NOT FORGETTING

1 WLBT station files, 1993.

2 Fermaglich, "Never," 8–10.

3 Ibid.

4 Hewitt Griffin, interview by author, Jackson, Miss., 17 August 1992, 27.

5 I found letters complaining about WLBT programming practices and the fact that the station was being "given to the Negroes" even into the 1980s in the mothballed station-complaint files of the FCC in Washington, D.C.

6 Fermaglich, "Never," 8–10.

7 Ibid., 1.

8 Legal proceedings often "break down" complicated, complex events
   and moments in life in order to further scrutinize them via law's technical apparatus. However, these "broken down" parts are not only ab-
   stractions of life lived whole but are also inevitably rearranged and
   pieced together by various social agents, all of whom are using their
   senses of "common sense" and life narratives. For more discussion of
   this observation along with an interesting application, see Nancy Isenberg's "Not 'Anyone's Daughter': Patty Hearst and the Postmodern
   Legal Subject," *American Quarterly* 52, no. 4 (2000): 639–81.

9 This is not to say that there were no focused civil rights campaigns
   aimed specifically at media change and reform. In fact, in the personal
   archives of Jan Hillegas in Jackson I found multiple duplicated petitions, signed by Mississippi SNCC workers, asking the FCC to take
   action engaging the FCC's fairness doctrine against specific stations
   in the state, including WLBT. Most likely these petitions followed
   guidelines suggested by a broadcast complaint primer distributed by
   Washington-based civil rights attorney William Higgs. Higgs was a
   former Mississippian and director of the Washington Human Rights
   Project — including Operation Mississippi (a student-directed voter
   registration drive) — and he urged activists to "actively press complaints against radio and television stations." The primer, titled "Radio
   and Television Programming and Editorializing: The FCC's Fairness
   Doctrine," was promoted by Higgs as possibly playing a key role in "a
   massive legal defense" in fall 1964. ("Primer for Negro Complaints
   against Radio-TV," *Broadcasting* [20 July 1964]: 40.) Certainly, as
   earlier chapters have shown, some Mississippians did press complaints. However, I found no evidence that this petition drive received
   significant attention from the Jackson movement or from other local
   integrationist efforts.

10 Noriega, *Shot in America*, 174.

11 Ibid., 94.

12 Ibid.

13 See Willard Rowland's excellent analysis of the seventies broadcast
   reform movement in his 1982 monograph "The Illusion of Fulfillment."

14 In the realm of communication policy studies Andrew Calabrese has
   attempted to address the local-global tension in his prescriptions
   for furthering democratic citizen participation and localism in U.S.
   broadcasting. He speaks of "translocalism" as a localism "not confined to the spacial boundaries of the local," by its use, for example,

of new computer technologies to build "local communities" in different ways. He concludes that "if a new politics of participation is to become relevant and vital, it will have to be a politics that can enable the members of place-bound, local communities to understand the world from a multiplicity of perspectives, part of which must be rooted in a politics of place and part of which must transcend place" (Calabrese, "Why Localism? On Renewing a Public Interest Theme in U.S. Communications Policy," paper presented at the annual conference of the International Communication Association, Washington, D.C., 1993, 15).

15 Marc Raboy, S. Proulx, and R. Welters, "Media Policy, Audiences, and Social Demand: Research at the Interface of Policy Studies and Audience Studies," *Television and New Media* 2, no. 2 (2001): 99.

16 Ibid.

17 William J. Clinton, *Public Papers of the Presidents of the United States: William J. Clinton, January 1 to December 31, 1996* (Washington, D.C.: GPO, 1996), 188, 190.

18 Ibid.

19 Even if an interested citizen makes the efforts required to be fully informed and fairly heard by the FCC, or perhaps contacts one of the agency's commissioners or top staff, they face enormous competition for commission attention. As a top FCC staffer told me recently, the citizens may be heard but professional lobbyists inevitably have the final access and opportunities to shape the agency's decisions.

20 Robert W. McChesney, *Corporate Media and the Threat to Democracy* (New York: Seven Stories Press, 1997), 44.

21 Quoted in Patricia Aufderheide, *Communications Policy and the Public Interest: The Telecommunications Act of 1996* (New York: Guilford Press, 1999), 107.

22 Managing economies and social risks through a reliance on a select sphere of business, scientific, and political expertise is a hallmark of what Streeter and others have identified as corporate liberalism. This historical movement is complicated and multifaceted but has primarily centered political, cultural, and economic leadership in big business. Motivating this leadership is the desire "to reconcile traditional liberal democratic notions of individualism, self-reliance, free enterprise, and anti-statism with corporate-capitalist and scientific-technological demands for order, stability, and social efficiency" (Streeter, *Selling the Air*, 35). This leadership — its values and pri-

orities, including industrial efficiency — typically lead to the co-optation of moderate reform and the marginalization of radical agents or agendas.

23 Especially in today's antistatist climate, "regulation" and "deregulation" are common, very slippery terms brimming with political agendas and priorities at the moment of their utterance. Certainly what is touted in recent years as "industry deregulation," is, as other scholars have noted, simply reregulation under a different name. It is, in essence, the state reformalizing the ways in which it will control and relate to a variety of entities. Rarely, if ever, does such "deregulation" benefit all commercial interests equally, and thus corporations fight for advantageous government regulation and protections under a variety of names while publicly praising the abstract virtues of the "open unregulated marketplace." Noriega puts it well when he states that "deregulation must be seen as a regulatory policy, not the absence of regulation" (*Shot in America*, 180). This point, as well as the state's essential role in the legal establishment of American broadcasting structures and property claims, is also given an excellent discussion in Streeter's *Selling the Air*.

24 Aufderheide, *Communications Policy and the Public Interest*, 67.

25 As I write this chapter, no fewer than six key media ownership rules are being "reviewed" by the FCC after most of them were suspended or challenged by the conservative U.S. Court of Appeals for the District of Columbia. These rules include the national television ownership cap, newspaper-broadcast cross-ownership, cable-broadcast cross-ownership, local television duopoly, cable horizontal ownership, and cable vertical ownership.

26 Aufderheide, *Communications Policy and the Public Interest*, 102.

27 U.S. Department of Commerce, *Changes, Challenges and Charting New Courses*, 32.

28 Ibid., 32–33.

29 While I find the statements of the minority station owners compelling, it is also reasonable to ask whether or not the variable of ethnicity in ownership correlates with programming diversity. Exactly this question is addressed in the aforementioned NTIA report, as it references a recent study establishing a link between the race or ethnicity of broadcast owners and the viewpoint diversity offered in programming content. Federally commissioned researchers concluded that "minority owned radio stations and, to a lesser extent, television stations tended to select a format that appealed to a minority audience and delivered

more news and public affairs programming focused on minority interests" (U.S. Department of Commerce, *Changes, Challenges and Charting New Courses*, 24). For further discussion of broadcast licensing as a construction of private property, see Streeter, *Selling the Air*.

30 U.S. Department of Commerce, "Commerce Secretary Mineta Releases Report Finding Gains in Minority Broadcast Ownership," Press Release (16 January 2001): 1.

31 Liberty Corporation should not be confused with Liberty Media, the huge multinational media conglomerate with interests in video programming, cable, satellite, telephone, and internet services. Liberty Corporation is a company based in South Carolina that has attempted in recent years to convert itself from an insurance firm to a broadcast station group owner. Liberty's subsidiary, Cosmos Broadcasting, claims ownership of fifteen network-affiliated television stations, most of which are in southern states such as Texas, Louisiana, and Mississippi.

32 Patrice Sawyer, "WLBT Changing Hands," *Jackson Clarion-Ledger* (20 June 2000): C1.

33 Streeter, *Selling the Air*, 37.

34 *Clarion-Ledger* (20 June 2000): C1–2.

35 Ibid., C1–2.

36 Streeter, *Selling the Air*, 287.

37 Ibid., 304, 307.

38 Ibid., 302.

39 Aufderheide, *Communications Policy and the Public Interest*, 6. "Consumers," as many industries and policymakers conceive them, are not proactive as much as reactive. They react to the provided programming, content, and offerings of commercial television, rather than engage industries in discussions of what programming and content might represent or address. In their monitoring and measuring of what viewers choose to consume, the commercial industries declare they are listening to their audiences and engaging the public. But, of course, "consumers" can only choose among products that are offered, and ratings never measure what citizens truly want or wish to have but rather what they select given a cultural menu not of their own making. The productive work that is entailed in listening, watching, reading, and interpreting is effaced in the production/consumption dichotomy and in the choices of consumers represented as "consumer sovereignty" but in fact limited to choices of consumption.

Thus, within a commercial system that runs on advertising dollars, advertisers and marketers are listening not to persons "but thin voices choosing from among a set of predetermined options. . . . The consumer is not simply a person, but a very particular way of understanding a person. Advertisers address their audience strictly as *consumers*, and only consumers" (Streeter, *Selling the Air*, 304).

40 Foucault, *Discipline and Punish*. For example, many within industry and academe, across political affiliations, sincerely hold to the view that those nominated as everyday "consumers" have very little, if anything, to say to the complicated issues and processes of, or policies governing, media production. Rather, it is presumed that they can only helpfully speak within their limited experiences to personalist evaluations of contemporary cultural consumption. Within scholarly circles I have regularly heard dismissals of ordinary citizen input that have consistently made me question not the citizen comments or perspectives as much as the questions asked, the language and knowledge assumed, and the fundamental approach taken to those questioned.

41 Particularly in recent decades the FCC has rarely even pretended to vigorously seek out nonindustry, outside-the-beltway, ordinary citizens on any large scale. Consumers can and do individually complain to the commission regarding excessive advertising, sex, violence, or cable rates, and the agency has established divisions designed to deal with such complaints, but it is very difficult to envision the FCC complaints division usurped by a citizen advisory division with the clout to significantly reconfigure U.S. radio and television. The commission has long held, explicitly or implicitly, that those in existing industries are best suited to envision how cultural production and policy is structured and designed.

42 Mukherjee, "Regulating Race in the California Civil Rights Initiative," 42.

43 Michael Curtin and Thomas Streeter, "Media," in *Culture Works: The Political Economy of Culture*, ed. Richard Maxwell (Minneapolis: University of Minnesota Press, 2001), 243–45. Also see George Yúdice, "Civil Society, Consumption, and Governmentality in an Age of Global Restructuring: An Introduction," *Social Text* 14, no. 4 (winter 1995): 1–25.

44 Raboy, "Media Policy, Audiences, and Social Demand," 101, 111.

45 Quoted in Sitkoff, *The Struggle for Black Equality, 1954–1992*, 86.

46 Quoted in Manning Marable, "An Idea Whose Time Has Come," *Time* (27 August 2001): 22.

47 Streeter, *Selling the Air*, 321.

48 In *Faces at the Bottom of the Well: The Permanence of Racism* (New York: Basic Books, 1992), Derrick Bell writes about this ongoing struggle and about living beyond the despair that comes from the reality and permanence of racism. Bell, a law professor, encourages the call for new stories or narratives that will interact with and inform law and that find inspiration less in defunct ideals of a postracist state than "in the lives of an oppressed people who defied social death as slaves and freedmen, insisting on their humanity" (197). In the end, he concludes, it is not a matter of choosing between the pragmatic recognition that racism is permanent no matter what we do, or an idealism based on the long-held dream of attaining a society free of racism. Rather, it is a question of "both/and": both the recognition of the futility of action — "where action is more civil rights strategies destined to fail — and the unalterable conviction that something must be done, that action must be taken" (199). Those I have talked with have echoed this same point, telling me that while racism endures and continues its destructive disaggregative work, their struggle against it must continue. It is within this context of struggle that the fight for control of Jackson television, as well as memories of it, must be placed.

APPENDIX

1 This observation is offered by Melissa Fay Greene in the initial pages of *Praying for Sheetrock: A Work of Nonfiction* (Reading, Mass.: Addison-Wesley, 1991), her beautifully written "chronicle of large and important things happening in a very little place" (x).

2 Richard Cuoto, *Lifting the Veil: A Political History of Struggles for Emancipation* (Knoxville: University of Tennessee Press, 1993), xvii.

3 For this timeline I have drawn heavily on secondary materials addressing Mississippi in the 1960s as well as surveys of the civil rights movement — in particular, Rhonda L. Blumberg, *Civil Rights: The 1960s Freedom Struggle*, rev. ed. (Boston: Twayne, 1991); John Dittmer, *Local People*; and Vollers, *Ghosts of Mississippi*. Other chronological entries come from the news articles of the *Jackson Daily News*, *Jackson Clarion-Ledger*, *New York Times*, and *Washington Post*.

4 FCC, Memorandum of Broadcast Bureau, 1959, accession no. 173–82–20, box 7.

BIBLIOGRAPHY

ARCHIVAL COLLECTIONS CONSULTED

FCC   Federal Communications Commission, National Archives, Washington, D.C. Includes records pertaining to WLBT-TV: Accession number 173-76-12, Docket 16663, Boxes 55–59; Accession number 173-81-67, Docket 18845, Boxes 18–36; Accession number 173-82-20, WLBT file, Boxes 6–7; Accession number 72-1-451, WLBT file, Box 494.

MDAH   Mississippi Department of Archives and History, Jackson, Mississippi. Includes files of the Mississippi State Sovereignty Commission, abbreviated as SCF.

NAACP   National Association for the Advancement of Colored People, Library of Congress, Washington, D.C.

SHSW   State Historical Society of Wisconsin, Madison, Wisconsin. Includes papers of NBC, Kenneth Cox, E. William Henry, Lee Loevinger, Newton Minow, and John Salter.

TC   Lillian Pierce Benbow Room of Special Collections, Zenobia Coleman Library, Tougaloo College, Tougaloo, Mississippi. Includes papers of R. Edwin King Jr., Aaron Henry, and R. L. T. Smith.

INTERVIEWS BY THE AUTHOR

Alexander, Margaret Walker. Jackson, Miss., 3 August 1992
Bailey, Ben. Tougaloo, Miss., 3 August 1993
Bailey, Sam. Jackson, Miss., 4 August 1993
Barber, Barbara. Jackson, Miss., 19 August 1993
Coker, Frances. Jackson, Miss., 29 July 1993
Collins, Corrice. Jackson, Miss., 5 August 1993
Cox, Kenneth. Washington, D.C., 17 June 1993
Evers, Charles. Jackson, Miss., 25 August 1993
Geller, Henry. Washington, D.C., 17 June 1993

Griffin, Hewitt. Jackson, Miss., 17 August 1992
Henderson, Gordon. Richmond, Ind., 18 April 1993
Henderson, Mary Ann. Richmond, Ind., 18 April 1993
Henry, Aaron. Clarksdale, Miss., 17 August 1992
Henry, E. William. Washington, D.C., 17 June 1993
Hines, Hosea. Jackson, Miss., 17 August 1993
Jefferson, Juanita. Jackson, Miss., 5 August 1993
King, Jeanette. Jackson, Miss., 11 August 1993
King, R. Edwin, Jr. Jackson, Miss., 16 July 1992
Kirksey, Henry. Tougaloo, Miss., 18 August 1993
Kirkwood, Alexander. Jackson, Miss. (telephone), 16 August 1993
Krystal, Elaine. Jackson, Miss., 14 August 1992
Lewis, Willie. Jackson, Miss., 13 August 1993
Loevinger, Lee. Washington, D.C., 24 June 1993
Logan, A. M. E. Jackson, Miss., 16 August 1993
Lyells, Ruby Stutts. Jackson, Miss., 13 August 1992
May-Pittman, Ineva. Jackson, Miss., 25 August 1993
McBride, Eddie. Jackson, Miss., 30 July 1992
Middleton (Forsythe), Jeanne. Jackson, Miss., 19 August 1993
Minor, Bill. Jackson, Miss., 13 August 1992
Moore, Austin C. III. Jackson, Miss., 21 July 1993
Nolan, Fred. Jackson, Miss., 3 August 1993
Owens, George. Jackson, Miss., 5 August 1992
Owens, Ruth. Jackson, Miss. (telephone), 30 August 1992
Parker, Everett. New York, N.Y., 21 October 1993
Redmond, Jessie. Jackson, Miss., 4 August 1993
Saddler, Walter. Jackson, Miss., 12 December 2000
Shirley, Aaron. Jackson, Miss., 1 August 1992
Taylor, Wendell. Jackson, Miss., 21 July 1992
Washington, James. Jackson, Miss., 3 August 1992
Young, Aurelia. Jackson, Miss., 18 August 1992

BOOKS AND ARTICLES

Aaker, David A., and George S. Day, eds. *Consumerism: Search for the Consumer Interest*. New York: Free Press, 1971.
"ACLU Wants Hearings on Jackson TV Station." *Broadcasting* (1 March 1965): 57.
"Airport to Industry (Jackson)." *Broadcasting* (17 June 1963): 98–100.
American Masters Presents. Rod Serling: Submitted for Your Consideration. CBS Video, 1998.
Andreasen, A. *The Disadvantaged Consumer*. New York: Free Press, 1975.

Ang, Ien. *Living Room Wars: Rethinking Media Audiences for a Postmodern World*. London: Routledge, 1996.

———. "Wanted: Audiences. On the Politics of Empirical Audience Studies." In *Media Studies: A Reader*, 2nd ed., edited by Paul Marris and Sue Thornham, 482–91. New York: New York University Press, 2000.

"Another Performer Cancels Show Here." Jackson *Daily News* (26 January 1964): 1.

"Appeals Court: What's It Up To?" *Broadcasting* (12 April 1965): 8.

Archer, Chalmers, Jr. *Growing Up Black in Rural Mississippi: Memories of a Family, Heritage of a Place*. New York: Walker and Company, 1992.

"Ask Bonanza Blackout." *Jackson Daily News* (31 January 1964): 1.

Aufderheide, Patricia. *Communications Policy and the Public Interest: The Telecommunications Act of 1996*. New York: Guilford Press, 1999.

Baker, Houston. "Scene . . . Not Heard." In *Reading Rodney King/ Reading Urban Uprising*, edited by Robert Gooding-Williams, 38–48. New York: Routledge, 1993.

Baughman, James L. *Television's Guardians: The FCC and the Politics of Programming, 1958–1967*. Knoxville: University of Tennessee Press, 1985.

Bell, Derrick A. *And We Are Not Saved: The Elusive Quest for Racial Justice*. New York: Basic Books, 1987.

———. *Faces at the Bottom of the Well: The Permanence of Racism*. New York: Basic Books, 1992.

Benjamin, Walter. *Illuminations: Essays and Reflections*. Translated by H. Zohn. New York: Schocken Books, 1969.

Blauner, Bob. *Black Lives, White Lives: Three Decades of Race Relations in America*. Berkeley: University of California Press, 1989.

Blumberg, Rhonda L. *Civil Rights: The 1960s Freedom Struggle*. Rev. ed. Boston: Twayne, 1991.

Boddy, William. *Fifties Television: The Industry and Its Critics*. Champaign: University of Illinois Press, 1990.

"Bonanza Family Will Appear Here." Jackson *Clarion-Ledger* (9 January 1964): 2.

"Bonanza Family Won't Come Here." Jackson *Daily News* (23 January 1964): 6.

Branch, Taylor. *Parting the Waters: America in the King Years, 1954–63*. New York: Simon and Schuster, 1988.

———. *Pillar of Fire: America in the King Years, 1963–65*. New York: Simon and Schuster, 1998.

Branscomb, Anne W., and M. Savage. "The Broadcast Reform Movement: At the Crossroads." *Journal of Communication* 28, no. 4 (1978): 25–34.

Brauer, Ralph, with Donna Brauer. *The Horse, the Gun and the Piece of Property: Changing Images of the TV Western.* Bowling Green: Bowling Green State University Popular Press, 1975.

Brooks, Tim, and Earle Marsh. *The Complete Directory to Prime Time Network TV Shows, 1946 to Present.* 5th ed. New York: Ballantine, 1992.

"Burden of Proof in WLBT Case in Court." *Broadcasting* (17 October 1966): 58.

Cagin, Seth, and Philip Dray. *We Are Not Afraid: The Story of Goodman, Schwerner, and Chaney and the Civil Rights Campaign for Mississippi.* New York: Bantam 1991.

Calabrese, Andrew. "Why Localism? On Renewing a Public Interest Theme in U.S. Communications Policy." Paper presented at the annual conference of the International Communication Association, Washington, D.C., 1993.

Calhoun, Craig, Edward LiPuma, and Moishe Postone, eds. *Bourdieu: Critical Perspectives.* Chicago: University of Chicago Press, 1993.

Calweti, John G. *The Six-Gun Mystique.* 2nd ed. Bowling Green: Bowling Green State University Popular Press, 1984.

Campbell, Clarice T., and Oscar A. Rogers. *Mississippi: The View from Tougaloo.* Jackson: University Press of Mississippi, 1979.

"Challenge in the South." *Newsweek* (29 May 1967): 63.

Chalmers, David M. *And the Crooked Place Made Straight: The Struggle for Social Change in the 1960s.* Baltimore: Johns Hopkins University Press, 1991.

"Church Aims at Southern TV's." *Broadcasting* (20 April 1964): 44.

"Church to Appeal Mississippi Renewals." *Broadcasting* (14 June 1965): 71–72.

Clift, Charles E., III. "The WLBT-TV Case, 1964–1969: An Historical Analysis." Ph.D. diss., Indiana University, 1976. University Microfilms, no. 72-04612.

Clinton, William J. *Public Papers of the Presidents of the United States: William J. Clinton, January 1 to December 31, 1996.* Washington, D.C.: GPO, 1996.

Cohen, Lizabeth. *A Consumer's Republic: The Politics of Mass Consumption in Postwar America.* New York: Knopf, 2003.

———. "Consumption and Civil Rights." Paper presented at the annual conference of the American Studies Association, Costa Mesa, Calif., 1992.

Cole, Barry, and Mal Oettinger. *The Reluctant Regulators: The FCC and the Broadcast Audience.* Reading, Mass.: Addison-Wesley, 1978.

Conley, Dalton. "40 Acres and a Mule: The Black-White Wealth Gap in America." *National Forum* 80, no. 2 (2000): 21–24.

"The Consumer's Rights." *Nation* (11 April 1966): 412–13.

Cooper, Caryl A. "Percy Greene and the *Jackson Advocate.*" In *The Press and Race: Mississippi Journalists Confront the Movement*, edited by David Davies, 55–83. Jackson: University Press of Mississippi, 2001.

Cose, Ellis. "The Good News about Black America." *Newsweek* (7 June 1999): 28–40.

"Court Raises Its Eyebrow." *Broadcasting* (30 August 1965): 55.

Cover, Robert. "The Supreme Court, 1982 Term — Foreword: Nomos and Narrative." *Harvard Law Review* 97, no. 4 (1983): 4.

Crawford, Vicki, Jacqueline Rouse, and Barbara Woods, eds. *Women in the Civil Rights Movement: Trailblazers and Torchbearers, 1941–1965.* Bloomington: Indiana University Press, 1990.

Creighton, Lucy B. *Pretenders to the Throne: The Consumer Movement in the United States.* Lexington, Mass.: D. C. Heath, 1976.

Crenshaw, Kimberlé. "Race, Reform, and Retrenchment: Transformation and Legitimation in Antidiscrimination Law." *Harvard Law Review* 101, no. 7 (1988): 1331–87.

Crenshaw, Kimberlé, and Gary Peller. "Reel Time/Real Justice." In *Reading Rodney King/Reading Urban Uprising*, edited by Robert Gooding-Williams, 56–70. New York: Routledge, 1993.

Cuoto, Richard. *Lifting the Veil: A Political History of Struggles for Emancipation.* Knoxville: University of Tennessee Press, 1993.

Curtin, Michael. *Redeeming the Wasteland: Television Documentary and Cold War Politics.* New Brunswick: Rutgers University Press, 1995.

Curtin, Michael, and Thomas Streeter. "Media." In *Culture Works: The Political Economy of Culture*, edited by Richard Maxwell, 225–49. Minneapolis: University of Minnesota Press, 2001.

Dahlgren, Peter. "Media, Citizenship, and Civic Culture." In *Mass Media and Society*, 3rd ed., edited by James Curran and Michael Gurevitch, 310–28. London: Arnold, 2000.

Danielson, Dan, and Karen Engle, eds. *After Identity: A Reader in Law and Culture.* New York: Routledge, 1995.

Dates, Jannette, and William Barlow, eds. *Split Image: African Americans in the Mass Media.* Washington, D.C.: Howard University Press, 1990.

Davies, David R., ed. *The Press and Race: Mississippi Journalists Confront the Movement.* Jackson: University Press of Mississippi, 2001.

Davies, David R., and Judy Smith. "Jimmy Ward and the *Jackson Daily News.*" In *The Press and Race: Mississippi Journalists Confront the Movement*, edited by David Davies, 85–109. Jackson: University Press of Mississippi, 2001.

de Certeau, Michel. "History and Science Fiction." In *Heterologies*, translated by B. Massumi. Minneapolis: University of Minnesota Press, 1986.

———. *The Practice of Everyday Life*. Translated by S. Rendall.
Berkeley: University of California Press, 1984.

Denard, Deborah L. "Womanpower Unlimited: A Case Study." Master's
thesis, Jackson State University, 1976.

"Dislikes Sullivan and the Cartwrights." Jackson *Daily News*
(28 January 1964): 6.

Dittmer, John. *Local People: The Struggle for Civil Rights in Mississippi*.
Urbana: University of Illinois Press, 1994.

Donovan, Robert J., and Ray Scherer, eds. *Unsilent Revolution:
Television News and American Public Life*. Cambridge: University of
Cambridge Press, 1992.

Ellison, Ralph. *Invisible Man*. New York: Vintage, 1990.

Entmann, Robert. "Modern Racism and the Images of Blacks in Local
Television News." *Critical Studies in Mass Communication* 7, no. 4
(1990): 332–45.

Entmann, Robert, and Andrew Rojecki. *The Black Image in the White
Mind: Media and Race in America*. Chicago: University of Chicago
Press, 2000.

Ethridge, Tom. "Mississippi Notebook." Jackson *Clarion-Ledger*
(6 February 1964): 8; (24 January 1964): 8.

Evers, Charles. *Evers*. New York: World, 1971.

Evers, Myrlie, with William Peters. *For Us, the Living*. Garden City,
N.Y.: Doubleday, 1967.

Ewald, François. "Norms, Discipline, and the Law." In *Law and the
Order of Culture*, edited by Robert Post, 138–61. Berkeley: University
of California Press, 1991.

Faulkner, William. *Requiem for a Nun*. New York: Random House,
1950.

"FCC Is Scorched by Burger." *Variety* (25 June 1969): 33.

"FCC Revisits WLBT-TV Renewal Case." *Broadcasting* (10 June 1968):
46–47.

FCC v. Sanders Brothers Radio Station, 309 U.S. 470 (1940).

Femia, Joseph V. *Gramsci's Political Thought: Hegemony,
Consciousness, and the Revolutionary Process*. Oxford: Clarendon,
1987.

Fermaglich, Kirsten. "Never: WLBT-TV and the Changing Public Sphere
of Jackson, Mississippi, 1962–1978." Paper presented at the
Conference Telling about the South, Charlottesville, Va., 1995.

Fish, Stanley. *There's No Such Thing as Free Speech . . . and It's a Good
Thing, Too*. New York: Oxford University Press, 1994.

Fisher, Paul L., and Ralph L. Lowenstein. *Race and the News Media*.
New York: Praeger, 1967.

Fiske, John. *Introduction to Communication Studies*. London: Routledge,
1982.

———. "The Culture of Everyday Life." In *Cultural Studies*, edited by Lawrence Grossberg, Cary Nelson, and Paul Treichler, 154–73. New York: Routledge.

———. *Power Plays, Power Works*. London: Verso, 1993.

———. *Media Matters: Everyday Culture and Political Change*. Minneapolis: University of Minnesota Press, 1994.

———. *Television Culture*. London: Methuen, 1987.

Fletcher, Michael. "Kerner Prophesy on Race Relations Came True; Report says Despite Progress, Foundation Finds 'Separate and Unequal' Societies More Deeply Rooted." *Washington Post* (1 March 1998): A6.

Foucault, Michel. *Discipline and Punish: The Birth of the Prison*. New York: Vintage, 1979.

Friendly, Fred W. *The Good Guys, the Bad Guys, and the First Amendment*. New York: Random House, 1976.

Frisch, Michael H. *A Shared Authority: Essays on the Craft and Meaning of Oral and Public History*. Albany: State University of New York Press, 1990.

Frug, Gerald. "The Ideology of Bureaucracy in American Law." In *Critical Legal Studies*, edited by Allan Hutchinson, 181–94. Totowa, N.J.: Rowman and Littlefield, 1989.

"Furor Grows Hotter over Hirt's Pullout." Jackson *Clarion-Ledger* (27 January 1964): 8.

Gaedeke, Ralph, and Warren Etcheson, eds. *Consumerism: Viewpoints from Business, Government, and the Public Interest*. San Francisco: Canfield, 1972.

Gellhorn, Ernest, and Ronald M. Levin. *Administrative Law and Process*. 3rd ed. St. Paul, Minn.: West, 1990.

Goldfield, David R. *Black, White, and Southern: Race Relations and Southern Culture, 1940 to the Present*. Baton Rouge: Louisiana State University Press, 1990.

Good, Paul. *The Trouble I've Seen: White Journalist/Black Movement*. Washington, D.C.: Howard University Press, 1974.

Gooding-Williams, Robert, ed. *Reading Rodney King/Reading Urban Uprising*. New York: Routledge, 1993.

Graham, Allison. *Framing the South: Hollywood, Television, and Race during the Civil Rights Struggle*. Baltimore: Johns Hopkins University Press, 2001.

Gramsci, Antonio. *Selections from the Prison Notebooks*. Translated and edited by Q. Hoare and G. N. Smith. New York: International, 1971.

Gray, Herman. *Watching Race: Television and the Struggle for Blackness*. Minneapolis: University of Minnesota Press, 1995.

Greene, Melissa Fay. *Praying for Sheetrock: A Work of Nonfiction*. Reading, Mass.: Addison-Wesley, 1991.

Grossberg, Lawrence, Cary Nelson, and Paula Treichler, eds. *Cultural Studies*. New York: Routledge, 1992.

Haight, Timothy R., and Laurie R. Weinstein. "Changing Ideology on Television by Changing Telecommunications Policy: Notes on a Contradictory Situation." In *Communication and Social Structure: Critical Studies in Mass Media Research*, edited by E. G. McAnany, J. Schnitman, and N. Janus, 110–44. New York: Praeger, 1981.

Halberstam, David. *The Fifties*. New York: Villard, 1993.

Hale, Grace E. *Making Whiteness: The Culture of Segregation in the South, 1890–1940*. New York: Pantheon, 1998.

Hall, Stuart. *Representation: Cultural Representations and Signifying Practices*. London: Sage, 1997.

———. "The Whites of Their Eyes: Racist Ideologies and the Media." In *The Media Reader*, edited by M. Alvarado and J. Thompson, 8–23. London: British Film Institute, 1990.

Hampton, Henry, and Steve Fayer, with Sarah Flynn. *Voices of Freedom: An Oral History of the Civil Rights Movement from the 1950s through the 1960s*. New York: Bantam, 1990.

Harrington, Walt. *Crossings: A White Man's Journey into Black America*. New York: HarperCollins, 1992.

Harvey, Clarie Collins. Oral history interview by John Dittmer and John Jones. Mississippi Department of Archives and History, Jackson, Miss., 1981.

Haskett, D. L. "Locus Standi and the Public Interest." *Canada-United States Law Journal* 4 (1981): 39–89.

Hayakawa, S. I. "TV and the Negro Revolt." *Television Quarterly* 3, no. 3 (1964): 23–25.

Head, Sydney, and Christopher Sterling. *Broadcasting in America: A Survey of Television, Radio, and New Technologies*. 4th ed. Boston: Houghton Mifflin, 1982.

"Hearing Called For on Mississippi Case." *Broadcasting* (22 February 1965): 54.

Henderson, Gordon, and John Q. Adams. Oral history collection transcripts. Millsaps College, Jackson, Miss., 1965–1966.

Hill, George H., and Sylvia S. Hill. *Blacks on Television: A Selectively Annotated Bibliography*. Metuchen, N.J.: Scarecrow, 1985.

Hill, Herbert, and James E. Jones, eds. *Race in America: The Struggle for Equality*. Madison: University of Wisconsin Press, 1993.

"Hirt Hurts Sick Children by Runout." Jackson *Daily News* (28 January 1964): 6.

"Hollywood Stars Not Needed Here." Jackson *Daily News* (13 February 1964): 6.

Hooker, Robert. "Race and the Mississippi Press." *New South* (winter 1971): 55–62.

"Hootenany Called Off in Jackson." Jackson *Clarion-Ledger*
(16 November 1963): 2.

Horwitz, Robert B. "Broadcast Reform Revisited: Reverend Everett C.
Parker and the 'Standing' Case (*Office of Communication of the
United Church of Christ v. Federal Communications Commission*)."
Communication Review 2, no. 3 (1997): 311–48.

———. *The Irony of Regulatory Reform: The Deregulation of American
Telecommunications*. New York: Oxford University Press, 1989.

Hunt, Alan. *Explorations in Law and Society: Toward a Constitutive
Theory of Law*. New York: Routledge, 1993.

———. "The Ideology of the Law: Advances and Problems in Recent
Applications of the Concept of Ideology to the Analysis of Law." *Law
and Society Review* 19, no. 1 (1985): 11–37.

Hutchinson, Allan, ed. *Critical Legal Studies*. Totowa, N.J.: Rowman and
Littlefield, 1989.

Isenberg, Nancy. "Not 'Anyone's Daughter': Patty Hearst and the
Postmodern Legal Subject." *American Quarterly* 52, no. 4 (2000):
639–81.

"Issues Restated in WLBT Case." *Broadcasting* (7 August 1967): 61.

"It's a Question of 'Standing.' " *Broadcasting* (30 August 1965):
54–55.

"Jackson Citizens' Council." *Aspect* (February 1964): 1.

Jacoway, Elizabeth. "An Introduction: Civil Rights and the Changing
South." In *Southern Businessmen and Desegregation*, edited by
Elizabeth Jacoway and David Colburn, 235–56. Baton Rouge:
Louisiana State University Press, 1982.

Jaffe, L. "Standing to Secure Judicial Review: Private Actions." *Harvard
Law Review* 75, no. 2 (1961): 255–58.

Johnston, Erle. *Mississippi's Defiant Years, 1953–1973: An Interpretive
Documentary with Personal Experiences*. Forest, Miss.: Lake Harbor,
1990.

Jones, E. 1984. "WLBT-TV, 1964–1979: A Case History of Progress."
Master's thesis, Iowa State University, Ames, Iowa.

Kairys, David, ed. *The Politics of Law: A Progressive Critique*. New
York: Pantheon, 1982.

———. *With Liberty and Justice for Some: A Critique of the Conservative
Supreme Court*. New York: New Press, 1993.

Keller, K. R. "The Law of Administrative Standing and the Public Right
of Intervention." *Federal Communications Bar Journal* 21, no. 3
(1967): 134–61.

Kelmar, Mark. *A Guide to Critical Legal Studies*. Cambridge: Harvard
University Press, 1987.

Kennedy, Duncan. "Political Power and Cultural Subordination: A Case
for Affirmative Action in Legal Academia." In *After Identity: A*

Reader in Law and Culture, edited by Dan Danielson and Karen
Engle, 83–102. New York: Routledge, 1995.

————. *Sexy Dressing Etc.: Essays on the Power and Politics of Cultural
Identity*. Cambridge: Harvard University Press, 1993.

Kennedy, John F. *Public Papers of the Presidents of the United States:
John F. Kennedy, January 1 to December 31, 1962*. Washington, D.C.:
GPO, 1962.

King, Mary. *Freedom Song: A Personal Story of the 1960s Civil Rights
Movement*. New York: Quill–William Morrow, 1987.

Krasnow, Erwin, Lawrence Longley, and Herbert Terry. *The Politics of
Broadcast Regulation*. 3rd ed. New York: St. Martin's Press, 1982.

Kupcinet, Irv. "Kup's Column." *Chicago Sun-Times* (22 January 1964):
44.

Lampman, Robert. "JFK's Four Consumer Rights: A Retrospective
View." In *The Frontier of Research in the Consumer Interest*, edited
by E. S. Maynes, 19–33. Columbia, Mo.: American Council on
Consumer Interests, 1988.

Leonard, Jerry D. "Foucault: Genealogy, Law, Praxis." *Legal Studies
Forum* 14, no. 1 (1993): 3–25.

Levine, Lawrence. *Black Culture and Black Consciousness: Afro-
American Folk Thought from Slavery to Freedom*. New York: Oxford
University Press, 1977.

"Licensing." *Time* (11 July 1968): 68.

Lipsitz, Geoge. *The Possessive Investment in Whiteness: How White
People Profit from Identity Politics*. Philadelphia: Temple University
Press, 1998.

————. *Time Passages: Collective Memory and American Popular
Culture*. Minneapolis: University of Minnesota Press, 1990.

López, Ian F. Haney. *White by Law: The Legal Construction of Race*.
New York: New York University Press, 1996.

Lord, Walter. *The Past That Would Not Die*. New York: Harper and Row,
1965.

MacDonald, J. Fred. *Blacks and White TV: Afro-Americans in Television
since 1948*. Chicago: Nelson-Hall, 1983.

Marable, Manning. "An Idea Whose Time Has Come." *Time* (27 August
2001): 22.

————. *Race, Reform and Rebellion: The Second Reconstruction in Black
America, 1945–1982*. Jackson: University Press of Mississippi, 1984.

Marris, Paul, and Sue Thornton, eds., *Media Studies: A Reader*. 2nd ed.
New York: New York University Press, 2000.

Marsh, Charles. *God's Long Summer: Stories of Faith and Civil Rights*.
Princeton: Princeton University Press, 1997.

————. "Jesus in Mississippi: The Civil Rights Movement as Theological
Drama." *Books and Culture* (March/April 1998): 16–19.

Massey, Douglas, and Nancy Denton. *American Apartheid*. Cambridge: Harvard University Press, 1993.

Matsuda, Mari J. "Public Response to Racist Speech: Considering the Victim's Story." *Michigan Law Review* 87 (1989): 2320–34.

Maxwell, Richard, ed. *Culture Works: The Political Economy of Culture*. Minneapolis: University of Minnesota Press, 2001.

McChesney, Robert W. *Corporate Media and the Threat to Democracy*. New York: Seven Stories Press, 1997.

———. *Rich Media, Poor Democracy: Communication Politics in Dubious Times*. Urbana: University of Illinois Press, 1999.

———. *Telecommunications, Mass Media, and Democracy: The Battle for Control of U.S. Broadcasting, 1928–1935*. Oxford: Oxford University Press, 1994.

McMillen, Neil R. *The Citizens' Council: Organized Resistance to the Second Reconstruction, 1954–1964*. Urbana: University of Illinois Press, 1971.

Mercer, Kobena. "1968: Periodizing Postmodern Politics and Identity." In *Cultural Studies*, edited by Lawrence Grossberg, Cary Nelson, and Paula Treichler, 424–49. New York: Routledge, 1992.

Mississippi Advisory Committee to the United States Commission on Civil Rights. *1963 Report on Mississippi*. Washington, DC: GPO, 1963.

Mississippi Department of Archives and History. Oral history interviews with John R. Salter Jr. and Reverend R. Edwin King Jr., 6 January 1981.

"Mississippi's TV's Defend Actions." *Broadcasting* (25 May 1964): 74.

Montgomery, Kathryn C. *Target: Prime Time; Advocacy Groups and the Struggle over Entertainment Television*. New York: Oxford University Press, 1989.

Moody, Anne. *Coming of Age in Mississippi*. New York: Dell, 1971.

Mosco, Vincent. "Toward a Theory of State and Telecommunications Policy." *Journal of Communication* 38, no. 1 (1989): 107–24.

Mukherjee, Roopali. "Regulating Race in the California Civil Rights Initiative: Enemies, Allies, and Alibis." *Journal of Communication* 50, no. 2 (2000): 27–47.

Nadel, Mark V. *The Politics of Consumer Protection*. Indianapolis: Bobbs-Merrill, 1971.

National Broadcasting Corporation v. FCC, 132 F 2d 545 (1942).

"Negro Impact on Market." *Broadcasting* (17 June 1963): 96.

"The Negro on TV." *Nation* (22 November 1965): 374.

"Negroes Step Up Drives on Radio-TV." *Broadcasting* (12 August 1963): 62–63.

Nicolson, D. "Truth, Reason, and Justice: Epistemological Politics in Evidence Discourse." *Modern Law Review* 57, no. 5 (1994): 726–43.

"No More Bonanzas on Sunday Nights." Jackson *Daily News* (28 January 1964): 6.

Nonviolent Agitation Association of College Pupils. *Voice of the Movement* (27 March 1964): 5–6.

Noriega, Chon A. *Shot in America: Television, the State, and the Rise of Chicano Cinema*. Minneapolis: University of Minnesota Press, 2000.

"Notes — Responsible Representatives of the Listening Public Have Standing as 'Persons Aggrieved.' " *Wayne Law Review* 13, no. 2 (1967): 377–84.

"Now It's Beginning to Hurt Both Ways." *Mississippi Free Press* (1 February 1964): 2.

Oates, Stephen B. *Let the Trumpet Sound: The Life of Martin Luther King, Jr.* New York: Mentor, 1982.

Office of Communication of the United Church of Christ v. FCC, 359 F 2d 994 (1966).

Ong, Walter J. *Orality and Literacy: The Technologizing of the Word*. London: Routledge, 1982.

Parker, Everett C. "The Impact of Public Interest Groups on Telecommunications Policy." Speech before the annual conference of Telecommunications Policy Research, Annapolis, Md., 1982.

———. "The Mississippi Television Station Cases." Unpublished manuscript, 1972.

Partner, Nancy. "Making Up Lost Time: Writing on the Writing of History." *Speculum* 61, no. 1 (1986): 90–117.

Payne, Charles M. *I've Got the Light of Freedom: The Organizing Tradition and the Mississippi Freedom Struggle*. Berkeley: University of California Press, 1995.

Peller, Gary. "Race Consciousness." In *After Identity: A Reader in Law and Culture*, edited by D. Danielson and K. Engle, 67–92. New York: Routledge, 1995.

Pertschuk, Michael. *Revolt against Regulation: The Rise and Pause of the Consumer Movement*. Berkeley: University of California Press, 1982.

Peters, John Durham. *Speaking into the Air: A History of the Idea of Communication*. Chicago: University of Chicago Press, 1999.

Phelps, Ernest E. "The Office of Communication: The Participant Advocate — Its Function as a Broadcast Citizen Group, March 1964–1971." Ph.D. diss., Ohio State University, 1971. University Microfilms, no. 72-4612.

Philco Corporation v. FCC, 257 F 2d 656 (1958).

"Pools of Experts on Access." *Broadcasting* (20 September 1971): 36.

Portelli, A. "The Peculiarities of Oral History." *History Workshop* 12 (autumn 1981): 96–107.

Post, Robert, ed. *Law and the Order of Culture*. Berkeley: University of California, 1991.

"Primer for Negro Complaints against Radio-TV." *Broadcasting*
(20 July 1964): 40.

Raboy, M., S. Proulx, and R. Welters. "Media Policy, Audiences, and
Social Demand: Research at the Interface of Policy Studies and
Audience Studies." *Television and New Media* 2, no. 2 (2001): 95–116.

Raines, Howell. *My Soul Is Rested: The Story of the Civil Rights
Movement in the Deep South*. New York: Penguin, 1983.

"Recent Decisions — Standing to Intervene before FCC — Granted to
Responsible Representatives of Listening Public Seeking to Vindicate
Broad Public Interest." *Albany Law Review* 31, no. 1 (1967): 133–36.

"Recent Developments — Administrative Law — Community
Representatives Have Standing to Challenge FCC License Renewal."
Michigan Law Review 65, no. 3 (1967): 518–31.

Reed, John Shelton. "Letter from the Lower Right: The Mississippi
Hippies and Other Denizens of the Deep (South)." *Chronicles* (July
1993): 47–48.

"Regulating Television." *New Republic* (13 July 1968): 8–9.

Reuther, Victor G. *The Brothers Reuther and the Story of the UAW*.
Boston: Houghton Mifflin, 1976.

Riggs, Karen E. *Mature Audiences: Television in the Lives of Elders*.
New Brunswick: Rutgers University Press, 1998.

Rowland, Willard D., Jr. "American Telecommunications Policy
Research: Its Contradictory Origins and Influences." *Media, Culture
and Society* 8, no. 2 (1986): 159–82.

——. "The Illusion of Fulfillment: The Broadcast Reform Movement."
Journalism Monographs (1982): 79.

——. "U.S. Broadcasting and the Public Interest in the Multichannel
Era: The Policy Heritage and Its Implications." *Studies in
Broadcasting*, no. 33 (1997): 89–130.

Rubin, Alissa. "Racial Divide Widens, Study Says." *Los Angeles Times*
(1 March 1998): A20.

Sallis, Charles, and John Q. Adams. "Desegregation in Jackson,
Mississippi." In *Southern Businessmen and Desegregation*, edited by
Elizabeth Jacoway and David Colburn, 236–56. Baton Rouge:
Louisiana State University Press, 1982.

Salter, John R., Jr. *Jackson, Mississippi: An American Chronicle of
Struggle and Schism*. Malabar, Fla.: Krieger, 1987.

——. "Thoughts on the Mississippi Free Press." *Mississippi Free Press*
(5 May 1963): 2.

Sanders, Richard L. Oral history interview by Baylor University Institute
for Oral History, 3 April 1987.

Sardar, Ziauddin, and Borin Van Loon. *Introducing Cultural Studies*.
New York: Totem Books, 1997.

Sawyer, Patrice. "WLBT Changing Hands." Jackson *Clarion-Ledger* (20 June 2000): C1–2.

Scheppele, Kim. "Facing Facts in Legal Interpretation." In *Law and the Order of Culture*, edited by R. Post, 42–77. Berkeley: University of California Press, 1991.

———. "Foreword: Telling Stories." *Michigan Law Review* 87 (1989): 2073–98.

Scripps-Howard Radio, Inc. v. FCC, 316 U.S. 4 (1942).

Sears, D. "Symbolic Racism." In *Eliminating Racism*, edited by P. A. Katz and D. A. Taylor. New York: Plenum, 1988.

Seiter, Ellen. *Television and New Media Audiences*. New York: Oxford University Press, 1999.

Shayon, Robert L. "The Public May Be Heard." *Saturday Review* (26 June 1965): 44.

———. "Rating the Broadcaster." *Saturday Review* (11 July 1964): 21.

"Short Renewals in Mississippi." *Broadcasting* (24 May 1965): 66–69.

Silver, James. *Mississippi: The Closed Society*. New York: Harcourt, Brace and World, 1963.

Sitkoff, Harvard. *The Struggle for Black Equality, 1954–1992*. New York: Hill and Wang, 1993.

Smith, J. C. "Toward a Pure Legal Existence: Blacks and the Constitution." *Howard Law Journal* 30 (1987): 921–36.

Southwestern Publishing Company v. FCC, 243 F. 2d 829 (1957).

Spigel, Lynn, and Michael Curtin, eds. *The Revolution Wasn't Televised: Sixties Television and Social Conflict*. New York: Routledge, 1997.

"Standing to Protest and Appeal the Issuance of Broadcasting Licenses: A Constricted Concept Redefined." *Yale Law Journal* 68, no. 4 (1959): 783–96.

Sterling, Christopher, and John Kitross. *Stay Tuned: A Concise History of American Broadcasting*. 3rd ed. Belmont, Calif.: Wadsworth, 2002.

Streeter, Thomas. "Beyond Freedom of Speech and the Public Interest: The Relevance of Critical Legal Studies to Communications Policy." *Journal of Communication* 40, no. 2 (1990): 43–63.

———. *Selling the Air: A Critique of the Policy of Commercial Broadcasting in the United States*. Chicago: University of Chicago Press, 1996.

Suggs, J. "Epistemology and the Law in Four African American Fictions." *Legal Studies Forum* 14, no. 2 (1990): 141–62.

Terkel, Studs. *Race: How Blacks and Whites Think and Feel about the American Obsession*. New York: Doubleday, 1992.

Thompson, Julius E. *The Black Press in Mississippi, 1865–1985*. Gainesville: University Press of Florida, 1993.

"Till Case TV Play Causes Big Uproar." *Pittsburgh Courier* (12 May 1956): n.p.

Torres, Sasha, ed. *Living Color: Race and Television in the United States.* Durham: Duke University Press, 1998.

Tushnet, Mark V. "The New Law of Standing: A Plea for Abandonment." *Cornell Law Review* 62, no. 4 (1977): 663–700.

U.S. Commission on Civil Rights. *Window Dressing on the Set: Women and Minorities in Television.* Washington, D.C.: GPO, 1977.

U.S. Department of Commerce. *Changes, Challenges, and Charting New Courses: Minority Commercial Broadcast Ownership in the United States.* Washington, D.C.: GPO, 2001.

———. "Commerce Secretary Mineta Releases Report Finding Gains in Minority Broadcast Ownership." Press Release (16 January 2001).

———. *1960 Census of Housing.* Vol. I, part 5, tables 26–10 and 26–15. Washington, D.C.: GPO, 1963.

Vogel, David. *Fluctuating Fortunes: The Political Power of Business in America.* New York: Basic Books, 1989.

Voice of the People. Jackson *Clarion-Ledger* (28 January 1964): 6; (20 February 1964): 10; (24 February 1964): 13.

Vollers, Maryanne. *Ghosts of Mississippi: The Murder of Medgar Evers, the Trials of Byron De La Beckwith, and the Haunting of the New South.* Boston: Little, Brown, 1995.

Waldinger, Roger, and Mehdi Bozorgmehr, eds. *Ethnic Los Angeles.* New York: Russell Sage Foundation, 1996.

Wall, T. H., and J. B. Jacob. "Communication Act Amendments, 1952 — Clarity or Ambiguity." *Georgetown Law Journal* 41, no. 2 (1953): 135–81.

Watson, Mary Ann. "Eleanor Intervenes: A Phone Call from the First Lady Jolts the FCC to Action." *Television Quarterly* (2001): Retrieved from http://www.emmyonline.org/tvq/articles/32-23-8.asp, 15 July 2002.

———. *The Expanding Vista: American Television in the Kennedy Years.* New York: Oxford University Press, 1990.

Weill, Susan M. "Mississippi's Daily Press in Three Crises." In *The Press and Race: Mississippi Journalists Confront the Movement,* edited by David Davies, 17–53. Jackson: University Press of Mississippi, 2001.

Welty, Eudora. *The Collected Stories of Eudora Welty.* New York: Harcourt Brace Jovanovich, 1980.

———. *Losing Battles.* New York: Vintage, 1970.

"What's Not Said." *Mississippi Free Press* (26 October 1963): 2.

"Where, Might We Ask, Is the FCC?" *Consumer Reports* (January 1960): 9–11.

White, Hayden. *Metahistory: The Historical Imagination in Nineteenth-Century Europe.* Baltimore: Johns Hopkins University Press, 1973.

———. *Tropics of Discourse: Essays in Cultural Criticism.* Baltimore: Johns Hopkins University Press, 1978.

Whitfield, Stephen. *The Culture of the Cold War*. Baltimore: Johns Hopkins University Press, 1991.

Williams, J. "Improper Conduct: WLBT Programming and Operations, 1955–65." Master's thesis, University of Florida, 1987.

Williams, Patricia J. *The Alchemy of Race and Fights*. Cambridge: Harvard University Press, 1991.

———. "Spirit-Murdering the Messenger: The Discourse of Finger-Pointing as the Law's Response to Racism." *University of Miami Law Review* 42, no. 1 (1987): 127–57.

"WJTV Will Alter the Patterns in Jackson Life." Jackson *Clarion-Ledger* (22 October 1952): n.p.

Yates, Gayle G. *Mississippi Mind: A Personal Cultural History of an American State*. Knoxville: University of Tennessee Press, 1990.

Yúdice, George. "Civil Society, Consumption, and Governmentality in an Age of Global Restructuring: An Introduction." *Social Text* 14, no. 4 (1995): 1–25.

Zeidenberg, Leonard. "Struggle over Broadcast Access II." *Broadcasting* (27 September 1971): 24.

ism of, 40; on *Brown v. Board of Education*, response to, 32; on Medgar Evers, 42, 45

Harvey, Paul, 31
Haughton, G. R., 54
Hayakawa, S. I., 149, 236 n.21
Hayden, J. Roger, 35
Hearin, Robert, 35
Hederman family, 34–36, 40
Henderson, Gordon, 61, 216 n.61, 219 n.35, 220 n.36, 236 n.36; as white supporter of civil rights movement, 159–161
Henderson, Mary Ann, 61, 142, 219 n.35, 236 n.36; as white supporter of civil rights movement, 159–161; as woman leader, 162
Henry, Aaron: activism of, 40, 177; on boycotts, 53–54; on identity of broadcasting stations, 171–172; and licensing challenges, 51, 61; and ownership of WLBT-TV, 203–204; as part of "minority controlled" group, 167–168; testimony of, 130; and UCC, 60
Henry, E. William, 51, 69, 73, 121, 211 n.45, 217 n.70, 220 n.39, 222 n.63
Higgs, William, 81, 238 n.9
High, Arrington, 78–79
Hirt, Al, 86, 100; canceled appearance by, 90–91, 98, 105; concert by, 89
Histories, oral. *See* Oral histories
History: race scholarship on, 17–18; writing of, 14–19
Home, 198
Homicide rates, in Jackson, 7–8
Honeysucker, Robert, 88
Hooker, Robert, 224 nn.8, 15
Hootenanny cast: activism against, 85; canceled appearance by, 88, 91, 105, 159; integrated concert by, 89
Hoover, J. Edgar, 31
Horwitz, Robert, 13, 208 n.27, 209 n.35, 219 n.32, 220 nn.37–38, 40

Howard, T. R. M., 40
"Human dignity" ("Black dignity"), activists' call for, 56–58, 123, 163–164
Hunt, Alan, 17, 206 n.7, 209 n.37
Hunter, Edward, 38
Hurley, Ruby, 40, 142, 146

Identity, of broadcasting stations, 171–172
Inferential racism, 8–9, 24, 138–139, 206 n.14
Information, mediated, 153–155
Inquiry, 174
Interviews, about oral history, 234 nn.2–3, 235 n.13
Invisible Man (Ellison), 138
Isenberg, Nancy, 238 n.8
I Spy, 108

Jackson, economic conditions in, 23–24
Jackson activists. *See* Tougaloo College: students and staff; *and under names of individual activists*
Jackson Advocate, 78, 80
Jackson *Clarion-Ledger*: on boycotts, 55; as dominant press, 78; practices of, compared with television, 147–148; response to Medgar Evers' broadcast, 5; and Sovereignty Commission, 39–40; and surveillance, 157
Jackson *Daily News*: on boycotts, 55; as dominant press, 78; practices of, compared with television, 147–148; and Sovereignty Commission, 39–40; and surveillance, 157
Jackson Movement: "bill of rights" for consumers, 58–59; "Black Christmas" campaign, 94–95; boycott organized by, 54–56, 200; characteristics of, 59; and

1934 Communications Act, 181, 182
1948–1952 FCC licensing freeze, 34
1950s: activism in, 31–33, 112, 146–147; broadcasting practices in, 42–43, 109; chronology of civil rights movement in, 197–204; media in Mississippi in, 11; prime-time programming in, 108; television set ownership in, 71
1960s: and African American testimony, 117–125; broadcast reform in, 73–74, 177–179; chronology of civil rights movement in, 197–204; and consumerism, 26, 193; controversial materials in broadcasting in, 109; FCC's investigation of southern stations in, 50; as historical moment, 6; media in Mississippi in, 11; prime-time programming in, 108; and 1990s compared, 7–9, 24; television as instrument of activism in, 112, 149; television set ownership in, 71, 148, 214 n.22
1963 March on Washington for Freedom and Jobs, 217 n.1
1964 petition to FCC, 113–117, 220 n.39
1965 licensing decision, 127–128, 130
1966 licensing decision, 26–27, 63–67; broadcasting before, 68; and consumerism, 67, 71–72, 191; and context of civil rights movement, 73–74; impact on broadcast reform, 73–74; and legal standing, 63–67, 191; and television consumers, 70–71, 74; texts surrounding, 69
1968 licensing decision, 129–130
1970s broadcast reform, 73–74, 180–181, 208 n.25; achieve-

ments in, 174–195; decline of, 12; and employees of WLBT-TV and WJTV, 180
1990s, and 1960s compared, 7–8, 9, 24
Nonviolent Agitation Association of College Pupils, 88
Noriega, Chon A., 118, 178, 210 n.44, 232 nn.30–31, 238 nn.10–12, 240 n.23
North Jackson Action, 54
North Jackson Youth Council of the NAACP, 54

Offensive language, used by newscasters, 112–113, 123, 231 n.17
Offensive programming, 112. *See also* Censorship, of local programming
Office of Communication of the United Church of Christ, 11–12, 51, 115. *See also* United Church of Christ
Office of Communication of the United Church of Christ v. FCC, 220 nn.43, 45–49, 222 nn.68, 70, 223 nn.77, 80
"Official" accounts, in licensing challenges, 14, 117–118
Omission, of blacks on local programming, 52–53, 118–122, 147
Ong, Walter J., 134–135, 142, 233 nn.65–68, 234 n.76, 235 nn.8–9
Oral histories, 142–145, 235 n.13; historical context of, 140–142; and literacy, tensions between, 134–135; and memory, dependence on, 143–144; "outsider" impact on, 19–29; and "patterns of truth," 233 n.69; views on research based on, 143. *See also under names of individual interviewees*
Orality and Literacy (Ong), 134–135

of, 185–189; scholarship on, 10–11

WLBT-TV licensing challenges, 11, 27, 51, 62, 121; circumstances surrounding, 59–60; and FCC, 19, 125–126; impact of, 11; and legal standing (*see* "Standing," legal); and United Church of Christ, 60, 225 n.21; and use of courtesy titles, 132; and WJTV, 35–36. *See also under individual court decisions*

WMPR-FM, 167

Womanpower Unlimited, 83–84, 162–163

Women, in local civil rights movement, 141–142, 161–163

Woods, Barbara, 215 n.39

"Written communication," FCC on, 116

Yarbrough, Glenn, 88–89

Young, Andrew, 130–131

Young, Aurelia, 84, 164

Young, Charles, 204

STEVEN D. CLASSEN

is an assistant professor of Communication

Studies at California State University,

Los Angeles.

Library of Congress Cataloging-in-Publication Data

Classen, Steven D.
Watching Jim Crow : the struggles over Mississippi TV,
1955–1969 / Steven D. Classen.
p. cm. — (Console-ing passions)
Includes bibliographical references and index.
ISBN 0-8223-3329-5 (acid-free paper)
ISBN 0-8223-3341-4 (pbk. : acid-free paper)
1. African Americans — Civil rights — Mississippi —
Jackson — History — 20th century. 2. Civil rights
movements — Mississippi — Jackson — History — 20th
century. 3. African Americans in television broadcasting —
Mississippi — Jackson — History — 20th century. 4. African
Americans on television — History — 20th century. 5. WLBT
(Television station : Jackson, Miss.) — History. 6. Jackson
(Miss.) — Race relations. 7. Jackson (Miss.) — Economic
conditions — 20th century. 8. African American consumers —
Mississippi — Jackson — Political activity — History — 20th
century. 9. Consumer satisfaction — Mississippi — Jackson —
History — 20th century. I. Title. II. Series.
F349.J13C58 2004
323.1196'073076212 — dc22   2003021426